France

MER DU NORD

Pays-Bas

Angleterre

Allemagne

Dunkerque

Calais

Belgique

NORD-PAS-DE-CALAIS

Lille

Valenciennes

coal mine

Luxembourg

LA MANCHE – *the sleve*

Amiens

Cherbourg

HAUTE-NORMANDIE

Le Havre

Rouen

PICARDIE

Seine

Reims

Metz

LORRAINE

ALSACE

Caen

Saint-Malo

BASSE-NORMANDIE

Versailles

★ **Paris**

ÎLE-DE-FRANCE

CHAMPAGNE-ARDENNE

Nancy

coal

Strasbourg

Meuse

Moselle

Rhin

VOSGES

Brest

Fougères

BRETAGNE

Rennes

Le Mans

Troyes

PAYS DE LA LOIRE

Angers

Orléans

Blois

Chambord

Seine

BOURGOGNE

Dijon

Mulhouse

St-Nazaire

Loire

Tours

Chenonceaux

Besançon

JURA

Nantes

Chinon

Azay-le-Rideau

Bourges

Chalon-sur-Saône

FRANCHE-COMTÉ

Suisse

Nevers

CENTRE

Loire

Poitiers

OCÉAN

ATLANTIQUE

La Rochelle

LIMOUSIN

Vichy

Clermont-Ferrand

Rhône

Annecy

Lyon

POITOU-CHARENTES

Limoges

Saint-Étienne

RHÔNE-ALPES

Italie

Périgueux

AUVERGNE

Grenoble

ALPES

Bordeaux

Garonne

MASSIF CENTRAL

Rodez

Rhône

PROVENCE-ALPES-CÔTE-D'AZUR

AQUITAINE

MIDI-PYRÉNÉES

Avignon

Monte-Carlo

Nîmes

Tarascon

Grasse

Monaco

Biarritz

Bayonne

Montpellier

Aix-en-Provence

Pau

Toulouse

Béziers

Marseille

Toulon

Nice

Cannes

PYRÉNÉES

Carcassonne

Narbonne

denim

Espagne

Andorre

Perpignan

LANGUEDOC-ROUSSILLON

MER MÉDITERRANÉE

0   75 km

CORSE

Ajaccio

©1993 Magellan Geographix

D1291000

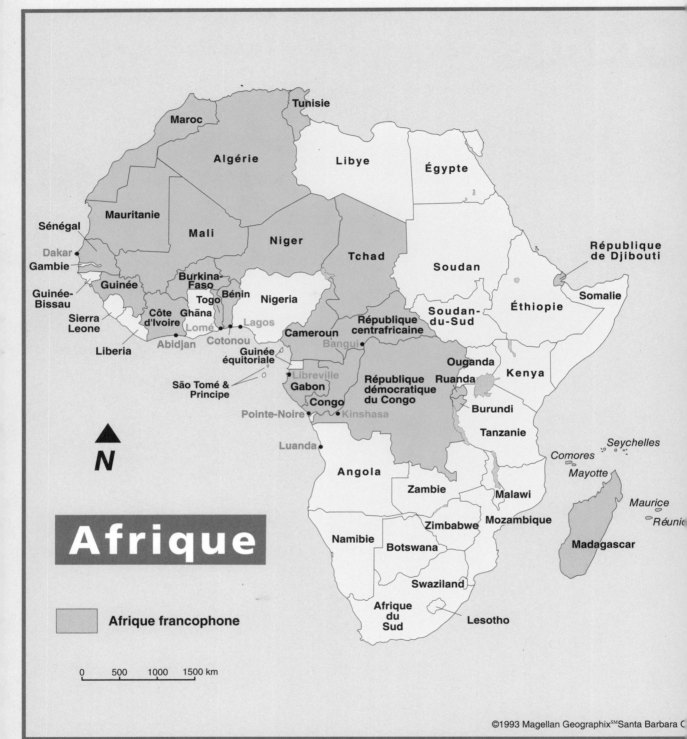

Maroc

Tunisie

Algérie

Libye

Égypte

Mauritanie

Sénégal

Dakar

Gambie

Mali

Niger

Tchad

Soudan

République
de Djibouti

Guinée

Burkina-
Faso

Bénin

Somalie

Guinée-
Bissau

Togo

Nigeria

Éthiopie

Sierra
Leone

Côte
d'Ivoire

Ghana

Lomé

Lagos

Soudan-
du-Sud

Liberia

Abidjan

Cotonou

Cameroun

République
centrafricaine

Guinée
équitoriale

Bangui

São Tomé &
Principe

Libreville

Gabon

Congo

République
démocratique
du Congo

Ouganda

Ruanda

Kenya

Burundi

Pointe-Noire

Kinshasa

Tanzanie

Luanda

Comores

Seychelles

Mayotte

Angola

Zambie

Malawi

Maurice

Réunion

Mozambique

Madagascar

Namibie

Zimbabwe

Botswana

N

Swaziland

Afrique

Afrique
du
Sud

Lesotho

Afrique francophone

0   500   1000 1500 km

Entre Amis/FLF 151

Michael D. Oates | Larbi Oukada

CENGAGE
Learning·

Australia • Brazil • Japan • Korea • Mexico • Singapore • Spain • United Kingdom • United States

CENGAGE
Learning

Entre Amis/FLF 151

Entre Amis: An Interactive Approach, Sixth Edition
Michael D. Oates | Larbi Oukada

© 2013, 2006 Heinle, Cengage Learning. All rights reserved.

Senior Project Development Manager:
Linda deStefano

Market Development Manager:
Heather Kramer

Senior Production/Manufacturing Manager:
Donna M. Brown

Production Editorial Manager:
Kim Fry

Sr. Rights Acquisition Account Manager:
Todd Osborne

For product information and technology assistance, contact us at
Cengage Learning Customer & Sales Support, 1-800-354-9706

For permission to use material from this text or product,
submit all requests online at **cengage.com/permissions**
Further permissions questions can be emailed to
permissionrequest@cengage.com

This book contains select works from existing Cengage Learning resources and was produced by Cengage Learning Custom Solutions for collegiate use. As such, those adopting and/or contributing to this work are responsible for editorial content accuracy, continuity and completeness.

Compilation © 2013 Cengage Learning
ISBN-13: 978-1-285-55299-6

ISBN-10: 1-285-55299-7

Cengage Learning
5191 Natorp Boulevard
Mason, Ohio 45040
USA

Cengage Learning is a leading provider of customized learning solutions with office locations around the globe, including Singapore, the United Kingdom, Australia, Mexico, Brazil, and Japan. Locate your local office at:
international.cengage.com/region.
Cengage Learning products are represented in Canada by Nelson Education, Ltd.
For your lifelong learning solutions, visit **www.cengage.com/custom.**
Visit our corporate website at **www.cengage.com.**

Printed in the United States of America

Table des matières

Table des matières

CHAPITRE 6 VOS ACTIVITÉS 161

Table des matières

CHAPITRE PRÉLIMINAIRE

Au départ

Nikada/iStockphoto.com

John Elk III/Alamy

BUTS COMMUNICATIFS

- Understanding basic classroom commands
- Understanding numbers
- Understanding basic expressions of time
- Understanding basic weather expressions

CULTURE

Il y a un geste
- Frapper à la porte
- Compter avec les doigts
- Comment? Pardon?

Vlad Ghiea/Shutterstock.com

Buts communicatifs

Grasping the meaning of spoken French is fundamental to learning to communicate in French. Developing this skill will require patience and perseverance, but your success will be enhanced if you associate a mental image (e.g., of a picture, an object, a gesture, an action, the written word) with the expressions you hear. This preliminary chapter will focus on establishing the association of sound and symbol in a few basic contexts: classroom expressions, numbers, time, and weather.

This material is recorded and available on the Premium Website. Practice with the recording as part of your homework.

I. UNDERSTANDING BASIC CLASSROOM COMMANDS

Dans la salle de classe

Track 1-1

Listen carefully and watch the physical response of your teacher to each command. Once you have learned to associate the actions with the French sentences, take turns with a partner practicing them and responding appropriately.

—Levez-vous.
—Allez à la porte.
—Ouvrez la porte.
—Sortez.
—Frappez à la porte.
—Entrez.
—Fermez la porte.

—Allez au tableau.
—Prenez la craie.
—Écrivez votre nom.
—Mettez la craie sur la table.
—Donnez la craie à ...
—Donnez-moi la craie.
—Asseyez-vous!

le tableau
la craie
la porte
la table

© Cengage Learning

Il y a un geste

Frapper à la porte. When knocking on a door (**toc, toc, toc**), the French often use the back of the index finger.

2. UNDERSTANDING NUMBERS

Track 1-2

01234 56789

Les nombres

0	zéro	16	seize
1	un	17	dix-sept
2	deux	18	dix-huit
3	trois	19	dix-neuf
4	quatre	20	vingt
5	cinq	21	vingt et un
6	six	22	vingt-deux
7	sept	23	vingt-trois
8	huit	24	vingt-quatre
9	neuf	25	vingt-cinq
10	dix	26	vingt-six
11	onze	27	vingt-sept
12	douze	28	vingt-huit
13	treize	29	vingt-neuf
14	quatorze	30	trente
15	quinze		

© Cengage Learning

Il y a un geste

Compter avec les doigts. When counting, the French normally begin with the thumb, then the index finger, etc. For instance, the thumb, index, and middle fingers are held up to indicate the number three, as a child might indicate when asked his/her age.

3. UNDERSTANDING BASIC EXPRESSIONS OF TIME

Quelle heure est-il?

Track 1-3

Il est une heure.

Il est une heure dix.

Il est une heure quinze.

1 hr 30

Il est une heure trente.

Il est deux heures moins vingt.

3 hr

Il est deux heures moins dix.

desert

Il est deux heures.

Il est trois heures.

PRONONCIATION

MASCULIN OU FÉMININ?

Track 1-4

► Nouns do not have gender in English, but they do in French. You will learn to identify nouns and adjectives as masculine or feminine.

Often, the feminine form ends in a consonant sound while the masculine form ends in a vowel sound.

Listen and repeat:

Féminins		*Masculins*	
Françoise	Louise	François	Louis
Jeanne	Martine	Jean	Martin
Laurence	Simone	Laurent	Simon
chaude	froide	chaud	froid
française	intelligente	français	intelligent
anglaise	petite	anglais	petit

L'alphabet français

prononciation

A	*Ah*	J	*ji*	S	*esse*		
B	*bé*	K	*ka*	T	*té*		
C	*cé*	L	*elle*	U	*u*		
D	*dé*	M	*emme*	V	*vé*		
E	*euh*	N	*enne*	W	*double vé*		
F	*effe*	O	*oh*	X	*iks*		
G	*jé*	P	*pé*	Y	*i grec*		
H	*ashe*	Q	*ku*	Z	*zed*		
I	*i*	R	*erre*				

Comment est-ce qu'on écrit **merci**?
Merci s'écrit M-E-R-C-I.

How do you spell "merci"?
"Merci" is spelled M-E-R-C-I.

À vous. Work with a partner to practice the French alphabet with the expressions you have learned so far. Spell an expression out loud from your book. Your partner will write it down.

Guyane is one of France's overseas **départements.**

4. UNDERSTANDING BASIC WEATHER EXPRESSIONS

Quel temps fait-il?

Track 1-5

Il fait du soleil (handwritten)

Il fait beau.
Il fait du soleil. — *the sun. its hot* (handwritten)
beautiful day (handwritten)

Il fait du vent.
It is windy (handwritten)

Il fait froid.

Il fait chaud.

Il pleut.
It rains (handwritten)

Il neige.
It snows (handwritten)

Réalités culturelles

Le français: la langue de toutes les saisons

WHEN WE THINK OF where the French language is spoken, we often think of France. But actually, France's territory extends beyond **l'Hexagone** (the hexagon-shaped mainland of France). In the forthcoming chapters, we will examine many French-speaking countries, but for now, here are some selected French-speaking regions from around the world, representing various climate zones during the month of October.

À Tahiti (en Polynésie française), il pleut. *Tahiti in Polynese french it rains* (handwritten)
À Bruxelles (en Belgique), il fait du vent. — *In Brussels in Belgium int* (handwritten)
En Antarctique, il neige. *In Antarctica its snow* (handwritten)
En Guyane (en Amérique du Sud), il fait du soleil. *In Guyan in SA its summy* (handwritten)
À Québec (au Canada), il fait froid. *it is cold* (handwritten)
À Port-au-Prince (en Haïti), il fait beau. *Haiti it is hot* (handwritten)
À Dakar (au Sénégal), il fait chaud.

Source: www.meteo.fr

Noël = two dots they break apart vowel (handwritten)

Cultural Activities

Jennifer Waddell Photography

Il y a un geste

Comment? Pardon? An open hand, cupped behind the ear, indicates that the message has not been heard and should be repeated.

Vocabulaire

Quelques expressions pour la salle de classe

Pardon?	*Pardon?*
Comment?	*What (did you say)?*
Répétez, s'il vous plaît.	*Please repeat.*
Encore.	*Again.*
En français.	*In French.*
Ensemble.	*Together.*
Tout le monde.	*Everybody, everyone.*
Fermez le livre.	*Close the book.*
Écoutez.	*Listen.*
Répondez.	*Answer.*
Comment dit-on «*the teacher*»?	*How do you say "the teacher"?*
On dit «le professeur».	*You say "le professeur."*
Que veut dire «le tableau»?	*What does "le tableau" mean?*
Ça veut dire «*the chalkboard*».	*It means "the chalkboard."*
Je ne sais pas.	*I don't know.*
Je ne comprends pas.	*I don't understand.*

Cultural Activities

Réalités culturelles

La France

"EVERY MAN HAS TWO COUNTRIES: his own and France." (Thomas Jefferson)

Official name	**République française**
Capital	**Paris**
Area (continental France)	**551,500 square kilometers**
Area (with overseas regions)	**643,427 square kilometers**
Population (January, 2010)	**64,700,000**
Monetary unit	**Euro**
Official religion	**None**
National holiday	**July 14**
Motto	**Liberté, Égalité, Fraternité**

CHAPITRE I

Bonjour

BUTS COMMUNICATIFS

- Exchanging personal information
- Identifying nationality
- Describing physical appearance

STRUCTURES UTILES

- Les pronoms sujets
- Le verbe **être**
- L'accord des adjectifs
- La négation
- L'accord des adjectifs (suite)

CULTURE

Zoom sur la politesse

- **Vidéo buzz:** Monsieur, Madame et Mademoiselle
- **Vu sur le web:** Les formules de politesse
- **Repères:** Les mots magiques
- **Insolite:** Les salutations dans le monde francophone
- **Article:** Le premier contact

Il y a un geste

- Le contact physique
- Faire la bise
- Assez

Lecture

- Profils d'un réseau social

Owen Franke/Stock Boston

RESOURCES

🔊 Audio	**iLrn** iLrn Heinle Learning Center	🌐 Premium Website
👥 Pair Work	👥 Group Work	▶ *Entre amis* Video Program

Coup d'envoi

🔊 **PRISE DE CONTACT: LES PRÉSENTATIONS**
Track 1-6

Mademoiselle Becker

Je m'appelle° Lori Becker.
J'habite à° Boston.
Je suis° américaine.
Je suis célibataire°.

Monsieur Davidson

Je m'appelle James Davidson.
J'habite à San Francisco.
Je suis américain.
Je suis célibataire.

My name is
I live in
I am
single

Review the Helpful Hints found in the To the Student section in the front of your text.

*Be sure to learn the vocabulary in **Prise de contact** and **Conversation**.*

Madame Martin

Je m'appelle Anne Martin.
J'habite à Angers.
Je suis française.
Je suis mariée°.

Monsieur Martin

Je m'appelle Pierre Martin.
J'habite à Angers.
Je suis français.
Je suis marié.

married

💬 **Et vous?** Qui êtes-vous?°

And you? Who are you?

CONVERSATION: DANS UN HÔTEL À PARIS

Maurice Savage/Alamy

Deux hommes sont au restaurant de l'hôtel Ibis à Paris.

Pierre Martin:	Bonjour°, Monsieur! Excusez-moi de vous déranger.°	*Hello* *Excuse me for bothering you.*
James Davidson:	Bonjour. Pas de problème.°	*No problem.*
Pierre Martin:	Vous permettez?° *(He touches the empty chair.)*	*May I?*
James Davidson:	Certainement. Asseyez-vous là°.	*there; here*
Pierre Martin:	Vous êtes anglais?°	*Are you English?*
James Davidson:	Non, je suis américain. Permettez-moi de me présenter.° Je m'appelle James Davidson. *(They stand up and shake hands.)*	*Let me introduce myself.*
Pierre Martin:	Martin, Pierre Martin. *(A cell phone rings. James Davidson answers the call.)*	
James Davidson:	Excusez-moi, s'il vous plaît, Monsieur.	
Pierre Martin:	Oui, certainement. Au revoir, Monsieur. *(They shake hands again.)*	
James Davidson:	Bonne journée°, Monsieur.	*Have a good day*
Pierre Martin:	Merci°, vous aussi°.	*Thank you / also; too*

👥 © **Jouez ces rôles.** Role-play the conversation with a partner. Use your own identities.

Zoom sur la politesse

Premium Website

PETIT TEST

Why does Pierre Martin say *Bonjour, Monsieur* instead of just *Bonjour*?

a. He likes variety; either expression will do.

b. **Bonjour** alone is a bit less formal than **Bonjour, Monsieur.**

c. He is trying to impress James Davidson.

(Only one answer is culturally accurate. Read the note and watch the clips referenced in *Vidéo buzz* to find out which one.)

Le premier contact (*Breaking the ice*)

THE FRENCH ARE USUALLY more reticent to "break the ice" than are Americans or Canadians. The fact that Pierre Martin introduces himself to a stranger and asks if he can take a seat is unusual. He most likely is used to working with foreign businessmen.

The French usually give their last name first in formal or professional situations and continue to use last names until told to do otherwise. Americans and French Canadians are much quicker to use first names. A good rule of thumb is to wait until invited to use a French speaker's first name, regardless of his or her nationality.

VIDÉO BUZZ

Monsieur, Madame et Mademoiselle

IN BUSINESS and many social settings, a certain amount of formality is in order when initial contact is made with French speakers. It is more polite to add **Monsieur, Madame,** or **Mademoiselle** when addressing someone than simply to say **Bonjour.** James Davidson catches on toward the end of the conversation when he remembers to say **Bonne journée, Monsieur.** Among university students, however, or young professionals who meet outside of business, French speakers often simply say **Bonjour** or **Salut.** Watch video clips about greetings to find out more on the *Premium Website.*

REPÈRES

Les mots[1] magiques...

• Bonjour

• Au revoir

• S'il vous plaît

• Merci

...sont des mots souvent oubliés[2]; faisons[3] l'effort de les utiliser!

[1]*words,* [2]*all too often forgotten,* [3]*let's make*

INSOLITE

Les salutations dans le monde francophone

GREETINGS PLAY an essential role in all forms of social interaction in French-speaking cultures. At social gatherings or business meetings in France and in the province of Quebec, you should greet and say goodbye to each person individually. It is also very important to say **Bonjour** before asking for something in a store or restaurant, and sometimes even when you simply enter a place where people are gathered, such as a waiting room or fitness club locker room.

In North and West Africa, every conversation begins with a greeting, and it is considered rude not to do so. Greetings also take a considerable amount of time because speakers not only ask about each other's well-being, but that of family members and friends. To not greet someone in some countries, such as Senegal, can be seen as an expression of anger.

Beryl Goldberg

VU SUR LE WEB

Les formules de politesse

ACCORDING TO Polly Plat (1927–2008), an American writer who published several books about French culture, the five most important words in French are **Excusez-moi de vous déranger.** This is a polite way to interrupt someone in France and a valuable formula for students and tourists who need to ask for directions or get permission to do something. Remaining polite, even in the face of adversity, is an important survival technique. Learn more **formules de politesse** (*polite expressions*) in *Vocabulaire* and by clicking on the links on the *Premium Website*.

Vocabulaire

La politesse

Au revoir, Monsieur.	*Goodbye, sir.*
Bonjour, Madame.	*Hello, madam.*
Bonne journée, Mademoiselle.	*Have a good day, miss.*
Enchanté(e).	*Delighted (to meet you).*
Excusez-moi.	*Excuse me.*
Excusez-moi de vous déranger.	*Excuse me for bothering you.*
Je vous demande pardon ...	*I beg your pardon ...*
Merci. De même.	*Thanks. Same to you.*
Merci. Vous aussi.	*Thanks. You too.*
Pardon.	*Pardon me.*
Permettez-moi de me présenter ...	*Please allow me to introduce myself ...*
S'il vous plaît.	*Please.*
Vous permettez?	*May I?*

À vous. How would you respond to the following?

1. Je m'appelle Alissa. Et vous?
2. Vous êtes français(e)?
3. J'habite à Paris. Et vous?
4. Excusez-moi, s'il vous plaît.
5. Bonne journée.

Il y a un geste

Le contact physique. James Davidson and Pierre Martin shake hands during their conversation, a normal gesture for both North Americans and the French when meeting someone. However, the French and people from other Francophone countries would normally shake hands with friends, colleagues, and their neighbors each time they meet and, if they chat for a while, at the end of their conversation as well. Physical contact plays a very important role in Francophone cultures and forgetting to shake hands with a friend would be rude.

Faire la bise. Among friends and family members, the French will exchange kisses on the cheek to greet and say goodbye to each other. Depending on the region, people will exchange two, three, or four **bises**.

jennifer waddell photography

photos © Cengage Learning

 ENTRE AMIS   **Permettez-moi de me présenter.**

1. Greet your partner.
2. Find out if s/he is French.
3. Give your name and tell where you live.
4. Can you say anything else? (Be sure to shake hands when you say goodbye.)

PRONONCIATION

L'ACCENT ET LE RYTHME

Track 1-8

► There is an enormous number of related words in English and French. We inherited most of these after the Norman Conquest, but many are recent borrowings. With respect to pronunciation, these are the words that tend to reveal an English accent the most quickly.

Compare:

Anglais	*Français*	*Anglais*	*Français*
CER-tain	cer-TAIN	MAR-tin	Mar-TIN
CER-tain-ly	cer-taine-MENT	A-MER-i-can	A-mé-ri-CAIN

► Even more important than mastering any particular sound is the development of correct habits in three areas of French intonation.

1. *Rhythm:* French words are spoken in groups, and each syllable but the last is said very evenly.
2. *Accent:* In each group of words, the last syllable is lengthened, thus making it the only accented syllable in the group.
3. *Syllable formation:* Spoken French syllables end in a vowel sound much more often than English ones do.

Counting is an excellent way to develop proper French rhythm and accent. Repeat after your instructor:

un DEUX	*un deux TROIS*	*un deux trois QUATRE*
mon-SIEUR	s'il vous PLAÎT	le té-lé-PHONE
mer-CI	cer-taine-MENT	A-sse-yez-VOUS
fran-ÇAIS	té-lé-PHONE	Mon-sieur Mar-TIN

LES CONSONNES FINALES

► A final (written) consonant is normally not pronounced in French.

Françoi~~s~~	permette~~z~~	s'il vou~~s~~ plaî~~t~~
George~~s~~	françai~~s~~	troi~~s~~
Il fai~~t~~ froi~~d~~	américai~~n~~	deu~~x~~

► There are some words whose final consonant is always pronounced (many words ending in **c, f, l,** or **r,** for instance).

Frédéri**c**	neu**f**	Miche**l**	bonjou**r**

► When a consonant is followed by **-e** within the same word, the consonant is always pronounced. A single **-s-** followed by **-e** is pronounced as [z]. Two **-ss-** followed by **-e** are pronounced [s].

Françai**s**e	Sui**ss**e	américai**n**e	j'habi**t**e	je m'appe**ll**e

These are the same as the consonants in the English word CaReFuL

► When a final silent consonant is followed by a word beginning with a vowel, it is often pronounced with the next word. This is called **liaison.**

vou~~s~~ *(silent)*	vou~~s~~ [z]êtes
deu~~x~~ *(silent)*	deu~~x~~ [z]hommes

Buts communicatifs

I. EXCHANGING PERSONAL INFORMATION

Track 1-9

Comment vous appelez-vous?°
Je m'appelle Nathalie Lachance.

Où habitez-vous?°
J'habite à Laval. J'habite près de° Montréal.

Êtes-vous célibataire?
Non, je suis mariée.

What is your name?

Where do you live?

near

*Learn all the words in each **But communicatif**.*

*Pronounce **appelle** [apɛl] and **appelez** [aple].*

Et vous, Monsieur (Madame, Mademoiselle)?

REMARQUE

1. **Je m'appelle** and **Comment vous appelez-vous?** should be memorized for now. Note that in **Comment vous appelez-vous?** there is only one **l**, while in **Je m'appelle,** there are two.
2. Use **J'habite à** to identify the city in which you live.
3. Use **J'habite près de** to identify the city you live *near*.
4. **M., Mme,** and **Mlle** are the abbreviations for **Monsieur, Madame,** and **Mademoiselle.**

I Les inscriptions (Registrations). You are working at a conference in Geneva. Greet the following people and find out their names and the city where they live. Your partner will provide the answers.

MODÈLE: M. Robert Perrin (Lyon)
—**Bonjour, Monsieur. Comment vous appelez-vous?**
—**Je m'appelle Perrin, Robert Perrin.**
—**Où habitez-vous?**
—**J'habite à Lyon.**

1. Mlle Marie Dupont (Metz)
2. Mme Anne Vermette (Montréal)
3. M. Joseph Guy (Lausanne)
4. Mlle Jeanne Delon (Paris)
5. le professeur de français
6. le président français
7. le président américain
8. le premier ministre canadien

A. Les pronoms sujets

See App. C, Glossary of Grammatical Terms, for an explanation of any terms with which you are not familiar.

► The subject pronouns in French are:

Singular forms		Plural forms	
je (j')	*I*	nous	*we*
tu	*you*		
vous	*you*	vous	*you*
il	*he; it*	ils	*they*
elle	*she; it*	elles	*they*
on	*one; someone; people; we*		

► Before a vowel sound at the beginning of the next word, **je** becomes **j'**. This happens with words that begin with a vowel, but also with most words that begin with **h-,** which is silent.

J'adore Québec, mais j'habite à New York.

► **Tu** is informal. It is used to address one person with whom you have a close relationship. **Vous** is the singular form used in other cases. To address more than one person, one always uses **vous.**

Tu es à Paris, Michel?

Vous êtes à Lyon, Monsieur?

Marie! Paul! **Vous** êtes à Bordeaux?

NOTE Whether **vous** is singular or plural, the verb form is always plural.

▶ There are two genders in French: masculine and feminine. All nouns have gender, whether they designate people or things. **Il** stands for a masculine person or thing, **elle** for a feminine person or thing. The plural **ils** stands for a group of masculine persons or things, and **elles** stands for a group of feminine persons or things.

le tableau = **il**   les téléphones = **ils**

la porte = **elle**   les tables = **elles**

▶ For a group that includes both masculine and feminine nouns **(Nathalie, Karine, Paul et Marie), ils** is used, even if only one of the nouns is masculine.

Karine et Éric? **Ils** sont à Marseille.

▶ **On** is a subject pronoun used to express generalities or unknowns, much as do the English forms *one, someone, you, people.* In informal situations, **on** is often used to mean *we.*

On est à San Francisco.   *We are in San Francisco.*

On est riche en Amérique?   *Are people in America rich?*

B. Le verbe être

Grammar
Tutorial

Il est à Québec.
Je suis à Strasbourg.
Nous sommes à Besançon.

▶ The most frequently used verb in French is **être** *(to be).*

je	**suis**	*I am*	nous	**sommes**	*we are*
tu	**es**	*you are*	vous	**êtes**	*you are*
il	**est**	*he is; it is*	ils	**sont**	*they are (m. or m. + f.)*
elle	**est**	*she is; it is*	elles	**sont**	*they are (f.)*
on	**est**	*one is; people are; we are*			

Review the use of **liaison** *on p. 13.*

▶ Before a vowel sound at the beginning of the next word, the silent final consonant of many words (but not all!) is pronounced and is spoken with the next word. This is called **liaison. Liaison** is necessary between a pronoun and a verb.

Vous [z]êtes à Montréal.   On [n]est où?

▶ Liaison is possible after all forms of **être,** but is common *only* with **est** and **sont.**

Il est [t]à Paris.   Elles sont [t]à Marseille.

2 **Où sont-ils?** *(Where are they?)* Identify the cities where the following people are. Use a subject pronoun in your answer.

MODÈLES: tu (Los Angeles) **Tu es à Los Angeles.**
vous (Québec) **Vous êtes à Québec.**

1. Lori (Boston)
2. Lise et Elsa (Bruxelles)
3. Thierry (Monte Carlo)
4. je (...)
5. Pierre et Anne (Angers)
6. nous (...)
7. Sylvie (Paris)

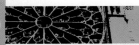

Réalités culturelles
Paris

Mikhail Zahranichny/Shutterstock.com

PARIS, the "city of lights," has long been a crossroads of ideas, trade, and scientific discovery. France's capital is also one of the world's most popular tourist destinations, home to well over 100 museums, including the world-renowned art museums of the **Louvre,** the **Musée d'Orsay,** and the **Centre Georges-Pompidou,** as well as famous monuments and churches like the **Tour Eiffel** and **Notre-Dame.**

Paris offers an amazing array of things to see and do. There are large public squares, such as the **Place Beaubourg,** where singers, jugglers, dancers, and mimes entertain audiences; large avenues, such as the **Champs-Élysées** and the **Boulevard Saint Michel,** where shops, theaters, and cafés keep people strolling through the night; open-air markets, where Parisians buy flowers, fresh vegetables, meat, and cheese; and extensively landscaped parks, such as the **Jardin du Luxembourg,** where people of all ages can escape from the hectic pace of city life or surf the Internet using the free wifi access available in many of Paris's parks. To get around, visitors need only access the city's efficient public transportation system, consisting of city buses, the **métro** (the second oldest subway system in the world, inaugurated in 1900), tramway, and bicycles. The latter is part of a commitment to make Paris a "greener" city. The **Vélib'** program offers thousands of bicycles for short-term rental in stations across the city.

C. L'accord des adjectifs

Grammar Tutorial

► Most adjectives have two pronunciations: one when they refer to a feminine noun and one when they refer to a masculine noun. From an oral point of view, it is usually better to learn the feminine form first. The masculine pronunciation can often be found by dropping the last consonant *sound* of the feminine.

Review Prononciation, p. 4.

Barbara est **américaine.**   Bob est **américain** aussi.
Christine est **française.**   David est **français** aussi.

► Almost all adjectives change their spelling depending on whether the nouns they refer to are masculine or feminine, singular or plural. These spelling changes may or may not affect pronunciation.

Il est américain.   Elle est américaine.
Ils sont américains.   Elles sont américaines.

Il est marié.   Elle est mariée.
Ils sont mariés.   Elles sont mariées.

► The feminine adjective often ends in a written **-e.** A number of masculine adjectives end in **-e** also. In this case, masculine and feminine forms are identical in pronunciation and spelling.

célibataire   fantastique   optimiste

► The plural is usually formed by adding a written **-s** to the singular. However, since the final **-s** of the plural is silent, the singular and the plural are pronounced in the same way.

américain   américains
américaine   américaines

NOTE

If the masculine singular ends in **-s,** the masculine plural is identical.

un homme français   deux hommes français

► Adjectives that describe a group of both masculine and feminine nouns take the masculine plural form.

Bill et Judy sont **mariés.**

Vocabulaire

L'état civil *(marital status)*

Femmes	Hommes	Women/men
célibataire(s)	célibataire(s)	single
mariée(s)	marié(s)	married
fiancée(s)	fiancé(s)	engaged
divorcée(s)	divorcé(s)	divorced
veuve(s)	veuf(s)	widowed

With the exception of **veuve(s) [vœv]** *and* **veuf(s) [vœf],** *the spelling changes in the adjectives listed in* **Vocabulaire** *do not affect pronunciation.*

❸ Quelle coïncidence! *(What a coincidence!)* State that the marital status of the second person or group is the same as that of the first.

MODÈLES: Léa est fiancée. Et Marc?   Pierre est marié. Et Zoé et Max?
          Il est fiancé aussi.   **Ils sont mariés aussi.**

1. Élise et Paul sont fiancés. Et Marie?
2. Nous sommes mariés. Et Monique?
3. Nicolas est divorcé. Et Sophie et Thérèse?
4. Je suis célibataire. Et Georges et Sylvie?
5. Madame Beaufort est veuve. Et Monsieur Dupont?

4 **Qui est-ce?** *(Who is it?)* Answer the following questions. Try to identify real people or famous fictional characters. Can you name more than one person? Make sure that the verbs and adjectives agree with the subjects.

MODÈLE: Qui est fiancé?
Olive Oyl est fiancée. ou
Olive Oyl et Popeye sont fiancés.

1. Qui est célibataire?
2. Qui est fiancé?
3. Qui est marié?
4. Qui est divorcé?
5. Qui est veuf?
6. Qui est français?
7. Qui est américain?

5 **Carte de débarquement** *(Arrival form).* When you travel overseas you are sometimes given an arrival form to fill out. Identify yourself by providing the information requested in the form below in French.

Carte de débarquement

Nom de famille: _____

Prénom(s): _____

Sexe: ❑ M ❑ F

Âge: _____ ans

Nationalité: _____

État civil: _____

Adresse: _____

_____

Code postal: _____

Numéro de passeport: _____

Motif du voyage: ❑ touristique ❑ professionnel
❑ transit ❑ visite privée

ENTRE AMIS **Dans un avion** *(In an airplane)*

Complete the following interaction with as many members of the class as possible.

1. Greet your neighbor in a culturally appropriate way.
2. Find out if s/he is French.
3. Find out each other's name.
4. Find out the city in which s/he lives.
5. What else can you say?

2. IDENTIFYING NATIONALITY

Track 1-10

Quelle est votre nationalité?°
  Moi, je suis canadienne.

What is your nationality?

Remember to learn all the words in each **But communicatif.**

Et vous? Vous êtes chinois(e)°?
  Pas du tout!° Je suis ...

Chinese

Not at all!

	Féminin	**Masculin**	
GB	anglaise	anglais	*English* ✶
F	française	français	*French* ✶
J	japonaise	japonais	*Japanese*
SN	sénégalaise	sénégalais	*Senegalese*
USA	américaine	américain	*American* ✶
MA	marocaine	marocain	*Moroccan*
MEX	mexicaine	mexicain	*Mexican*
CDN	canadienne	canadien	*Canadian*
I	italienne	italien	*Italian*
S	suédoise	suédois	*Swedish*
D	allemande	allemand	*German*
E	espagnole	espagnol	*Spanish*
B	belge	belge	*Belgian*
CH	suisse	suisse	*Swiss*
RUS	russe	russe	*Russian*

Remember to pronounce the final consonant in the feminine (see p. 4).

Ces amis habitent à Paris. Rachida est marocaine, Pierre est français et Amadou est sénégalais.

REMARQUE

In written French, some feminine adjectives are distinguishable from their masculine form not only by a final **-e**, but also by a doubled final consonant.

un homme canadien   *a Canadian man*
une femme canadie**nne**   *a Canadian woman*

6 **Quelle est votre nationalité?** A duty-free store at the airport is surveying customers to find out their nationalities. With a partner, take turns playing the role of the surveyor and the customers interviewed.

MODÈLES: Madame Jones et Mademoiselle Jones (GB)
  —Quelle est votre nationalité?   **—Nous sommes anglaises.**
  Maria Gomez (MEX)
  —Quelle est votre nationalité?   **—Je suis mexicaine.**

1. Jean-François (CDN)
2. Monsieur et Madame Smith (USA)
3. Mademoiselle Nakasone (J)
4. Madame et Mademoiselle Colon (E)
5. Mademoiselle Balke (D)
6. Bruno (SN)
7. Madame Volaro (I)
8. Marie-Christine (F)

7 **Qui êtes-vous?** *(Who are you?)* Assume the identity of each person below. Give your name, nationality, and the city you are from.

MODÈLE: Mademoiselle Brigitte Lapointe/Paris (F)
Je m'appelle Brigitte et je suis française. J'habite à Paris.

1. Monsieur Pierre La Vigne/Québec (CDN)
2. Madame Margaret Jones/Manchester (GB)
3. Madame Anne Martin/Angers (F)
4. Monsieur Yasuhiro Saya/Tokyo (J)
5. Madame Mary O'Leary/Boston (USA)
6. Monsieur Ahmed Zoubir/Casablanca (MA)
7. vous

Cultural Activities

Réalités culturelles
L'Organisation internationale de la francophonie

FRENCH is spoken by over 220 million people around the globe. In 1970, several French-speaking countries created the **Agence de la francophonie** *(Agency for French-speaking communities)*, now called **L'Organisation internationale de la francophonie (OIF)**. The word **francophonie** was coined in 1880 by geographer Onésime Reclus to describe the areas of the world where French is spoken by much of the population. The **OIF's** chief purpose is to use the French language in the service of peace and to promote cultural and economic cooperation among French-speaking countries. Today, the **OIF**, which consists of 75 states and governments, focuses on promoting the French language and cultural diversity; promoting peace, democracy, and human rights; supporting education, training, and research; and fostering sustainable development. It sponsors a French-language television station, **TV5,** and has created a French-speaking university, **l'université Senghor,** in Alexandria, Egypt. To find out more about **L'Organisation internationale de la francophonie** and its members, visit www.francophonie.org.

L'Organisation internationale de la Francophonie

Grammar
Tutorial

James Davidson **n'**est **pas** français. Il est américain. Il **n'**habite **pas** à Paris. Il habite à San Francisco.

▶ Two words, **ne** and **pas,** are used to make a sentence negative: **ne** precedes the conjugated verb and **pas** follows it.

Guy et Zoé **ne** sont **pas** mariés.	*Guy and Zoé aren't married.*
Il **ne** fait **pas** très beau.	*It's not very nice out.*

▶ Remember that both **ne** and **pas** are necessary in standard French to make a sentence negative.

ne + conjugated verb + **pas**

▶ **Ne** becomes **n'** before a vowel sound.

Je **n'**habite **pas** à Paris.	*I don't live in Paris.*
Nathalie **n'**est **pas** française.	*Nathalie is not French.*

8 Ils sont français? Ask your partner whether the following people are French. Choose the correct form of **être** and make sure that the adjective agrees. Your partner will first respond with a negative, and then state the correct information.

MODÈLE: —**Elles sont françaises?**
—**Non, elles ne sont pas françaises.**
  Elles sont anglaises.

1.   2.    3.   4.

5.    6.   7.   8.

ENTRE AMIS   **Je ne suis pas suisse.**

Pick a nationality from the list on page 19, but don't tell your partner which one you have chosen.

1. Your partner will try to guess your new nationality by asking you: **Vous êtes ...** [+ a nationality]**?**
2. Respond **"Pas du tout! Je ne suis pas ..."** if the guess is incorrect.
3. Continue until your partner has guessed your nationality, then switch roles.

*Learn all the words in each **But communicatif**.*

*Try to use **assez** and, in the case of a negative, **pas très** to avoid being overly categorical when describing people.*

Voilà° Christine.
Elle est jeune°.
Elle est assez grande°.
Elle n'est pas grosse°.
Elle est assez jolie°.

Voilà le Père Noël.
Il est assez° vieux°.
Il est assez petit°.
Il n'est pas très° mince°.

There is; Here is
young / rather / old
tall / short; small
fat / very / thin
pretty

🌀 **Et vous?** Vous êtes …

jeune	*ou*	vieux (vieille)?
petit(e)	*ou*	grand(e)?
gros(se)	*ou*	mince?
beau (belle)	*ou*	laid(e)?°

Décrivez votre meilleur(e) ami(e).°

attractive or ugly?
Describe your best friend.

Il y a un geste

Assez *(sort of, rather; enough).* The gesture for **assez** is an open hand rotated back and forth (palm down).

© Cengage Learning

E. L'accord des adjectifs (suite)

🌐 Grammar Tutorial

- The masculine forms of some adjectives are not like their feminine forms in either pronunciation or spelling, and so they must be memorized.

  belle **beau** vieille **vieux**

- The masculine plural of some adjectives is formed by adding **-x**. Pronunciation of the plural form remains the same as the singular.

  Robert et Paul sont très **beaux**.

*Some nouns form the plural in the same way: **le tableau, les tableaux.***

- Masculine singular adjectives that end in **-s** or **-x** keep the same form (and pronunciation) for the masculine plural.

  Bill est **gros**. Roseanne et John sont **gros** aussi.
  Je suis **vieux**. Georges et Robert sont très **vieux**.

Synthèse: l'accord des adjectifs

	FÉMININ		MASCULIN	
SINGULIER	PLURIEL		SINGULIER	PLURIEL
petite	petites		petit	petits
grande	grandes		grand	grands
jolie	jolies		joli	jolis
belle	belles		beau	beaux
laide	laides		laid	laids
jeune	jeunes		jeune	jeunes
vieille	vieilles		vieux	vieux
mince	minces		mince	minces
grosse	grosses		gros	gros

(handwritten margin notes: short, pretty, beautiful, ugly, young, thin, fat, same)

9 Oui, il n'est pas très grand. The French often tone down what they wish to say by using the opposite adjective and the word **très** in a negative sentence Use the opposite in a negative sentence to agree with the following descriptions.

MODÈLE: Tom Cruise est petit.
> **Oui, il n'est pas très grand.**

1. Abraham et Sarah sont vieux.
2. Marie-Christine est mince.
3. Frankenstein est laid.
4. Alissa est petite.
5. Dumbo l'éléphant est gros.
6. L'oncle Sam est vieux.
7. James et Lori sont jeunes.
8. Karine et Alix sont jolies.

10 Décrivez ... Describe the following people. If you don't know what they look like, guess. Pay close attention to adjective agreement.

MODÈLE: Décrivez James Davidson. **Il est grand, jeune et assez beau.**

1. Décrivez votre meilleur(e) ami(e).
2. Décrivez votre professeur de français.
3. Décrivez une actrice.
4. Décrivez un acteur.
5. Décrivez Minnie Mouse et Daisy Duck.
6. Décrivez le (la) président(e) des États-Unis.
7. Décrivez-vous.

ENTRE AMIS — Une personne célèbre

1. Choose a famous person and describe him/her.
2. If your partner agrees with each description s/he will say so.
3. If your partner disagrees, s/he will correct you.

iLrn
Self Test

Intégration

RÉVISION

A **Il y a plus d'une façon** *(There's more than one way).*

1. Give two ways to break the ice in French.
2. Give two ways to find out someone's name.
3. Give two ways to find out where someone lives.
4. Give two ways to find out someone's nationality.

B **L'inspecteur Clouseau.** A bumbling inspector is asking all the wrong questions. Correct him, using subject pronouns. Invent the correct answer if you wish.

MODÈLES: Vous êtes Madame Perrin?
Non, pas du tout, je ne suis pas Madame Perrin. Je suis Mademoiselle Smith.

Madame Perrin est française?
Non, pas du tout, elle n'est pas française. Elle est canadienne.

> Notice that #1 & 2 are plural. Use **nous** in your answer.

1. Vous êtes Monsieur et Madame Martin?
2. Vous *(pl.)* êtes belges?
3. Madame Martin est veuve?
4. Monsieur et Madame Martin sont divorcés?
5. James et Lori sont mariés?
6. Lori est italienne?
7. James est français?

C **À l'écoute.** Choose the image that corresponds to each of the following introductions you hear.

Track 1-12

a. hfng/iStockphoto.com   b. ©Travelshots.com/Alamy   c. ©itanistock/Alamy   d. Science Photo Library

D **À vous.** How would you respond to the following?

1. Bonjour, Monsieur (Madame, Mademoiselle).
2. Excusez-moi de vous déranger.
3. Vous êtes Monsieur (Madame, Mademoiselle) Dupont?
4. Comment vous appelez-vous?
5. Vous n'êtes pas français(e)?
6. Quelle est votre nationalité?
7. Vous habitez près d'Angers?
8. Où habitez-vous?
9. Vous êtes marié(e)?
10. Bonne journée!

Communication and Communities. To learn more about the culture presented in this chapter, go to the Premium Website and click on the Web Search Activities.

NÉGOCIATIONS

Identifications. Work with your partner to prepare a new identity. First, decide with your partner whether you are describing a man or a woman. Then, complete the first half of the following form; your partner will complete the second half, using the form in Appendix D. Each of you will ask questions in French to complete the form.

MODÈLE: **Comment vous appelez-vous? Quel est votre nom de famille?**
Êtes-vous français(e)? Êtes-vous jeune?

A
Nom de famille: _____
Prénom: _____
Nationalité: _____

B
État civil: _____
Description 1: _____
_____
Description 2: _____
_____

LECTURE

LA MÉTHODO The reading below consists of two profile pages from a social networking website. It is not vital that you understand every word in order to grasp the general meaning of what you read. The context and cognates, words in French and English with similar meanings that have the same or nearly identical spelling, will help you guess the meaning.

A Le contexte. You can often predict the information a text will contain if you know what you are about to read before you begin. Making these predictions will improve your comprehension. List all the types of information you expect to find in an individual's profile on a social networking site.

B Trouvez les mots apparentés (cognates). Scan the two profiles that follow and find at least fifteen cognates.

PROFILS D'UN RÉSEAU SOCIAL

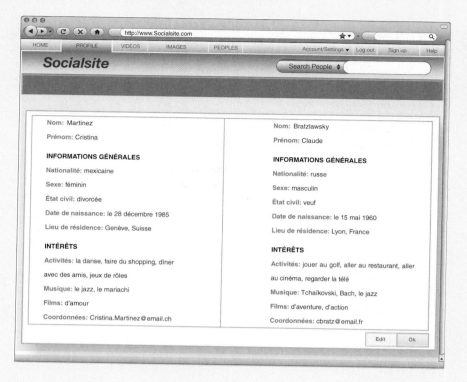

C **Les profils.** Read the above **profils** and answer the following questions.

1. What is the name and gender of each person?
2. Where are these two people from?
3. Where do they live now?
4. Who is older?
5. What is their marital status?
6. Do they share any common interests? If so, what?

D **Dans ces contextes (In these contexts).** Study context and cognates in the profiles above to help you guess the meaning of the following expressions.

1. date de naissance
2. lieu
3. faire du shopping
4. coordonnées
5. jouer
6. aller
7. regarder la télé
8. jeux de rôles

E **À vous.** With a partner, role-play a conversation between the two people from the reading in which you "break the ice" and find out a little bit about each other.

RÉDACTION

DES PORTRAITS

Write two brief descriptions: one of your best friend and one of a famous actor or actress. Include the following in each of your descriptions:

- who the person is (full name, profession or relationship)
- physical description
- marital status
- nationality

MODÈLE: **James Davidson est mon meilleur ami. Il est grand, jeune et assez beau. Il est aussi célibataire. Il est américain.**

A **Avant d'écrire.** Take a look at the list of **Vocabulaire actif** at the end of this chapter. Note the words and expressions that will be useful in writing descriptions. Next, go back and review the structures that will help you form sentences (subject pronouns, the verb **être**, and adjective agreement).

B **Écrire.** Review your notes from Activity A. Stick with these words and structures as you write.

C **Correction.** Exchange papers with a partner for proofreading. Check carefully for errors in spelling and agreement. Revise your descriptions based on your partner's feedback.

Vocabulaire Actif

Pour identifier les personnes Noms

un acteur / une actrice *actor / actress*
un(e) étudiant(e) *student*
une femme *woman*
un homme *man*
un(e) meilleur(e) ami(e) *best friend*
le Père Noël *Santa Claus*
une personne *person (male or female)*
un professeur *teacher (male or female)*
la nationalité *nationality*
un nom *name*
un nom de famille *family name*
un prénom *first name*

Description physique

beau (belle) *handsome (beautiful)*
grand(e) *big; tall*
gros(se) *fat; large*
jeune *young*
joli(e) *pretty*
laid(e) *ugly*
mince *thin*
petit(e) *small; short*
vieux (vieille) *old*

D'autres noms

un hôtel *hotel*
une porte *door*
un restaurant *restaurant*
une table *table*
un tableau *chalkboard*
un téléphone *telephone*
une université *university*

Prépositions

à *at; in; to*
de *from; of*
en *in*
près de *near*

Adjectifs de nationalité

allemand(e) *German*
américain(e) *American*
anglais(e) *English*
belge *Belgian*

canadien(ne) *Canadian*
chinois(e) *Chinese*
espagnol(e) *Spanish*
français(e) *French*
italien(ne) *Italian*
japonais(e) *Japanese*
marocain(e) *Moroccan*
mexicain(e) *Mexican*
russe *Russian*
sénégalais(e) *Senegalese*
suédois(e) *Swedish*
suisse *Swiss*

Pronoms sujets

je *I*
tu *you*
il *he, it*
elle *she, it*
on *one, people, we, they*
nous *we*
vous *you*
ils *they*
elles *they*

État civil

célibataire *single*
divorcé(e) *divorced*
fiancé(e) *engaged*
marié(e) *married*
veuf (veuve) *widowed*

Nombres

un *one*
deux *two*
trois *three*
quatre *four*

À propos de l'identité

Comment vous appelez-vous? *What is your name?*
Je m'appelle … *My name is …*
Madame (Mme) *Mrs.*
Mademoiselle (Mlle) *Miss*
Monsieur (M.) *Mr.; sir*
Permettez-moi de me présenter. *Allow me to introduce myself.*

Quelle est votre nationalité? *What is your nationality?*
Vous habitez … *You live, you reside …*
Où habitez-vous? *Where do you live?*
J'habite … *I live, I reside …*

La politesse

Au revoir. *Goodbye.*
Bonjour. *Hello.*
Bonne journée. *Have a good day.*
Enchanté(e). *Delighted (to meet you).*
Excusez-moi. *Excuse me.*
Excusez-moi de vous déranger. *Excuse me for bothering you.*
Je vous demande pardon … *I beg your pardon …*
Merci. Vous aussi. *Thanks. You too.*
Merci. De même. *Thanks. You too.*
Pardon. *Pardon me.*
Salut! *Hi!; Bye!*
S'il vous plaît. *Please.*
Vous permettez? *May I?*

Verbe

être *to be*

Adverbes

assez *sort of, rather; enough*
aussi *also, too*
certainement *surely, of course*
là *there; here*
ne … pas *not*
où *where*
très *very*

D'autres expressions utiles

Asseyez-vous. *Sit down.*
C'est … *It is …; This is …*
entre amis *between friends*
Et moi? *And me?*
Oui ou non? *Yes or no?*
Pas du tout! *Not at all!*
qui *who*
Voilà … *There is (are) …; Here is (are) …*

Qu'est-ce que vous aimez?

© David W. Hamilton/Alamy

BUTS COMMUNICATIFS
- Asking and responding to "How are you?"
- Giving and responding to compliments
- Offering, accepting, and refusing
- Expressing likes and dislikes

STRUCTURES UTILES
- Le verbe **aller**
- Les verbes en **-er**
- L'article défini: **le, la, l'** et **les**
- Les questions avec réponse **oui** ou **non**

CULTURE

Zoom sur les rencontres
- **Vidéo buzz:** Les rencontres entre amis et collègues
- **Vu sur le web:** Le kir
- **Repères:** Les rencontres amicales sur Internet
- **Insolite:** Dire *merci*
- **Article:** Les compliments

Il y a un geste
- À votre santé
- Non, merci
- Ça va

Lecture
- Votre signe du zodiaque et votre personnalité

RESOURCES

Audio

iLrn Heinle Learning Center

Premium Website

Pair Work

Group Work

Entre amis Video Program

Coup d'envoi

le café?

le coca?

le vin?

le thé?

Est-ce que is often placed at the start of a sentence to make it a question.

Est-ce que vous aimez ...°	*Do you like ...*
J'aime° le coca.	*I like (love)*
J'aime beaucoup° le thé.	*very much; a lot*
Je n'aime pas le café.	
Voulez-vous boire quelque chose?°	*Do you want something to drink?*
Non, merci.	*No thanks*
Oui, je veux bien.°	*Gladly; Yes, thanks.*
Je voudrais ...°	*I'd like ...*
une tasse de° café.	*a cup of*
une tasse de thé.	
un verre de° coca.	*a glass of*
un verre de vin.	

🕐 **Et vous?** Voulez-vous boire quelque chose?

Qu'est-ce que vous voulez?° — *What do you want?*

James Davidson étudie le français à Toulouse. Mais il vient de° San Francisco. Au cours d'une soirée°, il aperçoit° Karine Aspel, qui est assistante au laboratoire de langues.

he comes from / During a party / notices

James:	Bonsoir°. Quelle° bonne surprise! Comment allez-vous?°	*Good evening. / What a / How are you?*
Karine:	Ça va bien°, merci. Et vous-même?°	*Fine / And yourself?*
James:	Très bien ... Votre prénom, c'est Karine, n'est-ce pas?°	*isn't it?*
Karine:	Oui, je m'appelle Karine Aspel.	
James:	Et moi, James Davidson.	
Karine:	Est-ce que vous êtes américain? Votre français est excellent.	
James:	Merci beaucoup.	
Karine:	Mais c'est vrai!° Vous êtes d'où?°	*But it's true! / Where are you from?*
James:	Je viens de° San Francisco. Au fait°, voulez-vous boire quelque chose? Un coca?	*I come from / By the way*
Karine:	Non, merci, je n'aime pas beaucoup le coca.	
James:	Alors°, un kir, peut-être°?	*Then / perhaps*
Karine:	Je veux bien. Un petit kir, pourquoi pas°? *(James hands a glass of kir to Karine.)*	*why not*
James:	À votre santé°, Karine.	*To your health*
Karine:	À la vôtre°. Et merci, James.	*To yours*

Listen carefully to your instructor and/or the Audio while the conversation is presented. As soon as the presentation has ended, try to recall as many words as you can.

👥 ⓒ **Jouez ces rôles.** Role-play the above conversation with a partner. Use your own identities. Choose something else to drink.

Jennifer Waddell Photography

© Cengage Learning

Il y a un geste

À votre santé. The glass is raised when saying *To your health*. Among friends, the glasses are lightly touched and they look into each other's eyes.

Non, merci. The French often raise the index finger and move it from side to side to indicate *no*. They also may indicate *no* by raising a hand, palm outward, or by shaking their heads as do English speakers. In France, however, the lips are usually well rounded and often are pursed when making these gestures.

Zoom sur les rencontres

Premium Website

PETIT TEST

Why does Karine say *Mais c'est vrai!* when James says *Merci beaucoup?*

   a. She misunderstood what he said.

   b. She doesn't mean what she said.

   c. She feels that James doesn't really believe her when she tells him his French is good.

Read *Les compliments* to find out why.

Les compliments

THE FRENCH, like anyone else, enjoy receiving compliments. However, they may respond by playing it down, which could encourage more of the same. While Americans are taught from an early age to accept and say *thank you* to compliments, **merci,** when used in response to a compliment, is often perceived by the French as saying "you don't mean it." It is for this reason that Karine Aspel responds **Mais c'est vrai!,** insisting that her compliment was true. It is culturally more accurate, therefore, and linguistically enjoyable, to develop a few rejoinders such as **Oh, vraiment?** *(Really?),* **C'est gentil** *(That's kind),* or **Vous trouvez?** *(Do you think so?),* which one can employ in similar situations. In this case, a really French response on James's part might be **Mais non! Je ne parle pas vraiment bien. Mon accent n'est pas très bon.** *(Oh, no! I don't speak really well. My accent's not very good.)*

VU SUR LE WEB

Le kir

KIR is an **apéritif** *(before-dinner drink)* people often drink when they get together in France. Taking its name from **le Chanoine Kir,** a French priest and former mayor of Dijon, **kir** is made from four parts white wine and one part black currant liqueur. Two popular variations of **kir** are **kir royal,** made with champagne or sparkling wine, and **kir breton,** made with hard cider, a specialty of the Brittany region. To find out more about popular **apéritifs** in France and how to make them, click on the links found on the *Premium Website.*

© Owen Franken/Corbis

Les rencontres entre amis et collègues

A FAVORITE social activity among the French is to get together with friends at someone's home. Having people over or going to someone's house for dinner, an evening of board games, or to watch a movie is a weekly event for some people. More formal gatherings, such as **un cocktail** (*a cocktail party*) or **une soirée** (*a party*), provide opportunities to gather with work colleagues or other people in the extended community where one lives. Go to the *Premium Website* to watch videos showing how people interact with one another at these types of social gatherings.

© Xavier Arnau/iStockphoto.com

Dire *merci*

THE WORD **merci** is, of course, one of the best ways of conveying politeness, and its use is, by all means, to be encouraged. Its usage, however, differs from that of English in at least one important way: when one is offered something to eat, to drink, etc., the response **merci** is somewhat ambiguous and is often a way of saying *no, thank you.* One would generally say **je veux bien** or **s'il vous plaît** to convey the meaning *yes, thanks.* **Merci** is, however, the proper polite response once the food, the drink, etc., has actually been served.

Les rencontres amicales sur Internet

More and more people are turning to the Internet to meet people, as evidenced by the Parisian website "Just2meet". Read the following introduction to their website.

Faire une rencontre à Paris, une rencontre amicale[1], amoureuse[2] ou business avec **Just2meet.**

Just2meet: *[le] site de toutes les rencontres propose des lieux[3] exclusifs sur le net pour chatter et se rencontrer à Paris. Si vous êtes prêt[4] à rencontrer l'âme sœur[5], partager[6] des passions, élargir[7] votre cercle amical ou votre réseau[8] business à Paris, alors 'sortez sur le net' sur* **Just2meet**, *dans nos lieux de chat pour des rencontres à Paris 'made in Paris'.*

[1]*for friendship;* [2]*for love;* [3]*places;* [4]*ready;* [5]*soulmate;* [6]*to share;* [7]*enlarge;* [8]*network*

© Just2Meet: la cité des rencontres. Used with permission.

À **vous.** How would you respond to the following questions?

1. Comment allez-vous?
2. Est-ce que vous êtes français(e)?
3. Votre prénom, c'est ... ?
4. Vous êtes d'où?
5. Voulez-vous boire quelque chose?

ENTRE AMIS **À une soirée** *(At a party)*

Role-play the following conversation with a partner.

1. Greet another "invited guest."
2. Find out his/her name.
3. Find out his/her nationality.
4. Find out where s/he comes from.
5. What else can you say?

PRONONCIATION

 L'ALPHABET FRANÇAIS (SUITE)

Track 1-15

▶ English and French share the same 26-letter Latin alphabet and, although this is useful, it is also potentially troublesome.

▶ First, French and English cognates may not be spelled the same. French spellings must, therefore, be memorized.

adresse   personne   appartement

▶ Second, because the alphabet is the same, it is tempting to pronounce French words as if they were English. Be very careful, especially when pronouncing cognates, not to transfer English pronunciation to the French words.

téléphone   conversation   professeur

▶ Knowing how to say the French alphabet is not only important in spelling out loud, it is also essential when saying the many acronyms used in the French language.

le TGV   les USA   la SNCF

Quelques sigles. Read out loud the letters that make up the following acronyms.

1. **SVP**   S'il vous plaît
2. **RSVP**   Répondez, s'il vous plaît.
3. **La SNCF**   La Société nationale des chemins de fer français *(French railroad system)*
4. **La RATP**   La Régie autonome des transports parisiens *(Paris subway and bus system)*
5. **Les BD**   Les bandes dessinées *(comic strips)*
6. **Les USA**   Les United States of America (= Les États-Unis)
7. **La BNP**   La Banque nationale de Paris
8. **La CGT**   La Confédération générale du travail *(a French labor union)*
9. **BCBG**   Bon chic bon genre *(preppy)*
10. **Le RER**   Le Réseau Express Régional *(a train to the suburbs)*

LES ACCENTS

► French accents are part of spelling and must be learned. They can serve:

1. to indicate how a word is pronounced

   ç → [s]: français

   é → [e]: marié

   è → [ɛ]: très

   ê → [ɛ]: être

   ë → [ɛ]: Noël

2. or to distinguish between meanings

   ou *or* la *the (feminine)*

   où *where* là *there*

French names	Examples
´ **accent aigu**	américain; téléphone
` **accent grave**	à; très; où
^ **accent circonflexe**	âge; êtes; s'il vous plaît; hôtel; sûr
¨ **tréma**	Noël; coïncidence
¸ **cédille**	français
- **trait d'union**	Jean-Luc
' **apostrophe**	J'aime

Crème s'écrit C-R-E accent grave-M-E.

  Comment est-ce qu'on écrit ... ? Your partner will ask you to spell the words below. Give the correct spelling.

MODÈLE: être

  VOTRE PARTENAIRE: **Comment est-ce qu'on écrit «être»?**

  VOUS: *«Être» s'écrit E accent circonflexe-T-R-E.*

1. français
2. monsieur
3. belge
4. mademoiselle
5. professeur
6. vieux
7. hôtel
8. très
9. téléphone
10. j'habite
11. canadienne
12. asseyez-vous

Réalités culturelles

Cultural Activitie

TOULOUSE, LOCATED at the heart of southern France, is the capital of the country's largest region, the Midi-Pyrénées. Founded over 2,000 years ago by the Celts, Toulouse has long stood at a crossroads for European trade. It straddles the Garonne River and three canals come together there linking the Atlantic with the Mediterranean. The Canal du Midi, constructed in the seventeenth century, is the oldest canal still in operation in Europe. Today **La Ville Rose,** so-called because of the Roman brick from which many of its buildings are constructed, is home to some 89,000 students (making Toulouse France's third largest university town) and the country's aeronautical industry. Begun shortly after World War I with the establishment of the **Aéropostale** airmail service, it was built up by such important aviators as Antoine de Saint-Exupéry, who penned *Le Petit Prince.* It is in Toulouse that the first Concorde, Airbus, and giant A380 airplanes were produced.

Mikhail Plichard/iStockphoto.com

To learn more about Toulouse, consult http://www.toulouse-tourisme.com.

Buts communicatifs

Track 1-16

I. ASKING AND RESPONDING TO "HOW ARE YOU?"

Learn all the words in each But communicatif.

Salutations et questions

more formal	Bonjour, Madame (Monsieur, Mademoiselle). Comment allez-vous? Vous allez bien?
first-name basis	Salut, Lori (James, etc.). Comment ça va?° *How's it going?* Ça va?

Réponses

Je vais très bien°, merci.	*Very well, thanks.*
Ça va bien.	*I'm fine*
Pas mal.°	*Not bad.*
Oh! Comme ci, comme ça.°	*So-so.*
Oh! Pas trop bien.°	*Not too great.*
Je suis assez fatigué(e).°	*I'm rather tired.*
Je suis un peu malade.°	*I'm a little sick.*

 Et vous? Comment allez-vous?

1. It is very important to try to tailor your language to fit the situation. For example, with a friend or another student, you would normally ask **Ça va?** or **Comment ça va?** For someone whom you address as **Monsieur, Madame,** or **Mademoiselle,** you would normally say **Comment allez-vous?**

2. **Bonjour** and **bonsoir** are used for both formal (**Monsieur, Madame,** etc.) and first name relationships.

3. The family name (**le nom de famille**) is not used in a greeting. For example, when saying hello to Madame Martin, one says **Bonjour, Madame.**

4. **Salut** is used only in first-name relationships.

© Cengage Learning

Il y a un geste

Ça va. This gesture implies "so-so" and is very similar to **assez.** Open one or both hands, palms down, and slightly rotate them. This is often accompanied by a slight shrug, and the lips are pursed. One may also say **comme ci, comme ça.**

Vocabulaire

À quel moment de la journée? *(At what time of day?)*

à ... heure(s)	*at... o'clock*	l'après-midi	*afternoon, in the afternoon*
le jour	*day, daytime*	le soir	*evening, in the evening*
le matin	*morning, in the morning*	la nuit	*night, at night*

① Attention au style. Greet the following people at the indicated time of day and find out how they are. Adapt your choice of words to fit the time and the person being greeted. Be careful not to be overly familiar. If there is more than one response possible, give both.

MODÈLES: Monsieur Talbot (le matin à 8 h)
Bonjour, Monsieur. Comment allez-vous?

Anne (le soir à 7 h)
Salut, Anne. Comment ça va? *ou* **Bonsoir, Anne. Comment ça va?**

1. Paul (le soir à 7 h)
2. Mademoiselle Monot (le matin à 9 h 30)
3. Monsieur Talbot (l'après-midi à 4 h)
4. le professeur de français (le matin à 11 h)
5. votre meilleur(e) ami(e) (le soir à 10 h)
6. le (la) président(e) de votre université (l'après-midi à 1 h)

2 **Vous allez bien?** Ask the following people how they are doing. Be careful to choose between the familiar and the formal questions. Your partner will provide the other person's answer.

MODÈLE: Marie (a little sick)
   VOUS: **Comment ça va, Marie?**
  MARIE: **Oh! je suis un peu malade.**

1. Madame Philippe (tired)
2. Paul (not too great)
3. Monsieur Dupont (sick)
4. Mademoiselle Bernard (very well)
5. Anne (so-so)
6. votre professeur de français (...)
7. votre meilleur(e) ami(e) (...)
8. le (la) président(e) de l'université (...)

A. Le verbe aller

Grammar Tutorial ► One of the uses of the verb **aller** *(to go)* is to talk about one's health.

Nous **allons** bien.   *We are fine.*
Comment **vont** vos parents?   *How are your parents?*

aller (to go)			
je	**vais**	nous	**allons**
tu	**vas**	vous	**allez**
il/elle/on	**va**	ils/elles	**vont**

See Appendix C, Glossary of Grammatical Terms, for an explanation of any terms with which you are not familiar.

► You will study the verb **aller** again in Chapter 5. It is used, for example, with the infinitive to express the future.

Je **vais boire** une tasse de café.   *I am going to drink a cup of coffee.*

3 **À vous.** Answer the following questions.

MODÈLE: Comment vont vos parents?
Ils vont bien.   ou
Ils ne vont pas trop bien.

1. Comment va votre professeur?
2. Comment vont les étudiants?
3. Comment allez-vous?
4. Comment va votre meilleur(e) ami(e)?

  **ENTRE AMIS** **Au café**

Imagine you are in a sidewalk café at one o'clock in the afternoon and role-play the following conversation with as many members of the class as possible.

1. Greet your partner in a culturally appropriate manner.
2. Inquire how s/he is doing.
3. Offer him/her something to drink.
4. What else can you say?

Track 1-17

2. GIVING AND RESPONDING TO COMPLIMENTS

Quelques° compliments

	A few
Vous parlez très bien français.°	*You speak French very well.*
Vous dansez très bien.	
Vous chantez° bien.	*sing*
Vous skiez vraiment° bien.	*really*
Vous nagez comme un poisson.°	*You swim like a fish.*

Quelques réponses

Vous trouvez?°	*Do you think so?*
Pas encore.°	*Not yet.*
Oh! Pas vraiment.°	*Not really*
Oh! Je ne sais pas.°	*I don't know.*
C'est gentil mais vous exagérez.°	*That's nice but you're exaggerating.*
Je commence seulement.°	*I'm only beginning.*
Je n'ai pas beaucoup d'expérience.°	*I don't have a lot of experience.*

REMARQUE

There are several ways to express an idea. For instance, there are at least three ways to compliment someone's French:

Votre français est excellent.	*Your French is excellent.*
Vous parlez bien français.	*You speak French well.*
Vous êtes bon (bonne) en français.	*You are good in French.*

 4 Un compliment. Give a compliment to each of the people pictured below. Your partner will play the role of the person in the drawing and provide a culturally appropriate response. Then, switch roles.

MODÈLE: —**Vous parlez bien français.**
  —**Vous trouvez? Oh! je ne sais pas.**

1.

2.

3.

4.

Grammar
Tutorial

▶ All verb infinitives are made up of a **stem** and an **ending.** To use verbs in the present tense, one removes the ending from the infinitive and adds new endings to the resulting stem. Verbs that use the same endings are often classified according to the last two letters of their infinitive. By far the most common class of verbs is the group ending in **-er.**

parler *(to speak)*	STEM	ENDING
je	parl	**e**
tu	parl	**es**
il/elle/on	parl	**e**
nous	parl	**ons**
vous	parl	**ez**
ils/elles	parl	**ent**

tomber *(to fall)*	STEM	ENDING
je	tomb	**e**
tu	tomb	**es**
il/elle/on	tomb	**e**
nous	tomb	**ons**
vous	tomb	**ez**
ils/elles	tomb	**ent**

▶ Whether you are talking to a friend (**tu**), or about yourself (**je**), or about one or more other persons (**il, elle, ils, elles**), the verb is pronounced the same because the endings are silent.

Est-ce que tu **patines** bien?	*Do you skate well?*
Non, je ne **patine** pas du tout.	*No, I don't skate at all.*
Anne et Pierre **patinent** bien, n'est-ce pas?	*Anne and Pierre skate well, don't they?*
Elle **patine** bien.	*She skates well.*
Pierre **patine** souvent.	*Pierre skates often.*

▶ If you are using the **nous** or **vous** form, the verb is pronounced differently. The **-ez** ending is pronounced [e] and the **-ons** ending is pronounced [ɔ̃].

Vous **dansez** avec Marc?	*Do you dance with Marc?*
Nous ne **dansons** pas très souvent.	*We don't dance very often.*

▶ Remember that the present tense has only *one* form in French, while it has several forms in English.

je **danse**	*I dance, I do dance, I am dancing*
j'**habite**	*I live, I do live, I am living*

Remember to change **je** *to* **j'** *before a vowel sound. See p. 14.*

▶ Before a vowel sound, the final **-n** of **on** and the final **-s** of **nous, vous, ils,** and **elles** are pronounced and linked to the next word.

On [n]écoute la radio?	*Is someone listening to the radio?*
Nous [z]étudions le français.	*We are studying French.*
Vous [z]habitez ici?	*Do you live here?*

Activités

chanter (une chanson)	*to sing (a song)*
chercher (mes amis)	*to look for (my friends)*
danser (avec mes amis) *dance*	*to dance (with my friends)*
écouter (la radio)	*to listen to (the radio)*
enseigner (le français) *teacher*	*to teach (French)*
étudier (le français) *student*	*to study (French)*
jouer (au tennis)	*to play tennis*
manger [mãʒn]	*to eat*
nager	*to swim*
parler français	*to speak (French)*
patiner	*to skate*
pleurer	*to cry*
regarder (la télé)	*to watch, to look at (TV)*
tomber (quelquefois)	*to fall (sometimes)*
travailler (beaucoup)	*to work (hard)* *a lot*
voyager (souvent)	*to travel (often)*

NOTE

Verbs ending in **-ger** add an **-e-** before the ending in the form used with **nous: nous mangeons, nous nageons, nous voyageons.**

5 Comparaisons. Tell what the following people do and then compare yourself to them. Use **Et moi aussi, ...** or **Mais moi, ...** to tell whether or not the statement is also true for you.

MODÈLE: Pierre et Anne/habiter à Angers

Ils habitent à Angers. Mais moi, je n'habite pas à Angers.

1. vous/nager comme un poisson
2. James/parler bien français
3. Monsieur et Madame Dupont/danser très bien
4. tu/étudier le français
5. vous/chanter vraiment bien
6. tu/regarder souvent la télévision
7. le professeur/enseigner le français
8. Karine et James/travailler beaucoup
9. Sébastien/patiner/mais/il/tomber souvent

6 Non, pas du tout. Respond to each question in the negative, and then use the words in parentheses to follow up with an affirmative statement. Supply your own statements for items 5 and 6.

MODÈLES: Je danse *mal,* n'est-ce pas? (bien)
Non, pas du tout. Vous ne dansez pas mal. Vous dansez bien.

Vous *écoutez la radio?* (regarder la télé)
Non, pas du tout. Je n'écoute pas la radio. Je regarde la télé.

1. Vous *enseignez* le français? (étudier)
2. Le professeur *voyage* beaucoup? (travailler)
3. Est-ce que je chante *très mal?* (assez bien)
4. Vous *chantez* avec le professeur? (parler français)
5. Vous habitez *à Paris?* (...)
6. Est-ce que nous étudions *l'espagnol?* (...)

Vocabulaire

Des gens que je connais bien *(People that I know well)*

mon ami	*my (male) friend*
mon amie	*my (female) friend*
mes amis	*my friends*
ma mère	*my mother*
mon père	*my father*
le professeur	*the (male or female) teacher*
les étudiants	*the students*
ma colocataire	*my (female) roommate*
mon colocataire	*my (male) roommate*
ma petite amie	*my girlfriend*
mon petit ami	*my boyfriend*

7 Mes connaissances. Tell about your family and your acquaintances by choosing an item from each column to create as many factual sentences as you can. You may make any of them negative.

MODÈLES: **Nous ne dansons pas mal.**
Mon amie Mary n'étudie pas le français.

	chanter bien
les étudiants	travailler beaucoup
le professeur	écouter souvent la radio
je	étudier le français
nous	skier bien
ma mère	danser mal
mon père	patiner beaucoup
mes amis	habiter en France
mon ami(e)	parler français
mon petit ami	nager comme un poisson
ma petite amie	voyager souvent
	pleurer souvent
	regarder souvent la télévision

8 Tu parles bien français! Pay compliments to the following friends. Use **tu** for each individual; use **vous** for more than one person.

MODÈLES: Éric skie bien.
Tu skies bien!

Yann et Sophie dansent bien.
Vous dansez bien!

1. Alissa est très jolie.
2. Christophe parle très bien l'espagnol.
3. David est bon en français.
4. François et Michel parlent bien anglais.
5. Ils travaillent beaucoup aussi.
6. Anne et Marie sont vraiment bonnes en maths.
7. Elles chantent bien aussi.
8. Olivier est vraiment très beau.
9. Luc skie comme un champion olympique.

9 Identification. Answer the following questions as factually as possible.

MODÈLE: Qui parle bien français?
Le professeur parle bien français.
Mes amis parlent bien français.

1. Qui étudie le français?
2. Qui enseigne le français?
3. Qui ne skie pas du tout?
4. Qui chante très bien?
5. Qui joue mal au tennis?
6. Qui regarde souvent la télévision?
7. Qui écoute souvent la radio?

ENTRE AMIS Avec un(e) ami(e)

Role-play the following situation with as many members of the class as possible.

1. Pay your partner a compliment.
2. Your partner will give a culturally appropriate response to the compliment and then pay you a compliment in return.
3. Give an appropriate response.

3. OFFERING, ACCEPTING, AND REFUSING

Track 1-18

Pour offrir une boisson° — *To offer a drink*

Voulez-vous boire quelque chose?

Voulez-vous un verre d'orangina°? — *orange soda*

Voulez-vous un verre de (d') ...

bière°? — *beer*

eau°? — *water*

jus d'orange°? — *orange juice*

lait°? — *milk*

[handwritten: do you want a cup of ...]

Voulez-vous une tasse de ...

café?

chocolat chaud°? — *hot chocolate*

Qu'est-ce que° vous voulez? — *What*

Pour accepter ou refuser quelque chose° — *To accept or refuse something*

[handwritten: Oui,] Je veux bien.

[handwritten: Oui,] Volontiers.° — *Gladly.*

[handwritten: Oui,] S'il vous plaît.

Oui, avec plaisir.° — *Yes, with pleasure.*

Oui, c'est gentil à vous.° — *Yes, that's nice of you.*

Merci.

Non, merci.

Et vous? Est-ce que vous voulez boire quelque chose?

10 Voulez-vous boire quelque chose? Use the list of words below to create a dialogue in which one person offers a glass or a cup of something to drink and the other responds appropriately.

MODÈLES: Coca-Cola

—Voulez-vous un verre de coca?

—Volontiers.

coffee

—Voulez-vous une tasse de café?

—Non, merci.

1. water

2. tea

3. orange soda

4. wine

5. milk

6. orange juice

7. hot chocolate

8. beer

Note culturelle

Les jeunes Américains aiment beaucoup le lait. Mais, en général, les jeunes Français n'aiment pas le lait.

Réalités culturelles
Le café

A TIME-HONORED TRADITION in France is the outdoor café, a place with small tables on the sidewalk (**la terrasse**) where friends spend time talking and having drinks. Others come to the café to read their newspaper, work on their laptops using the free wi-fi services available in many cafés, or just watch people passing by. The French cafés are like mini-restaurants. You can order a drink, a sandwich or snack, or a simple meal during lunch and dinner hours. The cafés are open from early morning to very late in the evening. Smoking is not permitted inside, but still possible on the **terrasse,** except when closed in with glass partitions during the winter.

Robert Harding Picture Library Ltd./Alamy

When ordering in a café, you should use the expression **Je voudrais** *(I would like).*

For the French, especially Parisians, the cultural tradition of meeting others at the café is most likely due to the cramped nature of urban living in Paris, where apartments are usually small, as well as to the privacy the French reserve for their homes.

Two Parisian cafés popular with tourists are **Café de Flore** and **Les Deux Magots,** gathering spots in the early twentieth century for intellectuals and poets. Famous **habitués** included Pablo Picasso, Ernest Hemingway, Jacques Prévert, Jean-Paul Sartre, and Simone de Beauvoir. To find out more about these two cafés, visit their websites at: http://www.lesdeuxmagots.fr and http://www.cafedeflore.fr

⑪ Qu'est-ce que vous voulez?
Examine the drink menu of **La Bague d'or** *(The Golden Ring)* and order something.

MODÈLES: **Je voudrais une tasse de thé.**
Je voudrais un verre de coca-cola, s'il vous plaît.

La Bague d'or
BRASSERIE ALSACIENNE

Boissons

Vin rouge
Riesling (Vin d'Alsace)
Jus de fruits
Bière (pression)
Café
Thé
Chocolat chaud
Coca-cola
Orangina
Eau minérale (Perrier)

C. L'article défini: le, la, l' et les

Grammar Tutorial

You have already learned that all nouns in French have gender—that is, they are classified grammatically as either masculine or feminine. You also know that you need to remember the gender for each noun you learn. One of the functions of French articles is to mark the gender (masculine or feminine) and the number (singular or plural) of a noun.

FORMS OF THE DEFINITE ARTICLE	WHEN TO USE	EXAMPLES
le (l')	before a masculine singular noun	**le** thé, l'alcool
la (l')	before a feminine singular noun	**la** bière, l'eau
les	before all plural nouns, masculine or feminine	**les** boissons

► **Le** and **la** become **l'** when followed by a word that begins with a vowel sound. This includes many words that begin with the letter **h.**

le professeur
    but **l'**étudiant, **l'**ami, **l'**homme
la femme
    but **l'**étudiante, **l'**amie

► When they are used to refer to specific things or persons known to the speaker and the listener, **le, la, l',** and **les** all correspond to the English definite article *the.*

Le professeur écoute **les** étudiants.   *The teacher listens to the students.*
L'université de Paris est excellente.   *The University of Paris is excellent.*

Review nationalities, p. 19.

► **Le, la, l',** and **les** are also used before nouns that have a generic meaning, even when in English the word *the* would not be used.

Je n'aime pas **le** chocolat chaud.   *I don't like hot chocolate.*
Elle regarde souvent **la** télé.   *She often watches TV.*
J'étudie **le** chinois.   *I'm studying Chinese.*

► All languages are masculine. Many are derived from the adjective of nationality. All verbs except **parler** require **le** before the name of a language.

Ils **étudient le** russe.   *They are studying Russian.*
Ma mère **parle bien** français.   *My mother speaks French well.*

Vocabulaire

Pour répondre à «Comment?» (How?)

très bien	*very well*
(vraiment) bien	*(really) well*
assez bien	*rather well*
un peu	*a bit*
assez mal	*rather poorly*
(vraiment) mal	*(really) poorly*
ne … pas du tout	*not at all*

12 Parlez-vous bien français? For each language, describe how well you and a friend of yours (**mon ami(e)___**) speak it.

MODÈLE: l'allemand

Je ne parle pas du tout l'allemand mais mon ami Hans parle très bien l'allemand.

1. le russe   2. l'espagnol   3. l'anglais   4. le français

13 À vous. Take turns asking and answering the following questions with a partner.

1. Qu'est-ce que vous étudiez?
2. Étudiez-vous le français le matin, l'après-midi ou le soir?
3. Étudiez-vous aussi l'anglais?
4. Parlez-vous souvent avec le professeur de français?
5. Est-ce que le professeur chante avec la classe?
6. Est-ce que le professeur de français parle anglais?
7. Parlez-vous bien français?
8. Parlez-vous un peu espagnol?

> *Remember that* **Est-ce que...?** *just signals a question;* **Qu'est-ce que ...?** *means* What ...?

ENTRE AMIS   Une réception

Imagine you are at a reception for exchange students at a French university and role-play the following conversation with a partner.

1. Greet your partner and inquire how s/he is.
2. Offer him/her something to drink.
3. S/he will accept appropriately.
4. Toast each other.
5. Compliment each other on your ability in French.
6. Respond appropriately to the compliment.

4. EXPRESSING LIKES AND DISLIKES

Track 1-19

white wine	Qu'est-ce que tu aimes, Sophie? J'aime beaucoup le vin blanc°. J'adore voyager. J'aime bien danser.
Me too	Moi aussi°, j'aime voyager et danser.

Et qu'est-ce que tu n'aimes pas?
Je n'aime pas le vin rosé.
Je déteste le coca.
Je n'aime pas chanter.
Je n'aime pas beaucoup travailler.
Moi non plus°, je n'aime pas travailler.   *Me neither*

Et vous? Qu'est-ce que vous aimez?
Qu'est-ce que vous n'aimez pas?

REMARQUES

1. When there are two verbs in succession, the second is not conjugated. It remains in the infinitive form.

Mon ami **déteste nager** dans l'eau froide.	*My friend hates to swim in cold water.*
Les étudiants **aiment parler** français.	*The students like to speak French.*
Francis **désire danser.**	*Francis wants to dance.*

2. The use of **le, la, l',** and **les** to express a generality occurs particularly after verbs expressing preferences.

Marie adore **le** chocolat chaud.	*Marie loves hot chocolate.*
Elle aime **les** boissons chaudes.	*She likes hot drinks.*
Mais elle déteste **la** bière.	*But she hates beer.*
Et elle n'aime pas **l'**eau minérale.	*And she doesn't like mineral water.*

3. Be careful to distinguish between **j'aime** and **je voudrais.** Use **je voudrais** (*I would like*) when choosing something. Use **j'aime** or **je n'aime pas** to express whether or not you like it.

Je **voudrais** une tasse de thé.	*I'd like a cup of tea.*
Je n'**aime** pas le café.	*I don't like coffee.*

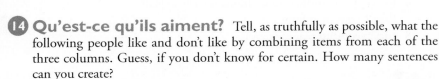

14 Qu'est-ce qu'ils aiment? Tell, as truthfully as possible, what the following people like and don't like by combining items from each of the three columns. Guess, if you don't know for certain. How many sentences can you create?

MODÈLES: **Mes amis détestent le lait.**
Je n'aime pas du tout skier.

		skier
		travailler
		la bière
		le français
		la télévision
	adorer	chanter
mes amis	aimer beaucoup	patiner
le professeur	ne pas aimer vraiment	danser
je	ne pas aimer du tout	le lait
nous	détester	l'université
		voyager
		nager
		enseigner

© Yadid Levy/Alamy

Ils aiment danser.

⑮ Vous aimez danser? Use the words below to interview the person sitting next to you. Find out if s/he likes to dance, to swim, etc. Use **aimer** in every question.

MODÈLE: dance

> VOUS: **Vous aimez danser?**
>
> VOTRE PARTENAIRE: **Oui, j'aime (beaucoup) danser.** ou
> **Non, je n'aime pas (beaucoup) danser.**

1. sing	6. study French
2. swim	7. work
3. watch television	8. travel
4. ski	9. play tennis
5. study	10. speak French

Vocabulaire

Quelques boissons populaires

le café	*coffee*	l'eau minérale *f.*	*mineral water*
le café au lait	*coffee with milk*	la limonade	*lemon-lime soda*
le (café) crème	*coffee with cream*	l'orangina *m.*	*orangina (an orange soda)*
le chocolat chaud	*hot chocolate*		
le thé	*tea*	la bière	*beer*
le citron pressé	*lemonade*	le kir	*kir*
le coca	*cola*	le vin (rouge, blanc, rosé)	*wine (red, white, rosé)*

(handwritten note in margin: only breakfast)

> **La limonade** *française ressemble beaucoup à la* boisson **7-Up.** *La boisson américaine* **lemonade** *est* **le citron pressé** *en France.*
>
> *Le café au lait est moitié* **(half)** *café, moitié lait chaud.*

⑯ Vous aimez le café? Use the preceding list of **boissons populaires** to order something, and take an (imaginary) sip. Your partner will ask if you like it. Respond.

MODÈLE: le café

> VOUS: **Je voudrais une tasse de café.**
>
> VOTRE PARTENAIRE: **Est-ce que vous aimez le café?**
>
> VOUS: **Oui, j'aime le café.** ou
> **Non, je n'aime pas le café.**

> *Remember to distinguish between* **un verre** *and* **une tasse.**

Vocabulaire

D'autres choses que les gens aiment ou n'aiment pas

le chocolat	*chocolate*	la politique	*politics*
le jogging	*jogging*	la radio	*the radio*
la pizza	*pizza*	les sports	*sports*

17 En général, les étudiants ... Decide whether you agree (**C'est vrai**) or disagree (**C'est faux**) with the following statements. If you disagree, correct the statement.

MODÈLE: En général, les étudiants détestent voyager.
C'est faux. En général, ils aiment beaucoup voyager.

1. En général, les étudiants n'aiment pas du tout danser.
2. En général, les étudiants détestent la pizza.
3. En général, les étudiants aiment beaucoup étudier.
4. En général, les étudiants n'aiment pas beaucoup regarder la télévision.
5. En général, les étudiants aiment nager.
6. En général, les étudiants aiment skier.
7. En général, les étudiants aiment beaucoup patiner.
8. En général, les étudiants détestent chanter.
9. En général, les étudiants aiment parler français avec le professeur.
10. En général, les étudiants désirent habiter à New York.

18 Comment trouvez-vous le café français? (What do you think of French coffee?) Your partner will ask you to give your opinion about something you have tasted. Use **aimer, adorer,** or **détester** in an answer that reflects your own opinion. Or make up an imaginary opinion. You might also say **Je ne sais pas, mais ...** and offer an opinion about something else that is related, instead.

MODÈLE: les tamalis mexicains

VOTRE PARTENAIRE: **Comment trouvez-vous les tamalis mexicains?**
VOUS: **J'aime beaucoup les tamalis mexicains.**   ou
Je ne sais pas, mais j'adore les enchiladas.

1. le thé anglais
2. le chocolat suisse
3. la pizza italienne
4. l'eau minérale française
5. le jus d'orange de Floride
6. le café de Colombie
7. la limonade française
8. la bière allemande
9. le vin français

D. Les questions avec réponse oui ou non

Grammar Tutorial

▶ In spoken French, by far the most frequently used way of asking a question that can be answered *yes* or *no* is by simply raising the voice at the end of the sentence.

Vous parlez français?　　　　　*Do you speak French?*

Hélène danse bien?　　　　　*Does Hélène dance well?*

▶ **Est-ce que** is often placed at the beginning of a sentence to form a question. It becomes **Est-ce qu'** before a vowel sound.

Est-ce que vous parlez français?　　*Do you speak French?*
Est-ce qu'Hélène danse bien?　　　*Does Hélène dance well?*

► The phrase **n'est-ce pas?** *(right?, aren't you?, doesn't he?, etc.)*, added at the end of a sentence, expects an affirmative answer.

Vous parlez français, **n'est-ce pas**?	*You speak French, don't you?*
Hélène danse bien, **n'est-ce pas**?	*Hélène dances well, doesn't she?*

► Another question form, which is used more often in written French than in speech and which is characteristic of a more formal speech style, is inversion of the verb and its pronoun subject. When inversion is used, there is a hyphen between the verb and the pronoun.

Parlez-vous français?	*Do you speak French?*
Aimez-vous chanter?	*Do you like to sing?*

NOTE

If the third person (**il, elle, on, ils, elles**) is used in inversion, there is always a [t] sound between the verb and the subject pronoun. If the verb ends in a vowel, a written **-t-** is added between the final vowel of the verb and the initial vowel of the pronoun. If the verb ends in **-t**, no extra **-t-** is necessary.

	Enseigne**-t**-il le français?	*Does he teach French?*
	Aime**-t**-elle voyager?	*Does she like to travel?*
But:	Aimen**t**-ils voyager?	*Do they like to travel?*
	Es**t**-elle française?	*Is she French?*
	Son**t**-ils américains?	*Are they American?*

For recognition only

If the subject is a noun, the inversion form can be produced by adding the pronoun of the same number and gender after the verb.

noun + verb + pronoun

Karen est-elle américaine?	*Is Karen American?*
Thierry aime-t-il la bière?	*Does Thierry like beer?*
Nathalie et Stéphane aiment-ils danser?	*Do Nathalie and Stéphane like to dance?*

 ⓭ Comment? *(What did you say?)* We often need to repeat a question when someone doesn't hear or understand us. For each question with inversion, ask a question beginning with **Est-ce que** and a question ending with **n'est-ce pas.**

iLrn
Self Test

MODÈLES: James habite-t-il à San Francisco?

> VOTRE PARTENAIRE: **Comment?**
> VOUS: **Est-ce que James habite à San Francisco?**
> VOTRE PARTENAIRE: **Comment?**
> VOUS: **James habite à San Francisco, n'est-ce pas?**

1. James est-il américain?
2. Étudie-t-il le français?
3. Parle-t-il bien le français?
4. Aime-t-il Karine Aspel?
5. Karine est-elle française?
6. Allez-vous bien?

20 **Une enquête entre amis** *(A survey among friends).* Use the following list to determine the likes and dislikes of two classmates. Be prepared to report back the results of your "survey" to the class. Are there any items on which all the students agree completely?

MODÈLES:　skier　　**—Est-ce que tu aimes skier?**
　　　　　　　　　　　　—Oui, j'adore skier.

　　　　　　　le jogging　**—Est-ce que tu aimes le jogging?**
　　　　　　　　　　　　—Non, je n'aime pas le jogging.　ou
　　　　　　　　　　　　Non, je déteste le jogging. Je n'aime pas le sport.

1. parler français
2. parler avec le professeur de français
3. voyager
4. regarder la télévision
5. chanter en français
6. la politique
7. l'université
8. étudier le français
9. nager
10. travailler beaucoup

21 **Les Dupont.*** Here are a few facts about the Dupont family. Interview a classmate to find out if this information is also true for him/her.

MODÈLES:　Les Dupont habitent à Marseille.

　　　　　　　　　VOUS:　**Habites-tu à Marseille aussi?**
　　　VOTRE PARTENAIRE:　**Non, je n'habite pas à Marseille.**

Gérard et Martine sont mariés.
　　　　　　　　　VOUS:　**Es-tu marié(e) aussi?**
　　　VOTRE PARTENAIRE:　**Non, je ne suis pas marié(e).**　ou
　　　　　　　　　　　Oui, je suis marié(e) aussi.

Review the verb **être,** *p. 15, and* **-er** *verbs, p. 40.*

1. Martine adore voyager.
2. Gérard Dupont aime la limonade.
3. Les Dupont sont malades.
4. Martine Dupont parle espagnol.
5. Monsieur et Madame Dupont aiment beaucoup danser.
6. Les Dupont voyagent beaucoup.

ENTRE AMIS　À une soirée

Role-play the following conversation with as many members of the class as possible. You are at a dance and are meeting people for the first time. Use **vous.**

1. Say good evening and introduce yourself.
2. Find out if your partner likes to dance.
3. Ask your partner if s/he wants to dance. (S/he does.)
4. Tell your partner that s/he dances well.
5. Offer your partner something to drink.
6. Toast each other.
7. Compliment each other on your ability in French.
8. Respond appropriately to the compliment.

---

*An **-s** *is not added to family names in French; the article* **les** *indicates the plural.*

Intégration

RÉVISION

A **Trouvez quelqu'un qui ... (Find someone who ...).**
Interview your classmates in French to find someone who ...

MODÈLE: speaks French **Est-ce que tu parles français?**

1. likes coffee
2. swims often
3. doesn't like beer
4. sings poorly
5. studies a lot
6. doesn't ski
7. is tired
8. hates to work
9. likes to travel
10. skates

Track 1-20 **B** **À l'écoute.** Listen to each of the following exchanges and decide whether it involves **a)** asking and responding to "How are you?", **b)** giving and receiving a compliment, **c)** offering, accepting, and refusing, or **d)** expressing likes and dislikes.

C **À vous.** How would you respond to the following questions and comments?

1. Parlez-vous français?
2. Comment allez-vous?
3. Où habitez-vous?
4. Voulez-vous boire quelque chose?
5. Qu'est-ce que vous désirez boire?
6. Vous parlez très bien français!
7. Vous étudiez l'espagnol, n'est-ce pas?
8. Aimez-vous voyager?
9. Est-ce que vous aimez danser?
10. Qu'est-ce que vous n'aimez pas?

NÉGOCIATIONS

Les activités. Use the expressions below to interview as many students as possible. Other students will use a form from Appendix D. Try to find people who answer the questions affirmatively then write their initials next to the appropriate expression. No student's initials should be used more than twice.

MODÈLE: —**Est-ce que tu détestes les hot-dogs?**
          —**Oui, je déteste les hot-dogs.** (*Write the person's initials and move to the next question.*)

or

          Non, je ne déteste pas les hot-dogs. J'aime les hot-dogs. (*Ask the next person.*)

A

écouter la radio le matin	jouer au tennis	parler espagnol
chanter une chanson française	aimer patiner	étudier l'anglais
tomber quelquefois	détester les hot-dogs	être célibataire
adorer skier	pleurer quelquefois	aimer étudier le français

Communication and Communities. To learn more about the culture presented in this chapter, go to the *Premium Website* and click on the Web Search Activities.

LECTURE

The following reading selection describes people's personality according to their astrological sign. It is not vital that you understand every word.

A **Les mots apparentés et les faux amis.** Skim the reading and list all the cognates you find. Then read the text a second time more carefully. Are any of the cognates you found really **des faux amis**?

B **Familles de mots** *(Word families).* You can use word families to help you understand what you read. Can you guess the meanings of the following words? One member of each word family is found in the reading.

1. comprendre, compréhensif, compréhensive, la compréhension
2. séducteur, séduire, séduisant, séduction
3. richesse, riche
4. lire, un lecteur, une lectrice, la lecture

Votre signe du zodiaque et votre personnalité

Capricorne: Flexibles et élégants. Ils aiment les compliments, mais s'attendent toujours à de mauvaises[1] surprises.

Verseau: Charmants, mais pas très beaux. Ils adorent parler.

Poisson: Très féminins (même les hommes!) Sincères. Ils n'aiment pas les conflits.

Bélier: Pas très beaux. Actifs. Esprit d'indépendance. Ils aiment rester seuls[2].

Taureau: Forts. Dominants. Musclés. Chefs de la famille. Le travail est leur raison d'être.

Gémeaux: Élégants. Esprit d'économie. Ils adorent la bonne cuisine.

Cancer: Physiquement, rien[3] de remarquable. Compréhensifs. Ils aiment le cercle familial et lire des romans[4] historiques.

Lion: Grands et minces. Charmants et autoritaires. Esprit d'indépendance. Ils n'aiment pas travailler en équipe[5].

Vierge: Traits fins et réguliers. Bonnes en relations publiques. Elles aiment parler des affaires sérieuses.

Balance: Très belles. Séductrices. Elles aiment la beauté dans la musique et les arts.

Scorpion: Minces. Sensibles aux compliments et aux critiques. Ils aiment collectionner les diplômes et les euros.

Sagittaire: Ni beaux, ni laids. Ils aiment la richesse et veulent toujours[6] arriver premier.

---

[1]*bad* / [2]*alone* / [3]*nothing* / [4]*novels* / [5]*team* / [6]*always want*

C **Votre signe du zodiaque.** Does the description given for your zodiac sign fit you? Why or why not? Describe *yourself* using five of the adjectives from the reading.

RÉDACTION

LA MÉTHODO Combining phrases or sentences with conjunctions, such as **et, ou,** or **mais** will help you express ideas, show relationships, and create greater variety when you write in French. After you write a draft of the assignment below, go back over your sentences to see which ones might be combined using a conjunction. Ask yourself how you might show similar or opposing relationships in your sentences. For example, you might combine the following two sentences using **mais** to show a contrast.

Marie-Christine n'aime pas les sports. Elle aime danser.
Marie-Christine n'aime pas le sport, mais elle aime danser.

FORUM D'AMITIÉS ET DE CORRESPONDANCE: MESSAGE

Imagine you have just logged on to **Forum d'amitiés et de correspondance** to find someone in a Francophone country with whom to practice your written French. Write a message in which you:

- greet forum users and introduce yourself
- say where you live
- briefly describe yourself
- tell two things you like and two things you don't like
- tell a few things you do with friends and how often you do them
- say goodbye

MODÈLE:

Votre nom:	**Beth Garner**
Votre adresse e-mail:	**bgarner@freemail.com**
Sujet:	**recherche amis et correspondants dans le monde francophone**

Message:

Bonjour!
Je m'appelle Beth Garner.
J'habite à Irvine, en Californie.
Je suis jeune, petite et mince. J'adore le français…

A **Avant d'écrire.** Make a list in French of the information you will include in your message.

B **Écrire.** Write a draft of your message.

C **Correction.** Exchange papers with a partner for proofreading. Check carefully for errors in spelling and agreement. Look for places where sentences would be more effective if combined with a conjunction. Then revise your message based on your partner's feedback.

Intégration *cinquante-cinq* **55**

Vocabulaire Actif

Quelque chose à boire

la bière *beer*
une boisson *drink*
le café (au lait) *coffee (with milk)*
le (café) crème *coffee with cream*
le chocolat chaud *hot chocolate*
le citron pressé *lemonade*
le coca *cola*
l'eau f. (minérale) *(mineral) water*
le jus d'orange *orange juice*
le kir *kir*
le lait *milk*
la limonade *lemon-lime soda*
l'orangina m. *orangina (an orange soda)*
le thé *tea*
le vin (rouge, blanc, rosé) *(red, white, rosé) wine*

Des gens que je connais bien

les étudiants *the students*
ma (mon) colocataire *my roommate*
ma mère *my mother*
ma petite amie *my girlfriend*
mes amis *my friends*
mon ami(e) *my friend*
mon père *my father*
mon petit ami *my boyfriend*

D'autres noms et pronoms

une chanson *song*
le chocolat *chocolate*
le jogging *jogging*
la pizza *pizza*
un poisson *fish*
la politique *politics*
quelque chose *something*
quelqu'un *someone*
la radio *radio*
une soirée *an evening party*
le sport *sport*
une tasse *cup*
la télévision (la télé) *television (TV)*
l'université f. *university*
un verre *glass*

Adjectifs

bon (bonne) *good*
chaud(e) *hot*
cher (chère) *dear*
excellent(e) *excellent*
fatigué(e) *tired*
faux (fausse) *false; wrong*
froid(e) *cold*
malade *sick*
vrai(e) *true*

Répondre à un compliment

Vous trouvez? *Do you think so?*
Pas encore. *Not yet.*
Oh! Pas vraiment. *Not really.*
Je ne sais pas. *I don't know.*
C'est gentil mais vous exagérez.
    That's nice but you're exaggerating.
Je commence seulement. *I'm only beginning.*
Je n'ai pas beaucoup d'expérience. *I don't have a lot of experience.*

Articles définis

le, la, l', les *the*

Verbes

aller *to go; to be + adverb (health)*
chanter *to sing*
chercher *to look for*
danser *to dance*
désirer *to want*
écouter *to listen to*
enseigner *to teach*
étudier *to study*
habiter *to live; to reside*
jouer (au tennis) *to play (tennis)*
manger *to eat*
nager *to swim*
parler *to speak*
patiner *to skate*
pleurer *to cry*
regarder *to watch; to look at*
skier *to ski*
tomber *to fall*
travailler *to work*
trouver *to find; to be of the opinion*
voyager *to travel*

Mots invariables

alors *then, therefore, so*
avec *with*
beaucoup *a lot*
bien *well; fine*
comme *like*
en général *in general*
ensemble *together*
mais *but*
mal *poorly; badly*
peut-être *maybe; perhaps*
pour *for; in order to*
pourquoi *why*
quelquefois *sometimes*
seulement *only*
souvent *often*
un peu *a little bit*
vraiment *really*

À quel moment?

à ... heure(s) *at ... o'clock*
le jour *day, daytime*
le matin *morning, in the morning*
l'après-midi *afternoon, in the afternoon*
le soir *evening, in the evening*
la nuit *night, at night*

Demander comment on va

Comment allez-vous? *How are you?*
Vous allez bien? *Are you well?*
(Comment) ça va? *How is it going?*
Je vais très bien. *Very well.*
Ça va bien. *(I'm) fine.*
Comme ci, comme ça. *So-so.*
Assez bien. *Fairly well.*
Je suis fatigué(e). *I am tired.*
Je suis un peu malade. *I am a little sick.*
Pas trop bien. *Not too well.*
Pas mal. *Not bad.*

Offrir, accepter et refuser

Voulez-vous boire quelque chose? *Do you want to drink something?*
Je veux bien. *Gladly. Yes, thanks.*
Volontiers. *Gladly.*
S'il vous plaît. *Please.*
Oui, avec plaisir. *Yes, with pleasure.*
Oui, c'est gentil à vous. *Yes, that's nice of you.*
Merci. *No, thank you.*
(Non,) merci. *(No,) thank you.*
Pourquoi pas? *Why not?*
Je voudrais ... *I would like ...*

Verbes de préférence

adorer *to adore; to love*
aimer *to like; to love*
détester *to hate; to detest*

D'autres expressions utiles

Bonsoir. *Good evening.*
Comment? *What (did you say)?*
Est-ce que ... ? *(question marker)*
n'est-ce pas? *right? are you? don't they?*
Comment est-ce qu'on écrit ... ? *How do you spell ... ?*
Qu'est-ce que ... ? *What ...?*
Vous êtes d'où? *Where are you from?*
Quelle bonne surprise! *What a good surprise!*
À votre santé! *(Here's) to your health!*
À la vôtre! *(Here's) to yours!*
Au fait ... *By the way ...*
Je ne sais pas. *I don't know.*
Je viens de ... *I come from ...*
même(s) *-self (-selves)*
moi aussi (...non plus) *me too (neither)*

Chez nous

PhotoAlto/John Dowland/Getty Images

BUTS COMMUNICATIFS
- Identifying family and friends
- Sharing numerical information
- Talking about your home

STRUCTURES UTILES
- L'article indéfini: **un**, **une** et **des**
- Le verbe **avoir**
- Les nombres (suite)
- Les expressions **il y a** et **voilà**
- Les adjectifs possessifs **mon, ton, notre** et **votre**
- La négation + **un (une, des)**
- La possession avec **de**
- Les adjectifs possessifs **son** et **leur**

CULTURE

Zoom sur la famille
- **Vidéo buzz:** Pour gagner du temps
- **Vu sur le web:** L'importance de la famille
- **Repères:** La composition des familles françaises
- **Insolite:** La langue et la culture
- **Article:** Les pronoms **tu** et **vous**

Il y a un geste
- Voilà

Lectures
- Maisons à vendre
- Charlotte Gainsbourg continue la tradition de sa famille

RESOURCES

🔊 Audio	iLrn Heinle Learning Center	🌐 Premium Website

Pair Work	Group Work	▶ *Entre amis* Video Program

Coup d'envoi

🔊 PRISE DE CONTACT: DES PHOTOS DE FAMILLE

Christophe

Monique

Ahmed

Marie

Marie:	Avez-vous des frères ou des sœurs?°	*Do you have any brothers or sisters? / I have*
Christophe:	J'ai° un frère et une sœur.	
Monique:	J'ai une sœur, mais je <u>n'ai pas de</u>° frère.	*I don't have any*
Ahmed:	Moi, je n'ai pas de frère ou de sœur.	
Marie:	Dans° ma famille il y a° cinq personnes. Il y a trois enfants°, deux filles° et un garçon°. Ma sœur s'appelle° Chantal et mon frère s'appelle Robert. Mes parents s'appellent Bernard et Sophie.	*In / there are* *children / girls* *boy / My sister's name is*

🌐 **Et vous?** Avez-vous des frères ou des sœurs?
Avez-vous <u>une</u> photo de votre famille?
Qui est sur la photo?°   *Who is in the picture?*

Lori Becker est une étudiante américaine qui vient° en France pour passer un an° dans une famille française. Elle descend du train à la gare° Saint-Laud à Angers. Anne Martin et sa fille°, Émilie, attendent° son arrivée.

who is coming
year
railroad station
daughter / are waiting for

Mme Martin: Mademoiselle Becker?

Lori: Oui. Bonjour, Madame. Vous êtes bien Madame Martin?°

You're Madame Martin, aren't you?

Mme Martin: Oui. Bonjour et bienvenue°, Mademoiselle. Vous êtes très fatiguée, sans doute°?

welcome

probably

Lori: Pas trop°. J'ai dormi° un peu dans le train.

too much / I slept

Mme Martin: Mademoiselle Becker, voilà ma fille.

Lori: Bonjour, tu t'appelles comment?

La petite fille: Émilie.

Lori: Et tu as quel âge?°
(*The child holds up her thumb and two fingers.*)

And how old are you?

Mme Martin: Elle a trois ans.

Lori: Elle est charmante.° Et vous avez un fils°?

She's charming / son

Mme Martin: Nous avons° six enfants°. Cinq sont à l'école° et Émilie est encore à la maison°. Voilà°.

have / children
school / still at home
There you have it.

Lori: Comment? Combien d'enfants dites-vous?°

How many children do you say?

Mme Martin: Six.

Lori: Oh là là! Vraiment?°

Wow! Really?

Mme Martin: Pourquoi? Qu'est-ce qu'il y a?°

What's the matter?

Lori: Euh … rien°. J'ai mal compris°. J'aime beaucoup les enfants.

nothing / I misunderstood

👥 ⓒ **Jouez ces rôles.** Role-play the conversation exactly as if you were Lori Becker and Mme Martin. Once you have practiced it several times, role-play the conversation using one partner's identity in place of Lori's.

Il y a un geste

Voilà. The open hand is extended, palm up, to emphasize that some fact is evident. **Voilà** is also used to conclude something that has been said or to express that's how things are.

© Cengage Learning

Zoom sur la famille

Premium Website

PETIT TEST

Why does Lori use *tu* with Émilie Martin?

  a. They have met before and are good friends.

  b. She is speaking to a child.

  c. Lori considers Émilie an inferior.

Read the side-bar article to find out the answer.

Les pronoms *tu* et *vous*

FRENCH HAS TWO WAYS of saying *you*. The choice reflects the nature of the relationship, including degree of formality and respect. **Tu** is typically used when speaking to one's family and relatives as well as to close friends, fellow students, and children. **Vous** is normally used when speaking to someone who does not meet the above criteria (e.g., employers, teachers, or business acquaintances). It expresses a more formal relationship, respect, or a greater social distance than **tu.** In addition, **vous** is always used to refer to more than one person.

Visitors to French-speaking countries would be well advised to use **vous** even if first names are being used, unless they are invited to use the **tu** form. In the ***Conversation,*** Lori correctly uses **vous** with Madame Martin and **tu** with Émilie.

INSOLITE

La langue et la culture

EACH LANGUAGE has its own unique way of expressing reality. The fact that French uses the verb **avoir** *(to have)* when expressing age, whereas English uses the verb *to be,* is only one of many examples that prove that languages are not copies of each other. In addition, one language may have separate expressions to convey two concepts, while another language uses the same expression for both.

English	French
parents/relatives	parents
girl/daughter	fille
there are	voilà/il y a

Photodisc Blue/Getty Images

L'importance de la famille

DESPITE SIGNIFICANT changes in the size and composition of households, the family continues to play an important role in the lives of the French and other French-speaking peoples, such as the **Québécois.** Branches of government exist to aid and support families in both France and Canada, and people place great importance on nurturing their relationships with friends and family, devoting much of their leisure time to social gatherings, such as reunions, picnics, and Sunday meals. They are often equally attached to the region in which they live. It is common to find homes in both France and Quebec that have been lived in by successive generations of the same family. To learn more about the importance of family in Quebec and France, explore the links provided on the *Premium Website.*

REPÈRES

The make-up of French families continues to change just as it has in the United States. Look at the chart below to see some of these changes.

La composition des familles françaises

EN MILLIERS

	1999	en %	2007	en %
Couples avec enfant(s)	8.061,5	48,8	7.773,5	44,4
Familles monoparentales	2.113,6	12,8	2.427,1	13,9
Femmes seules avec enfant(s)	1.806,5	10,9	2.050,4	11,7
Hommes seuls avec enfant(s)	307,1	1,9	376,7	2,2
Couples sans enfant	6.338,9	38,4	7.299,9	41,7
Ensemble des familles	16.514,1	100,0	17.500,6	100,0

Champ: France Source: Insee, RP1999 et RP2007 exploitations complémentaires, *Tableaux de l'Économie Française,* 2010

À vous. How would you respond to the following?

1. Comment s'appellent vos parents?
2. Vous avez des frères ou des sœurs?
3. (Si oui) Comment s'appellent-ils (elles)?
4. Où habitent-ils (elles)?

Pour gagner du temps *(To stall for time)*

A HELPFUL STRATEGY for the language learner is to acquire and use certain expressions and gestures that allow him or her to "buy time" to think without destroying the conversational flow or without resorting to English. Like the cup of coffee we sip during a conversation to give us a chance to organize our thoughts, there are a number of useful expressions for "buying time" in French. The number one gap-filler is **euh,** which is the French equivalent of the English *uh* or *umm.* Some useful expressions follow. To see them used in context, explore the links on the *Premium Website.* After watching the videos, decide which expressions can be used in any situation and which you should use only among family and friends.

Vocabulaire

Pour gagner du temps *(To stall for time)*

alors	*then; therefore, so*	euh	*uh; umm*
ben	*well*	mais …	*but*
bon	*good*	oui …	*yes*
eh bien	*well then*	Tiens!	*Well, well!*
et …	*and*	voyons	*let's see*

Euh *rhymes with* **deux. Ben [be]** *is derived from* **bien.**

ENTRE AMIS Des frères ou des sœurs?

Role-play the following conversation with a partner.

1. Introduce and tell what you can about yourself.
2. Find out what you can about your partner.
3. Find out if your partner has brothers or sisters.
4. If so, find out their names.

PRONONCIATION

🔊 L'ACCENT ET LE RYTHME (SUITE)

Track 1-23

Review the Prononciation section of Ch. 1.

▶ Remember: When pronouncing French sentences, it is good practice to pay particular attention to the facts that: (1) French rhythm is even (just like counting), (2) syllables normally end in a vowel sound, and (3) the final syllable of a group of words is lengthened.

Count before repeating each of the following expressions.

un, deux, trois, quatre, cinq, SIX
Je suis a-mé-ri-CAIN.
Elle est cé-li-ba-TAIRE.
Vous tra-va-illez beau-COUP?

un, deux, trois, quatre, cinq, six, SEPT
Je m'a-ppelle Ka-rine As-PEL.
Vous ha-bi-tez à Pa-RIS?
Je n'aime pas beau-coup le VIN.

LES SONS [e], [ɛ], [ə], [a] et [wa]

▶ The following words contain some important and very common vowel sounds.

Practice saying these words after your instructor, paying particular attention to the highlighted vowel sound.

[e]
- écrivez, zéro, répétez, écoutez, nationalité, téléphone, divorcé
- ouvrez, entrez, fermez, assez, asseyez-vous, excusez-moi
- présenter, habiter, écouter, arrêter, commencer, continuer
- et

[ɛ]
- personne, professeur, hôtel, université, espagnol, elle, canadienne
- crème, frère, chère, discrète
- être, êtes
- anglaise, française, célibataire, laide, certainement

[ə]
- le, levez-vous, prenez, regardez, que, de, je, ne, votre santé, me

encor¢, heur¢, femm¢, homm¢, un¢, ami¢, famill¢, entr¢ amis

[a] • **la, a**llez, **a**mie, **a**méricain, **a**ssez, m**a**tin, c**a**n**a**dien, qu**a**tre, s**a**lut, d'**a**ccord, **à,** voil**à**

[wa] • Fran**ç**ois, m**oi**, tr**oi**s, v**oi**là, Madem**oi**selle, au rev**oi**r, bons**oi**r, v**oy**age

Now go back and look at how these sounds are spelled and in what kinds of letter combinations they appear. What patterns do you notice?

It is always particularly important to pronounce **la** [la] and **le** [lə] correctly since each marks a different gender, and the meaning of a word may depend on which is used. Listen and repeat:

la tour=*tower*
la tour Eiffel

le tour=*tour, turn*
le Tour de France

Buts communicatifs

1. IDENTIFYING FAMILY AND FRIENDS

Track 1-24

—Je vous présente° mon amie, Anne Martin. Elle a° une   *I introduce to you / has*
sœur qui habite près d'ici.
—Votre sœur, comment s'appelle-t-elle?
—Elle s'appelle Catherine.
—Et vous êtes d'où?
—Je suis de Nantes.
—Tiens! J'ai des cousins à Nantes.
—Comment s'appellent-ils?
—Ils s'appellent Dubois.

Et vous? Présentez un(e) ami(e).

When you use **qui,** the verb that follows agrees with the person(s) to whom **qui** refers.

Elle a des cousins **qui habitent** à Nantes.

Arbre généalogique d'une famille française

Jean et Monique Martin   Marie et Georges Duhamel

Éric Bernard et Chantal   Michel   Pierre et Anne   Catherine et Alain Dubois

Christophe   Céline   David   Sylvie   Amélie   Benoît   Émilie   Nathalie   Stéphane

Vocabulaire

Une famille française

des parents	*parents; relatives*	
un mari et une femme	*a husband and a wife*	
un père et une mère	*a father and a mother*	
un(e) enfant	*a child (male or female)*	
un fils et une fille	*a son and a daughter*	
un frère et une sœur	*a brother and a sister*	
des grands-parents	*grandparents*	
un grand-père	*a grandfather*	
une grand-mère	*a grandmother*	
des petits-enfants	*grandchildren*	
un petit-fils et une petite-fille	*a grandson and a granddaughter*	

un oncle et une tante	*an uncle and an aunt*
un neveu et une nièce	*a nephew and a niece*
un(e) cousin(e)	*a cousin (male or female)*
des beaux-parents	*stepparents (or in-laws)*
un beau-père	*a stepfather (or father-in-law)*
une belle-mère	*a stepmother (or mother-in-law)*
un beau-frère	*a brother-in-law*
une belle-sœur	*a sister-in-law*
un demi-frère	*a stepbrother*
une demi-sœur	*a stepsister*

NOTES

1. Most plurals of nouns are formed by adding **-s.** In compound words for family members, an **-s** is added to both parts of the term: **des grands-pères, des belles-mères.**

2. The words **neveu** and **beau** form their plurals with an **-x: des neveux, des beaux-frères.**

3. The word **fils** is invariable in the plural: **des fils, des petits-fils.**

4. **C'est** (*He/She/It is*) and **Ce sont** (*They are/These are*) are often used with a noun phrase to identify someone or something.

    C'est la grand-mère d'Amélie.   *It's (She's) Amélie's grandmother.*
    Ce sont les grands-parents de Stéphane.   *They're Stéphane's grandparents.*

Add **arrière** *before* **petit** *or* **grand** *to convey the meaning great:* **un arrière-petit-fils; une arrière-grand-mère.**

I **Ce sont les parents de Pierre.** Study the genealogical chart on p. 64 and then use **C'est** and **Ce sont** to explain how the following people are related to Pierre.

MODÈLE: David?
   C'est le fils de Pierre.

1. Anne?
2. Jean et Monique Martin?
3. Christophe?
4. Céline et Sylvie?
5. Marie et Georges Duhamel?

A. *L'article indéfini:* un, une et des

Grammar
Tutorials

▶ The French equivalent of the English article *a (an)* is **un** for masculine nouns and **une** for feminine nouns.

un frère	**un** train	**un** orangina
une sœur	**une** table	**une** limonade

▶ The final **-n** of **un** is normally silent. **Liaison** is required when **un** precedes a vowel sound.

un [n]étudiant

▶ The consonant **-n-** is always pronounced in the word **une.** If it precedes a vowel sound, it is linked to that vowel.

	une femme	[yn fam]
But:	une étudiante	[y ne ty djãt]

▶ The plural of **un** and **une** is **des.**

singulier:	un frère	une sœur
pluriel:	**des** frères	**des** sœurs

▶ **Des** corresponds to the English *some* or *any.* However, these words are often omitted in English. **Des** is not omitted in French.

J'ai **des** amis à Paris.   I have (some) friends in Paris.

▶ Liaison is required when an article precedes a vowel sound.

un [n]enfant	un [n]étudiant	un [n]homme
des [z]enfants	des [z]étudiants	des [z]hommes

▶ In a series, the article *must* be repeated before each noun.

un homme et **une** femme	*a man and (a) woman*
une mère et **des** enfants	*a mother and (some) children*

2 Présentations. Introduce the following people and tell where someone in their family lives.

MODÈLE: Mademoiselle Blondel / frère à New York
Je vous présente Mademoiselle Blondel.
Elle a un frère qui habite à New York.

1. Madame Brooks / sœur à Toronto
2. Mademoiselle Jones / parents près de Chicago
3. Monsieur Callahan / frère à Milwaukee
4. Monsieur Lefont / fils près d'ici
5. Madame Perez / petits-enfants près d'El Paso
6. Mademoiselle Keita / cousins à New York
7. un ami
8. une amie
9. votre père ou votre mère

3 Quelque chose à boire? Use an indefinite article to order each of the following items.

Review the list of boissons on p. 49.

MODÈLE: citron pressé
Je voudrais un citron pressé, s'il vous plaît.

1. thé
2. café
3. bière
4. verre d'eau
5. jus d'orange
6. chocolat
7. coca
8. limonade
9. orangina
10. café crème

B. Le verbe avoir

Grammar Tutorials

Je m'appelle Soléane. **J'ai** une grande famille. Nous habitons à Paris, mais **nous avons** des parents qui habitent en Guadeloupe. Et toi, **tu as** une grande famille?

michaeljung/Shutterstock.com

avoir (to have)	
j'**ai**	nous **avons**
tu **as**	vous **avez**
il/elle/on **a**	ils/elles **ont**

▶ Liaison is required in **on a, nous avons, vous avez, ils ont,** and **elles ont**.

on [n]a   nous [z]avons

▶ Do not confuse **ils ont** and **ils sont**. In liaison, the **-s** in **ils** is pronounced [z] and is linked to the following verb.

Ils [z]ont des enfants.   *They **have** children.*
But: Ils **sont** charmants.   *They **are** charming.*

▶ Use Je **n'ai pas de (d')** ... to say *I don't have a ...* or *I don't have any ...*
Je n'ai pas de père.   *I don't have a father.*
Je n'ai pas de frère.   *I don't have any brothers.*
Je n'ai pas d'enfants.   *I don't have any children.*

4 **Un recensement** *(A census).* A census taker is interviewing these people. Work with a partner to complete each interview, following the model.

MODÈLE: Mademoiselle Messin / 2 sœurs, 0 frère / Jeanne et Perrine
(frères ou sœurs?)

> LE RECENSEUR: **Avez-vous des frères ou des sœurs, Mademoiselle?**
> MLLE MESSIN: **J'ai deux sœurs mais je n'ai pas de frère.**
> LE RECENSEUR: **Comment s'appellent-elles?**
> MLLE MESSIN: **Elles s'appellent Jeanne et Perrine.**

1. Monsieur Dubois / 2 frères, 0 sœur / Henri et Luc
   (frères ou sœurs?)
2. Madame Bernard / 1 enfant: 1 fils, 0 fille / Christophe (enfants?)
3. Monsieur Marot / 2 enfants: 1 fils, 1 fille / Pascal et Hélène
   (enfants?)
4. vos parents (enfants?)
5. votre meilleur(e) ami(e) (frères ou sœurs?)
6. vos grands-parents (petits-enfants?)
7. vous (?)

5 **La famille de David.** Use the genealogical chart on page 64 to create sentences describing David's family ties.

MODÈLE: **David a des parents qui s'appellent Pierre et Anne.**

ENTRE AMIS **Votre famille**

Follow the steps below to interview your partner.

1. Find out if your partner has brothers or sisters.
2. If so, find out their names.
3. Find out where they live.
4. Find out if your partner has children and, if so, what their names are.
5. Introduce your partner to another person and share the information you have just found out.

2. SHARING NUMERICAL INFORMATION

Track 1-25

Combien de personnes y a-t-il dans ta famille, Christelle?	Il y a quatre personnes: mes parents, ma sœur et moi.
Quel âge ont tes parents?	Ils ont 50 ans et 47 ans.
Quel âge a ta sœur?	Elle a 18 ans.
Quel âge as-tu?	J'ai 20 ans.
En quelle année es-tu née°?	Je suis née° en mille neuf cent quatre-vingt-six.

were you born / I was born

Et vous? Combien de personnes y a-t-il dans votre famille? Quel âge ont les membres de votre famille? Quel âge avez-vous?

REMARQUES

1. The verb **avoir** is used when asking or giving someone's age.

   Quel âge **a** ta camarade de chambre? *How old is your roommate?*

   Quel âge **a** ton petit ami? *How old is your boyfriend?*

2. In inversion, remember to insert a **-t-** before the singular forms **il, elle,** and **on.**

   Quel âge ont-elles? *How old are they?*

   But: Quel âge a-**t**-elle? *How old is she?*

3. The word **an(s)** must be used when giving someone's age.

   J'ai vingt et un **ans.** *I am twenty-one.*

C. Les nombres (suite)

Review the numbers 0–29 on p. 3.

30	trente	
31	trente et un	
32	trente-deux	
33	trente-trois	
	etc.	

Numbers from 70 to 99 show a different pattern: 70 = 60 + 10; 80 = 4 × 20; 90 = 80 + 10.

40	quarante
41	quarante et un
42	quarante-deux
43	quarante-trois
	etc.
50	cinquante
51	cinquante et un
52	cinquante-deux
53	cinquante-trois
	etc.
60	soixante
61	soixante et un
62	soixante-deux
63	soixante-trois
	etc.
70	soixante-dix
71	soixante et onze
72	soixante-douze
73	soixante-treize
74	soixante-quatorze

75	soixante-quinze
76	soixante-seize
77	soixante-dix-sept
78	soixante-dix-huit
79	soixante-dix-neuf
80	quatre-vingts
81	quatre-vingt-un
82	quatre-vingt-deux
83	quatre-vingt-trois
	etc.
90	quatre-vingt-dix
91	quatre-vingt-onze
92	quatre-vingt-douze
	etc.
100	cent
101	cent un
200	deux cents
1000	mille
1.999	mille neuf cent quatre-vingt-dix-neuf
2.000	deux mille
2.006	deux mille six
100.000	cent mille
1.000.000	un million
1.000.000.000	un milliard

Numbers above 100 repeat the same pattern: **cent vingt et un, cent quatre-vingt-un, deux cent vingt** et un, *etc.*

► All numbers are invariable except **un.** Remember to replace the number **un** with **une** before a feminine noun, even in a compound number.

un oncle	trois oncles	vingt et un cousins
une tante	trois tantes	**vingt et une** cousines

▶ When numbers from 1 to 10 stand alone, the final consonants of **un, deux,** and **trois** are silent, but all others are pronounced. The **-x** at the end of **six** and **dix** is pronounced [s].

	un	deux	trois
But:	quatre	cin**q**	si**x**	sep**t**	hui**t**	neu**f**	di**x**

▶ Certain numbers have a different pronunciation when they precede a noun:

- The final consonant of **six, huit,** and **dix** is not pronounced before a consonant.

  six personnes   hui~~t~~ jours   di~~x~~ verres

- When the following noun begins with a vowel sound, the final consonant is always pronounced and linked to the noun. Note that with **quatre,** both final consonants are linked and the final **-e** is not pronounced.

  un [n]homme   cinq [k]hommes   huit [t]hommes

  deux [z]hommes   six [z]hommes   neuf [f]hommes

  trois [z]hommes   sept [t]hommes   dix [z]hommes

  quatre [tr]hommes   vingt [t]hommes

- The **-f** in **neuf** is pronounced as [v] only before the words **ans** *(years)* and **heures** *(hours)*.

  neuf [v]ans   neuf [v]heures

  But: neuf [f]enfants   neuf [f]hommes

- The final **-t** in **vingt** is silent when the number stands alone, but is pronounced in the compound numbers built on it.

  vin~~gt~~   [vɛ̃]

  vin~~gt~~ et un   [vɛ̃ te ɛ̃]

  vin~~gt~~-deux   [vɛ̃ dø]

▶ For numbers ending in 1, from 21 to 71, **et** is used. From 81 to 101 **et** is not used.

  vingt **et** un   *But:* quatre-vingt-un

▶ **Vingt** and **cent** do not add an **-s** if they are *followed* by a number.

  quatre-vingt**s** personnes   *But:* quatre-vingt-un

  trois cent**s** personnes   *But:* trois cent cinq

▶ **Mille** never adds an **-s.**

  mille personnes   deux **mille** personnes

▶ The words **million** and **milliard** are nouns and take an **s** in the plural. If they are followed by another noun, **de** is inserted between the nouns.

  deux millions d'euros

NOTE

In France, commas and periods used with numbers are the reverse of the system used in North America. Even more frequently, a space is used in the place of a period.

L'État a besoin de **2.000.000,00** d'euros. (deux millions)

ou L'État a besoin de **2 000 000,00** d'euros.

▶ There are five pairs of numbers in a French telephone number: **02.42.83.21.14.** The first pair indicates the general area of France.

6 **Les numéros de téléphone.** Read aloud the following phone numbers.

MODÈLE: 02.81.88.40.01
zéro deux / quatre-vingt-un / quatre-vingt-huit / quarante / zéro un

1. 02.41.93.21.80
2. 04.77.63.06.97
3. 04.42.08.98.89
4. 02.31.86.15.96
5. 04.71.83.61.91
6. 04.67.85.76.90
7. 05.61.10.99.02
8. 02.51.81.95.12
9. 03.88.19.82.43
10. 04.78.87.03.92

7 **Parlez-moi de votre famille** *(Tell me about your family).* Describe the people listed below. Use the model as a guide. If you don't have a brother, etc., say so.

MODÈLE: un frère
J'ai un frère qui s'appelle Bill. Il habite à Boston. Il est grand et assez beau. Il a vingt-trois ans.

1. une sœur
2. un frère
3. un oncle
4. une tante
5. des cousins
6. une cousine
7. un grand-père ou une grand-mère
8. des parents

Réalités culturelles
La France d'outre-mer

Cultural Activities 🌐

Find the places mentioned in this section on the map on the inside front cover.

FRANCE IS DIVIDED into 101 **départements**. **Départements** are administrative units created by the revolutionary government in 1790 to replace the old provinces. Among these are five overseas: **la Guadeloupe** and **la Martinique** (both in the Caribbean), **la Guyane** (in South America), and **la Réunion** and **Mayotte** (both in the Indian Ocean). These **départements d'outre-mer**, or **DOM** for short, have the same legal status as the continental departments, and their inhabitants enjoy the same rights of French citizenship.

vladoskan/Shutterstock.com

France also has a number of overseas possessions, **les territoires,** which do not have the same legal status as the departments. Their residents are, however, French citizens. These territories are **la Nouvelle-Calédonie** and its dependencies, **Wallis-et-Futuna,** and **la Polynésie française** (all in the Pacific Ocean), **Saint-Pierre-et-Miquelon** (off the coast of Canada), and **les Terres australes et antarctiques françaises** (French Antarctica). **Mayotte** and **Saint-Pierre-et-Miquelon** have a special status that is close to that of a department.

Note culturelle

En France il y à un **code départemental** pour indiquer où on habite. Le code pour Angers dans le Maine-et-Loire, par exemple, est 49, et pour Paris le code est 75. Le numéro forme les deux premiers chiffres *(numbers)* du **code postal.**

8 Codes postaux. The map above shows major cities and the first two numbers of the zip code for several French **départements.** Give the general zip code for the following cities by adding three zeros to the two numbers.

MODÈLE: Nantes

Le code postal pour Nantes est quarante-quatre mille (44000).

1. Dijon
2. Amiens
3. Tours
4. Besançon
5. Angers
6. Le Mans
7. Orléans
8. Grenoble
9. Paris
10. Brest
11. Rouen
12. Strasbourg

Voilà la famille Laplante.

Il y a combien de personnes dans la famille Laplante?

Il y a quatre personnes.

Il y a combien de garçons et **combien de** filles?

Il y a deux filles mais **il n'y a pas de** garçon.

► **Voilà** can mean either *there is (are)* or *here is (are)*. **Il y a** means *there is (are)*. While **voilà** and **il y a** are both translated *there is* or *there are* in English, they are used quite differently.

► **Voilà** and **voici** *(here is, here are)* point something out. They bring it to another person's attention. There is usually an accompanying physical movement—a nod of the head, a gesture of the hand toward the person or object, or a pointing of the finger to identify a specific object.

Voici mon fils et ma fille.	*Here are my son and daughter.*
Voilà ma voiture.	*There's my car.*

► **Il y a** simply states that something exists or tells how many there are.

Il y a un livre sur la table.	*There is a book on the table.*
Il y a quatre filles et deux garçons dans la famille Martin.	*There are four girls and two boys in the Martin family.*

► The negative of **il y a un (une, des)** is **il n'y a pas de.**

Il n'y a pas de voitures ici.	*There aren't any cars here.*

ATTENTION

Do not use **de** if **il n'y a pas** is followed by a number.

Il n'y a pas trois voitures dans le garage; il y a quatre voitures.	*There aren't three cars in the garage; there are four cars.*

► There are several ways to use **il y a** in a question.

Il y a un livre sur la table?
Est-ce qu'il **y a** un livre sur la table? } *Is there a book on the table?*
Y a-t-il un livre sur la table?

► **Il y a** is often used with **combien de.**

Il y a combien de garçons?
Combien de garçons **est-ce qu'il y a**?
Combien de garçons **y a-t-il**?

9 Lori parle avec Anne Martin. Complete the following sentences using either **il y a** or **voilà**.

MODÈLE: <u>Voilà</u> ma fille Émilie.

1. _____ deux enfants dans votre famille?
2. Non, Mademoiselle, _____ six enfants.
3. _____ une photo de ma famille.
4. _____ ma mère. Elle est jolie, n'est-ce pas?
5. _____ combien de filles dans votre famille?
6. Où sont-elles? Ah! _____ vos filles!

10 À vous. Answer the following questions as factually as possible.

1. Quel âge avez-vous?
2. Combien de personnes y a-t-il dans votre famille?
3. Quel âge ont les membres de votre famille?
4. Combien d'étudiants y a-t-il dans votre classe de français? Combien d'hommes et combien de femmes y a-t-il?
5. Quel âge a votre professeur de français? (Imaginez!)
6. Combien d'oncles et combien de tantes avez-vous? Quel âge ont-ils?

E. Les adjectifs possessifs mon, ton, notre, votre

Grammar
Tutorials

—Comment s'appellent **tes** parents?
—**Mes** parents s'appellent Jean et Stéphanie.
—Combien d'enfants y a-t-il dans **ta** famille?
—Il y a trois enfants dans **ma** famille: deux garçons et une fille.
—Quel âge a **ton** frère? Quel âge a **ta** sœur?
—**Mon** frère a 18 ans et **ma** sœur a 12 ans.
—Où habitent **vos** grands-parents?
—**Nos** grands-parents habitent à Saumur.

adjectifs possessifs

EN ANGLAIS	MASCULIN		FÉMININ		PLURIEL (M. ET F.)	
my	mon		ma		mes	
your	ton	père	ta	mère	tes	parents
our	notre		notre		nos	
your	votre		votre		vos	

► Possessive adjectives agree in gender and number with the nouns they modify (the "possessions"). **Notre** and **votre** are used for both masculine and feminine singular nouns.

Denise, **ton** père est gentil.	*Denise, your father is nice.*
Alain, **ta** mère est gentille aussi.	*Alain, your mother is nice also.*
Nathalie, **tes** parents sont très gentils.	*Nathalie, your parents are very nice.*

▶ In the singular, **ma** and **ta** become **mon** and **ton** when used directly before a feminine word beginning with a vowel sound.

ma meilleure amie

But: **mon** amie

ta tante

But: **ton** autre tante

▶ Liaison occurs if the word following **mon, ton, mes, tes, nos,** or **vos** begins with a vowel sound.

moɳ petit ami   voȿ bons amis

But: mon [n]ami   vos [z]amis

▶ As with **quatre,** the final **-e** of **notre** and **votre** is not pronounced before a vowel sound, but the final consonants are linked to the next word.

notrȩ [tR]ami

11 Qui? Try to identify people from among your friends and relatives who "fit" the following questions. Use possessive adjectives in each response. Be sure that verbs agree with subjects, and that adjectives agree with nouns.

MODÈLE: Qui chante bien?

Mes parents chantent bien. ou **Notre ami chante bien.**

1. Qui est grand?
2. Qui parle français?
3. Qui ne skie pas?
4. Qui adore le sport?
5. Qui n'aime pas beaucoup la bière?
6. Qui aime être étudiant?

12 À vous. Show a real (or imaginary) picture of your family and point out parents, brothers, sisters, cousins, uncles, and aunts. Give each person's age as well.

MODÈLE: **Voilà ma sœur, Kristen. Elle a 16 ans.**

ENTRE AMIS   Dans ta famille

Follow the steps below to interview your partner about his or her family. Use possessive adjectives whenever possible.

1. Ask your partner how many people there are in his/her family.
2. Find out the names of his/her brother, sister, etc.
3. Find out how old they are.
4. Find out where they live.
5. Ask if his/her brother, sister, etc. speaks French or studies French.
6. What else can you find out about his/her family members?

3. TALKING ABOUT YOUR HOME

Track 1-26

—Habitez-vous dans une maison° ou dans un appartement°, Lori?
   —*Nous habitons dans une maison.*

house
apartment

—Et combien de pièces° y a-t-il dans votre maison?
   —*Il y a sept pièces.*

rooms

—Et qu'est-ce qu'il y a chez vous°?
   —*Chez moi° il y a ...*

at your house
at my house

> **Bureau** *can mean either* desk *or* office. *The teacher's office* = **le bureau du professeur.** **Chambre** *implies* bedroom, *not* room *in general.*

... dans ma salle de séjour

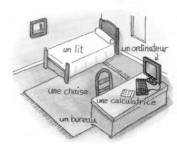

... dans ma chambre.

... dans ma cuisine.

... dans mon garage.

Et vous? Qu'est-ce qu'il y a chez vous?

⑬ Les renseignements *(Information).* Olivier is giving some information about people in his neighborhood. Complete his sentences, using the verb **avoir** and a number. Where no number is indicated, use **un, une,** or **des** as appropriate.

MODÈLE: Les Dufoix / deux enfants / chat
        Les Dufoix ont deux enfants et un chat.

1. Charles / radio antique
2. Je / enfants extraordinaires
3. Les Dubois / trois télévisions / stéréo / ordinateur
4. Madame Martin / mari / six enfants
5. Nous / petit appartement / voiture
6. Mes grands-parents / grande maison / quatre chambres
7. Les Martin / chat / chien / deux réfrigérateurs / cuisinière à gaz / lave-vaisselle
8. Madame Davis / voiture japonaise / vélo français

F. La négation + un (une, des)

Review the negative of **il y a,** *p. 72.*

▶ After a negation, indefinite articles (**un, une, des**) usually become **de (d')**.

Vous avez **un** ordinateur?   Non, je n'ai pas **d'**ordinateur.
Vous avez **une** voiture?   Non, je n'ai pas **de** voiture.
Vous avez **des** frères ou **des** sœurs?   Non, je n'ai pas **de** frère ou **de** sœur.
Y a-t-il **un** lave-vaisselle?   Non, il n'y a pas **de** lave-vaisselle.

This rule does not apply after **être.**

Christophe n'est pas **un** enfant.   *Christophe isn't a child.*
La voiture n'est pas **une** Ford.   *The car is not a Ford.*
Ce ne sont pas **des** amis.   *They're not friends.*

▶ Also, definite articles (**le, la, l', les**) and possessive adjectives (**mon, ma, mes,** etc.) do not change after a negation.

Je n'aime pas **le** thé.   Mon frère n'aime pas **notre** chien.

▶ When contradicting a negative statement or question, use **si** instead of **oui.**

Il n'y a pas de sandwichs ici.   **Si,** il y a des sandwichs.
Vous n'avez pas d'ordinateur?   **Si,** j'ai un ordinateur.
Vous n'aimez pas le café?   **Si,** j'aime le café.

14 Un riche et un pauvre. Guy has everything, but Philippe has practically nothing. Tell what Guy has and Philippe doesn't have.

MODÈLE: voiture
      Guy a une voiture, mais Philippe n'a pas de voiture.

1. appartement   4. ordinateur
2. lave-linge   5. amis
3. petite amie   6. chien

15 Bavardages *(Gossip).* Someone has made up gossip about you and your neighbors. Correct these falsehoods by making each statement negative.

MODÈLE: Monsieur Dupont a des filles.
      Mais non! Il n'a pas de fille.

1. Marie a un petit ami.
2. Il y a une moto dans votre garage.
3. Vous détestez le café.
4. Jean-Yves a des enfants.
5. Christophe et Alice ont un chien.
6. Votre voiture est une Renault.

16 As-tu … ? Your partner will interview you according to the model. If you have the item in question, say so. If not, give a negative answer and then name something that you do have.

MODÈLE: une voiture

    VOTRE PARTENAIRE: **As-tu une voiture?**

    VOUS: **Non, je n'ai pas de voiture mais j'ai une moto.**

1. une maison
2. un chien
3. un cousin à Lyon
4. un ordinateur
5. des amis qui habitent à Paris
6. un frère ou une sœur qui parle français

17 Une voyante. A fortune teller has made the following statements about you. Affirm or deny them. Remember to use **si** if you wish to contradict a negative statement.

MODÈLE: Vous n'avez pas de frère.
    Si, j'ai un frère (des frères).
    Oui, c'est vrai, je n'ai pas de frère.

1. Vous n'avez pas de sœur.
2. Vous n'habitez pas dans un appartement.
3. Vous n'avez pas de stéréo.
4. Vous n'étudiez pas beaucoup.
5. Le professeur n'est pas gentil.
6. Vous n'aimez pas étudier le français.

Vocabulaire

Les pièces d'une maison

un bureau	*office*	les toilettes	*restroom*
une chambre	*bedroom*	un salon	*living room*
une cuisine	*kitchen*	une salle de séjour	*den; living room*
une salle à manger	*dining room*	un sous-sol	*basement*
une salle de bain	*bathroom*	une véranda	*porch*

18 À vous. Answer the following questions.

1. Où habitez-vous?
2. Combien de pièces y a-t-il chez vous?
3. Quelles pièces est-ce qu'il y a?
4. Y a-t-il un fauteuil dans votre chambre?
5. Combien de chaises y a-t-il dans votre chambre?
6. Y a-t-il un chien ou un chat dans votre maison?
7. Qu'est-ce qu'il y a dans votre chambre?
8. Qu'est-ce qu'il y a dans le garage du professeur? (Imaginez!)

Grammar
Tutorials

C'est le mari **de** Mme Martin.	*It's Mme Martin's husband.*
Ce n'est pas la maison **de** René.	*It's not René's house.*
C'est la maison **des** parents **de** René.	*It's René's parents' house.*

▶ The preposition **de (d')** is used to indicate possession or relationship. French has no possessive *-'s* ending: *Marie's sister* has to be expressed in French as *the sister of Marie.*

la sœur **de** Marie	*Marie's sister*
la voiture **d'**Alain	*Alain's car*

▶ If the "owner" is indicated with a proper name, **de (d')** is used without an article or possessive adjective. When the word referring to the "owner" is not a proper name, an article or a possessive adjective precedes it: *The grand-mother's room* has to be expressed as *the room of the grandmother.*

la chambre de **la** grand-mère	*the grandmother's room*
la moto de **mon** ami	*my friend's motorcycle*

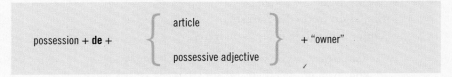

possession + **de** +   { article / possessive adjective }   + "owner"

▶ The preposition **de** contracts with the articles **le** and **les,** but there is no contraction with the articles **la** and **l'**.

de + le	→	**du**	du professeur
de + les	→	**des**	des étudiants
de + la	→	**de la**	de la femme
de + l'	→	**de l'**	de l'enfant

*Remember that **de l'** could be masculine or feminine.*

C'est une photo **du** professeur.	*It's a picture of the teacher.*
C'est la maison **des** parents d'Éric.	*It's Éric's parents' house.*
C'est le chat **de la** mère de Céline.	*It's Céline's mother's cat.*
C'est la voiture **de l'**oncle de Pascal.	*It's Pascal's uncle's car.*

19 J'ai trouvé une radio (*I found a radio*). A number of objects have been found. Ask a question to try to identify the owners. Your partner will answer negatively and will decide who *is* the owner.

MODÈLE: J'ai trouvé une radio. (Jeanne)

> VOUS: **J'ai trouvé une radio. C'est la radio de Jeanne?**
>
> VOTRE PARTENAIRE: **Non, ce n'est pas la radio de Jeanne. C'est la radio de Kévin.**

Remember to use only **de (d')** *with a proper name.*

1. J'ai trouvé une voiture. (Madame Dufour)
2. J'ai trouvé une radio. (professeur)
3. J'ai trouvé un chat. (Karine)
4. J'ai trouvé une moto. (l'ami de Michèle)
5. J'ai trouvé un chien. (les parents de Denis)
6. J'ai trouvé une calculatrice. (Frédérique)
7. J'ai trouvé un vélo. (la sœur de Sophie)

20 Nos possessions. Complete the following sentences with **de, du, de la, de l',** and/or **des.**

1. Le vélo _de_ Laurence est dans le garage.
2. La voiture _du_ père _d'_ Anne est bleue.
3. La photo _de l'_ oncle et _____ tante _de_ Guy est sur le bureau _des_ grands-parents _de_ Guy.
4. Le chat _du_ frère _de_ Chantal est sur le lit _____ parents _de_ Chantal.
5. Où est la calculatrice _de la_ sœur _de_ Sandrine?
6. C'est la stéréo _____ enfants _____ professeur.
7. La moto _de_ mon frère est dans notre garage.

↑ possessive adj

21 Où est-ce? Patrick's family has a number of possessions. Ask where each item is.

MODÈLE: La sœur de Patrick a un vélo.
> **Où est le vélo de la sœur de Patrick?**

1. Les sœurs de Patrick ont une télévision.
2. Le frère de Patrick a une voiture.
3. L'oncle de Patrick a un chien.
4. Les cousins de Patrick ont une stéréo.
5. Les enfants de Patrick ont un ordinateur.
6. La cousine de Patrick a un appartement.
7. Les parents de Patrick ont une voiture allemande.
8. Le père de Patrick a un bureau.
9. La tante de Patrick a un petit chat.
10. Les parents de Patrick ont une belle maison.

Grammar
Tutorials

As-tu une photo de la famille de Léa?	Voilà une photo de **sa** famille.
Où est le père de Léa?	Voilà **son** père.
Où est la mère de Léa?	Voilà **sa** mère.
Où sont les grands-parents de Léa?	Voilà **ses** grands-parents.
Où est la fille de M. et Mme Dupont?	Voilà **leur** fille. C'est Léa!
Où sont les cousins des Dupont?	Voilà **leurs** cousins.

▶ **Son, sa,** and **ses** can mean either *his* or *her*. As with **mon, ma,** and **mes,** the choice of form depends on whether the "possession" is masculine or feminine, singular or plural. It makes no difference what the gender of the "owner" is.

son lit	*his bed or her bed*
sa chambre	*his room or her room*
ses chaises	*his chairs or her chairs*

▶ **Leur** and **leurs** mean *their* and are used when there is more than one "owner." Both forms are used for either masculine or feminine "possessions."

leur lit	**leur** chambre
leurs lits	**leurs** chambres

NOTE

> Be sure not to use **ses** when you mean **leurs.**
>
> | | |
> |---|---|
> | **ses** parents | *his parents or her parents* |
> | **leurs** parents | *their parents* |

▶ In the singular, **sa** becomes **son** when used directly before a feminine word beginning with a vowel sound.

	sa meilleure amie
But:	**son** amie

▶ Liaison occurs if the word following **son, ses,** or **leurs** begins with a vowel sound.

	son petit ami	ses bons amis	leurs parents
But:	son [n]ami	ses [z]amis	leurs [z]amis

▶ Sometimes the identity of the "owner" would be unclear if a possessive adjective were used. In such cases, it is better to use the possessive construction with **de.**

Robert et Marie habitent avec **sa** mère.	*(Robert's mother? Marie's mother?)*
Robert et Marie habitent avec **la** mère **de Marie.**	*(clearly Marie's mother)*

Synthèse: les adjectifs possessifs *Starting w/ Vowel or h*

PRONOM	MASCULIN	FÉMININ	PLURIEL (M. ET F.)	
je	**mon**	**ma** / *m on* ★	**mes**	*my*
tu	**ton**	**ta** / *ton* ★	**tes**	*your*
il/elle/on	**son**	**sa** / *sa* ★	**ses**	*his/her*
nous	**notre**	**notre**	**nos**	*our*
vous	**votre**	**votre**	**vos**	*your*
ils/elles	**leur**	**leur**	**leurs**	*their*

22 La chambre de qui? Clarify the identity of the "owner" in each of the following phrases by completing the following expressions with the appropriate form of **de** + the definite article.

MODÈLE: sa chambre. La chambre de qui? La chambre **du** frère de Marc.

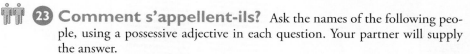

1. leur photo. La photo de qui? La photo *des* enfants de ma tante.
2. son nom. Le nom de qui? Le nom *de la* jeune fille.
3. sa moto. La moto de qui? La moto *du* mari d'Anne.
4. leurs livres. Les livres de qui? Les livres *des* étudiants.
5. son chien. Le chien de qui? Le chien *de l'* oncle d'Isabelle.
6. sa maison. La maison de qui? La maison *de l'* ami de Laurent.
7. ses amies. Les amies de qui? Les amies *de la* sœur de Denis.
8. son chat. Le chat de qui? Le chat *de la* petite amie de Jean-Luc.
9. son bureau. Le bureau de qui? Le bureau *du* professeur.

23 Comment s'appellent-ils? Ask the names of the following people, using a possessive adjective in each question. Your partner will supply the answer.

Be careful to distinguish between **son/sa/ses** and **leur(s)** when asking these questions.

MODÈLES: le cousin de Nathalie? (Stéphane)

VOUS: **Comment s'appelle son cousin?**
VOTRE PARTENAIRE: **Il s'appelle Stéphane.**

les cousines de Nathalie? (Christelle et Sandrine)

VOUS: **Comment s'appellent ses cousines?**
VOTRE PARTENAIRE: **Elles s'appellent Christelle et Sandrine.**

1. le père de Nathalie? (Michel)
2. la sœur d'Éric? (Isabelle)
3. la mère d'Éric et d'Isabelle? (Monique)
4. les frères de Nathalie? (Christophe et Sébastien)
5. les sœurs de Nathalie? (Sylvie et Céline)
6. le chien de Nathalie? (Fidèle)
7. les grands-parents de Nathalie? (Marie et Pierre Coifard; Louis et Jeanne Dupuis)
8. les parents de votre meilleur(e) ami(e)?
9. les amis de vos parents?

24 À vous. Interview your partner using the following questions. Use possessive adjectives in your answers.

Self Test

MODÈLE: Où est la maison de votre ami(e)?
Sa maison est à Denver.

1. Comment s'appelle votre meilleur(e) ami(e)?
2. Quel âge a votre ami(e)?
3. Combien de personnes y a-t-il dans la famille de votre ami(e)?
4. Comment s'appellent les parents de votre ami(e)?
5. Où habitent les parents de votre ami(e)?
6. Qu'est-ce qu'il y a dans la maison des parents de votre ami(e)?

ENTRE AMIS Dans ta chambre

Follow the steps below and use **tu** to interview your partner.

1. Find out where your partner lives.
2. Find out if your partner has a TV in his/her room.
3. Find out two other items that s/he has in his/her room.
4. Find out two other items that s/he does not have.
5. Find out if your partner has a roommate.
6. If so, find out his/her name and two items of information about the roommate.
7. Turn to another person and share what you found out.

Comment s'appellent leurs filles?

© Owen Franken/Corbis

Intégration

RÉVISION

 A **Chez mon professeur.** Imagine the home, garage, etc. of your French teacher. Make up five different sentences to state what s/he has or does not have.

MODÈLE: **Il y a une moto dans son garage.**

B **Trouvez quelqu'un qui ...** Interview your classmates in French to find someone who ...

MODÈLE: speaks French
Est-ce que tu parles français?

1. has a computer
2. has no brothers or sisters
3. has a dog or a cat or a fish
4. likes children a lot
5. is 21 or older
6. has a sister named Nicole
7. has a brother named Christopher
8. lives in an apartment
9. has grandparents who live in another state or province

C **À l'écoute.** Anne Martin is explaining who the people are in a family photo. Listen and complete each description to say how each person is related to Anne.

Track 1-27

MODÈLE: YOU HEAR: **Monique Martin est la mère de mon mari.**
YOU WRITE: **Monique Martin est _sa belle-mère_.**

1. Émilie est _____ et Benoît est _____.
2. Nathalie est _____.
3. Marie Duhamel est _____.
4. Alain est _____ et Georges Duhamel est _____.

D **À vous.** Answer the following questions.

1. Combien de personnes y a-t-il dans votre famille?
2. Comment s'appellent deux de vos ami(e)s?
3. Où habitent-ils/elles? Quel âge ont-ils/elles?
4. Sont-ils/elles étudiant(e)s? Si oui, ont-ils/elles une chambre à l'université? Étudient-ils/elles le français ou une autre langue?
5. Avez-vous des ami(e)s qui ont un appartement? Si oui, qu'est-ce qu'il y a dans leur appartement?
6. Avez-vous un ami qui est marié? Si oui, comment s'appelle sa femme? Quel âge a-t-elle?
7. Avez-vous une amie qui est mariée? Si oui, comment s'appelle son mari? Quel âge a-t-il?
8. Avez-vous des amis qui ont des enfants? Si oui, combien d'enfants ont-ils? Comment s'appellent leurs enfants? Quel âge ont-ils?

Communication and Communities. To learn more about the culture presented in this chapter, go to the Premium Website and click on the Web Search Activities.

NÉGOCIATIONS

C'est à qui? Each of the items below belong to one of David's relatives. Ask your partner questions to match each item with its correct owner. Complete the form with the missing information. Your partner's form is in Appendix D.

MODÈLE: **C'est la voiture du frère de David?**
          Non, ce n'est pas la voiture de David. C'est la voiture de son père.

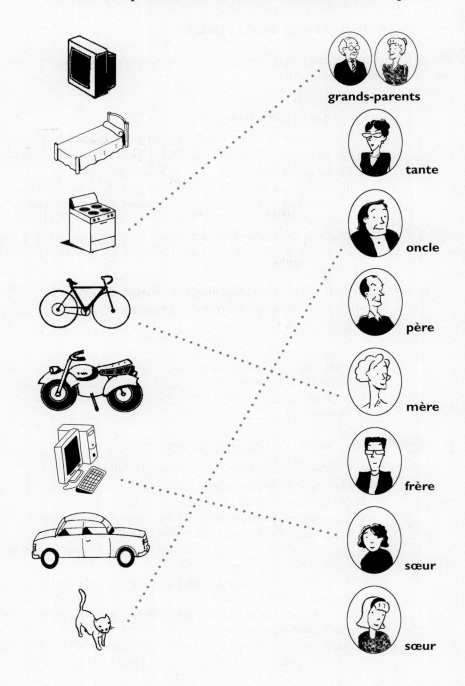

LECTURE 1

A Ma maison idéale. To review the vocabulary you have learned for housing, draw a sketch of a home that would be ideal for you. Then label each of the rooms in French.

B Étude du vocabulaire. Study the following sentences and choose the English words that correspond to the French words in bold print: *square meters, fireplace, planted with trees, in new condition, winter, landscaped lot, approximately, stone, in good taste, on one level, roof, country, house, set up/ready-to-use.*

1. Le **pavillon** est situé à la **campagne** à **environ** 30 kilomètres de Montréal.
2. Près de la maison il y a un jardin **arboré** et un beau **terrain paysagé** de 300 **mètres carrés.**
3. En **hiver**, s'il fait froid, il y a une belle **cheminée** en **pierre** dans la salle de séjour.
4. La cuisine est **aménagée** et équipée **avec goût.**
5. La **toiture** de la maison est **à l'état neuf.**
6. Les personnes handicapées n'ont pas de problème avec une maison de **plain-pied.**

C Les pièces. Read the four ads for houses in Québec in order to:

1. identify the number of rooms in each home, and
2. make a list of the rooms that are mentioned.

MAISONS À VENDRE

CADRE EXCEPTIONNEL Belle maison récente, agréable séjour-salle à manger en L 45 m² environ, cuisine aménagée et équipée, 3 chambres, belle salle de bain, garage et jardin, mérite visite!

ELLE VOUS SÉDUIRA Aux portes de Chicoutimi, agréable pavillon indépendant sur 500 m² de terrain, cuisine aménagée et équipée, beau séjour-salle à manger avec cheminée, 3 chambres, garage 2 voitures et jardin aménagé avec goût.

Image Source/Getty Images

Image Source/Getty Images

DE TOUTE BEAUTÉ Le charme de la campagne à 10 mn de Chicoutimi, belle cuisine aménagée et équipée, vaste pièce de réception 90 m² avec superbe cheminée en pierre, jardin d'hiver parfaitement exposé, 4 chambres, 2 sdb, bureau, grand garage, 1 700 m² de terrain paysagé, aménagement de goût et de qualité!

EXCEPTIONNELLE Plain-pied indépendant, séjour-salle à manger, 2 chambres, toiture état neuf, garage, jardin arboré. Affaire à saisir!

D Inférence. Reread the ads to try to determine the following information. Be ready to justify your answers by quoting the reading.

1. the newest home
2. the biggest home
3. the largest lot
4. the home that has been remodeled
5. the name of the closest Canadian city
6. the home you would choose and why

E À discuter. Aimez-vous ces maisons? Pourquoi ou pourquoi pas?

F Comparaisons culturelles. What similarities or differences between **Québécois** homes and those of your country can you infer from what you have read?

Réalités culturelles

Le Québec

Cultural Activities

Reuters/Jim Young

QUEBEC IS THE LARGEST of the ten Canadian provinces. The vast majority of people in **la belle province,** as the **Québécois** refer to it, speak French, while the majority language in the other provinces is English. However, sizable French-speaking minorities exist in Ontario and New Brunswick, and smaller French-speaking populations can be found in the other provinces. The history of Quebec goes back to the sixteenth century, when Jacques Cartier established a French colonial empire in North America called New France. In 1608, Samuel de Champlain founded the city of Quebec. (In 2008 the city celebrated its 400th birthday, and Canada as a nation celebrated its beginning.) In 1763, at the end of the Seven Years' War, England was granted possession of the whole province. Quebec's French-speaking population now faced the challenge of maintaining its distinct language and cultural heritage under British rule. Over the course of the next two centuries, the **Québécois'** tenacity has resulted in a vibrant French-speaking culture. By the beginning of the 1960s, French Canadians considered themselves not so much a *minority* in the Canadian Confederation as the Francophone *majority* in the province of Quebec. This situation culminated in the passage of the Charter of the French Language in 1977, known as **Loi 101,** which established French as the sole official language in the province of Quebec. Its goal was to "ensure the quality and influence of the French language" in North American civilization. Although many amendments have been added to **la Loi 101** since its inception, the major provisions of the law remain intact. To find out more, see http://www.oqlf.gouv.qc.ca/english/charter/index.html.

LECTURE II

A **Faire des prédictions.** The following text is a short biography of French actress-singer Charlotte Gainsbourg, who has followed in the footsteps of her famous parents. What kind of information would you expect to find in this kind of text? What vocabulary from the chapter might you find?

B **Étude du vocabulaire.** Study the following sentences and choose the English words that correspond to the French words in bold print: *makes, among, as well as, won, since, known.*

1. Charlotte grandit **parmi** des artistes.
2. Charlotte Gainsbourg est **connue** en France et aux États-Unis pour ses films et sa musique.
3. Elle commence sa carrière très jeune; elle **tourne** dans des films **depuis** les années 80.
4. Elle joue dans des films dramatiques **ainsi que** des comédies.
5. L'actrice **a remporté** plusieurs prix de cinéma.

C **Parcourez la lecture** *(Skim the reading).* Skim the following reading to identify:

1. the names of Charlotte's family members and their professions.
2. the names of the films Charlotte has acted in and the names of her albums.
3. how she has followed in the footsteps of her famous parents.

The Premium Website includes a link with information about Charlotte Gainsbourg.

Charlotte Gainsbourg
continue la tradition de sa famille

Robert Pitts/Landov

Charlotte Gainsbourg est une actrice et chanteuse française. Elle est la fille de deux grands artistes: Serge Gainsbourg, auteur-compositeur-chanteur français, et Jane Birkin, actrice-chanteuse britannique. Les passions de Charlotte et les langues qu'elle parle reflètent le talent et les cultures variées de ses parents célèbres. Aux États-Unis Charlotte est connue pour ses rôles dans *21 Grammes, The Science of Sleep, I'm Not There* et *Antichrist.* En France, elle est connue depuis les années 80 pour ses rôles dans des films dramatiques ainsi que des comédies. Elle a remporté trois César (l'équivalent d'un Oscar).

page suivante

Née à Londres en 1971, Charlotte grandit parmi des artistes. Elle étudie le piano et la peinture[1], tout comme son père. Mais sa jeunesse n'est pas toujours facile. Les enfants à l'école se moquent d'elle parce qu'elle est la fille de Serge Gainsbourg, une figure assez controversée. (La chanson que ses parents, Serge Gainsbourg et Jane Birkin, ont chantée en 1969, «*Je t'aime… moi non plus*»[2], a fait scandale.) En 1984, le grand public découvre[3] Charlotte quand elle chante «*Lemon Incest*» avec son père. Elle continue cette collaboration dans *Charlotte for Ever*. En même temps[4], sa mère l'encourage à devenir[5] actrice et elle débute dans le film *Paroles et musique* en 1984. Puis à l'âge de 15 ans, elle gagne le César du Meilleur espoir féminin pour son travail dans le film *L'Effrontée*. Elle joue le rôle d'une adolescente tourmentée et révoltée.

En 1991, Charlotte rencontre Yvan Attal qui devient son compagnon et avec qui elle tourne des films plus légers[6] que ceux de son adolescence. Elle change son image complètement avec les rôles qu'elle interprète dans les films d'Yvan Attal, tels que *Ma femme est une actrice* et *La Bûche*. Le couple, qui continue à collaborer sur des projets cinématographiques, a un fils né en 1997 qui s'appelle Ben et une fille née en 2002 qui s'appelle Alice Jane.

Bien que[7] Charlotte continue à tourner des films, en 2006 elle retourne à la musique et sort l'album *5:55*. En 2010 elle sort un deuxième album, *IRM*, collaborant avec Beck. Presque[8] toutes les chansons cette fois-ci sont en anglais. Elle dit[9] qu'elle aime bien le mélange[10]—une Française qui chante en anglais, un mélange qui continue la tradition bi-culturelle établie par ses parents.

The Premium Website includes a link with information about Charlotte Gainsbourg.

---

1. *painting* / 2. *"I love you… me neither"* / 3. *discovers* / 4. *At the same time* / 5. *to become* 6. *lighter* / 7. *Although* / 8. *Almost* / 9. *says* / 10. *mixture*

D Questions. Answer the following questions in French.

1. Comment s'appellent les parents de Charlotte?
2. Comment s'appelle son compagnon?
3. Comment s'appellent son fils et sa fille?
4. Où est-ce que Charlotte est née?
5. À quel âge est-ce que Charlotte chante avec son père?
6. À quel âge est-ce qu'elle rencontre Yvan, son compagnon?
7. Quel âge ses enfants ont-ils aujourd'hui?

E Inférence. Reread the passage to determine the following. Be ready to quote the reading to justify your answers.

1. how Charlotte's parents influenced her life
2. how Charlotte is a bicultural person

RÉDACTION

MA FAMILLE

Your new key-pal would like to know about your family. Write him or her an e-mail in which you:

- greet and ask how s/he is doing
- tell how you're doing
- tell how many people there are in your immediate family, what their names are, how old they are, and their relationship to you
- tell where your parents and siblings live
- describe one of their homes
- ask about your key-pal's family
- close the e-mail

MODÈLE:

> **Bonjour Christine,**
> **Comment ça va? Je vais bien ici à Chicago.**
> **Alors, il y a cinq personnes dans ma famille: mes parents, mon frère, ma sœur et moi. Mes parents s'appellent…**

Ⓐ Avant d'écrire. Read the instructions above, then ask yourself: What are the main topics I will address? What vocabulary do I need? What grammar concepts will I use? Create a list of topics and decide how you will order them in your e-mail. Then, create a list of French vocabulary to accompany each topic.

Ⓑ Écrire. Use your lists to draft your e-mail.

Ⓒ Correction. Read over your draft and check the content against your lists. Did you include everything you had intended to write about? Read your draft a second time, checking for any errors in agreement, spelling, or sentence structure. Make any corrections and revise your draft.

Vocabulaire Actif

Practice this vocabulary with the flashcards on **iLrn**.

Possessions

un bureau *desk*
une calculatrice *calculator*
une chaise *chair*
un chat *cat*   *une chatte / une chienne*
un chien *dog*
une cuisinière *stove*
un fauteuil *armchair*
un lave-linge *washing machine*
un lave-vaisselle *dishwasher*
un lit *bed*
un livre *book*
une moto *motorcycle*
un ordinateur *computer*
un réfrigérateur *refrigerator*
un scooter *scooter*
un sofa *sofa*
une stéréo *stereo*
un vélo *bicycle*
une voiture *car*

La maison ou l'appartement

un appartement *apartment*
un bureau *office*
une chambre *bedroom*
une cuisine *kitchen*
un garage *garage*
une maison *house*
une pièce *room*
un salon *living room*
une salle à manger *dining room*
une salle de bain *bathroom*
une salle de séjour *living room*
un sous-sol *basement*
les toilettes *(f.pl.) restroom*
une véranda *porch*

La famille

un beau-père *stepfather; father-in-law*
des beaux-parents *(m.pl.) stepparents; in-laws*
une belle-mère *stepmother; mother-in-law*
une belle-sœur *sister-in-law*
un(e) cousin(e) *cousin*
un(e) enfant *child*
une famille *family*
une femme *wife*
une fille *daughter*
un fils *son*
un frère *brother*
un demi-frère *stepbrother*
une (arrière-) grand-mère *(great) grandmother*
un (arrière-) grand-père *(great) grandfather*

des grands-parents *(m. pl.) grandparents*
un mari *husband*
une mère *mother*
un neveu *nephew*
une nièce *niece*
un oncle *uncle*
des parents *(m. pl.) parents; relatives*
un père *father*
une petite-fille *granddaughter*
un petit-fils *grandson*
des petits-enfants *(m. pl.) grandchildren*
une sœur *sister*
une demi-sœur *stepsister*
une tante *aunt*

D'autres noms

l'âge *(m.) age*
un an *year*
l'arrivée *(f.) arrival*
l'école *(f.) school*
un(e) étudiant(e) *student*
une fille *girl*
un garçon *boy*
la gare *(train) station*
un membre *member*
une photo *photograph*
un train *train*

Nombres

trente *thirty*
quarante *forty*
cinquante *fifty*
soixante *sixty*
soixante-dix *seventy*
soixante et onze *seventy-one*
soixante-douze *seventy-two*
quatre-vingts *eighty*
quatre-vingt-un *eighty-one*
quatre-vingt-dix *ninety*
quatre-vingt-onze *ninety-one*
cent *one hundred*
mille *one thousand*
un million *one million*
un milliard *one billion*

Adjectifs possessifs

mon, ma, mes *my*
ton, ta, tes *your*
son, sa, ses *his; her*
notre, nos *our*
votre, vos *your*
leur, leurs *their*

D'autres adjectifs

autre *other*

charmant(e) *charming*
gentil(le) *nice*

Verbes

avoir *to have*
passer (un an) *to spend (a year)*

Prépositions

chez *at the home of*
dans *in*
près *close*
sur *on*

Conjonction

si *if*

Articles indéfinis

un/une *a, an*
des *some; any*

Adverbes

combien (de) *how many; how much*
comment *how; what*
encore *still; again; more*
trop (de) *too much; too many*

Expressions utiles

Bienvenue! *Welcome!*
C'est *He/she/it is*
Ce sont *They are/There are*
chez moi *at my house*
chez nous *at our house; back home*
chez vous *at your house*
Comment s'appelle-t-il (elle)? *What's his (her) name?*
Comment s'appellent-ils (elles)? *What are their names?*
Il (elle) s'appelle … *His (her) name is …*
Ils (elles) s'appellent … *Their names are …*
il y a *there is (are)*
J'ai mal compris. *I didn't understand correctly.*
En quelle année es-tu né(e)? *What year were you born?*
Je suis né(e) *I was born*
Je vous présente … *Let me introduce you to …*
Qu'est-ce qu'il y a … ? *What is there … ?*
Qu'est-ce qu'il y a? *What's the matter?*
Quel âge avez-vous? (a-t-il?, etc.) *How old are you? (is he?, etc.)*
sans doute *probably*
Si! *Yes!*
sur la photo *in the picture*
voici *here is; here are*
voilà tout *that's all*
vous dites *you say*

CHAPITRE 4

L'identité

Mike Watson Images/Jupiter Images

BUTS COMMUNICATIFS
- Describing personal attributes
- Describing clothing
- Describing people and things
- Describing what you do at home
- Identifying someone's profession

STRUCTURES UTILES
- Quelques groupes d'adjectifs
- **Ne ... jamais**
- Les adjectifs de couleur
- L'adjectif démonstratif
- La place de l'adjectif
- Le verbe **faire**
- Les mots interrogatifs **qui, que** et **quel**

CULTURE
Zoom sur l'Internet
- **Vidéo buzz:** Être au pair
- **Vu sur le web:** L'e-commerce
- **Repères:** La netiquette
- **Insolite:** Le franglais
- **Article:** L'internet: un moyen de perfectionner votre français
- **Petit lexique de l'Internet**

Il y a un geste
- Paresseux
- Ennuyeux
- C'est cher!

Lectures
- Offres d'emploi
- «Familiale»

RESSOURCES

 Audio

 iLrn Heinle Learning Center

Premium Website

 Pair Work

 Group Work

 Entre amis Video Program

Coup d'envoi

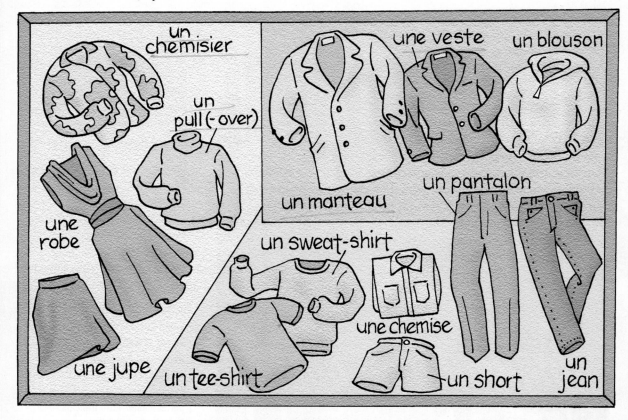

🔊 PRISE DE CONTACT: **LES VÊTEMENTS°**   *clothes*

Track 1-28

Qu'est-ce que vous portez en cours?   *What clothes do you wear to class?*

Je porte …

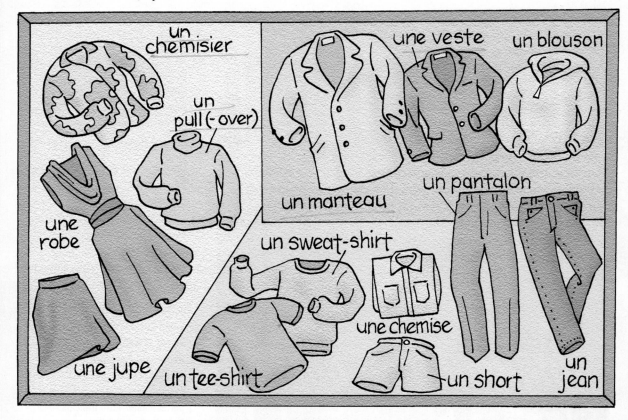

un chemisier

un pull (- over)

une robe

une jupe

une veste

un blouson

un manteau

un sweat-shirt

un pantalon

une chemise

un tee-shirt

un short

un jean

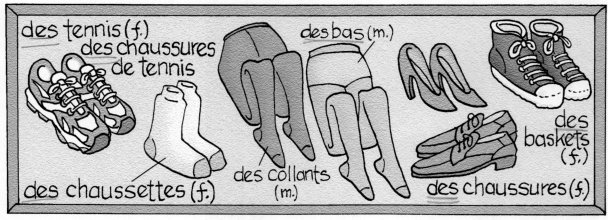

des tennis (f.)
des chaussures de tennis

des bas (m.)

des chaussettes (f.)

des collants (m.)

des chaussures (f.)

des baskets (f.)

🌐 **Et vous?** Qu'est-ce que vous portez aujourd'hui°?   *today*

Moi, je porte …

Lori Becker envoie° un e-mail à son professeur de français aux États-Unis. sends

---

To:	
CC:	
BCC:	
Sub:	

Cher Professeur,   *Angers, le 2 octobre*

Me voilà au pair chez les Martin. J'aime bien cette[1] famille! Je garde[2] deux des enfants et je fais quelquefois le ménage.[3] Ça me donne[4] beaucoup de travail mais c'est Mme Martin qui fait la cuisine.[5] Et puis[6] les enfants font la vaisselle[7] le soir.

Quelle belle ville[8]! Et les gens[9] sont vraiment charmants! Comme chez nous, beaucoup d'étudiants portent un jean et un tee-shirt ici[10] pour aller en cours. Je suis heureuse[11] d'être en France, mais il faut[12] beaucoup étudier! Chaleureusement[13],

Lori

PS: Ci-joint[14] une photo de moi avec les enfants.

---

1. this 2. look after 3. do housework sometimes 4. That gives me 5. who does the cooking 6. then
7. do the dishes 8. city 9. people 10. here 11. happy 12. it is necessary; I have to 13. Warmly
14. Attached

ⓒ Compréhension. Taking turns, read the following statements with your partner. Decide whether they are true (**C'est vrai**) or false (**C'est faux**). If a sentence is false, correct it.

1. Lori Becker habite à Angers.
2. Elle habite chez ses parents.
3. Elle travaille pour les Martin.
4. Elle fait la cuisine et la vaisselle.
5. Elle est contente d'être en France.
6. Les vêtements des jeunes Français sont très différents des vêtements des jeunes Américains.

ⓒ À vous Describe to your partner what your classmates are wearing.

MODÈLE: **VOTRE PARTENAIRE: Qu'est-ce que Sean porte aujourd'hui?**
          VOUS: **Il porte ...**

Zoom sur l'Internet

Premium
Website

VIDÉO BUZZ

Être au pair

MANY YOUNG WOMEN from foreign countries work as **jeunes filles au pair** *(nannies)* in France. They are able to spend a year abroad by agreeing to work in a French home, in exchange for room and board and a token salary. They do some light housework and help to take care of the children. Lori is **au pair chez les Martin.** To learn more about the **au pair** experience, go to the *Premium Website* and click on the links.

Olive Images/Jupiter Images

INSOLITE

Le franglais

BORROWING INEVITABLY takes place when languages come into contact. The Norman Conquest in 1066 introduced thousands of French words into English and many English words found their way into the French language. French words borrowed from English are particularly common in certain fields, such as technology, business, and fashion. They may be nouns, verbs, or expressions **(le chewing-gum, un tee-shirt, l'e-mail, le business, formater, "Allez go!").** Borrowed words that have similar forms and similar meanings are called *cognates*. Words that have smilar forms but different meanings are called **faux amis** or *false friends*. An example is **un smoking**, which means a *tuxedo* in French. Official measures have been adopted in France to try to stem the flow of English expressions into the French language. Currently, for example, the terms **le logiciel espion** and **diffuser** are being encouraged rather than the borrowed words **le spyware** and **podcaster.**

VU SUR LE WEB

L'e-commerce

E-COMMERCE is on the rise in France. According to **FEVAD (la Fédération du e-commerce et de la vente à distance),** over 80% of Internet users consult web sites before making a purchase. The products most often bought on line include electronic merchandise, cultural products (books, music, DVDs), and clothing. Around 45% of Internet users in France buy clothing and accessories on line.

Among the top ten sites are **La Redoute, Les 3 Suisses,** and **Carrefour.** To find out what types of products these three companies offer, browse the links on the *Premium Website.*

Source: http://www.fevad.com

La netiquette

The Internet is perhaps the most important communication tool of our times. To promote courteous behavior on the Internet, the **Association des Fournisseurs d'Accès et de Services Internet** (The Association of Internet Access Suppliers) suggests that all internautes (users of cyberspace) *adhere to a set of rules called* **la netiquette.**

La netiquette est un guide de bonne conduite[1] pour les gens qui communiquent avec d'autres personnes sur l'Internet. Voici une "petite" liste des règles.

- Répondez rapidement aux messages, dans les 24 heures.
- Soyez[2] toujours poli.
- N'utilisez pas de termes extrêmes.
- À l'exception de la première lettre d'une phrase et pour les noms propres[3], n'écrivez jamais de texte en majuscules[4].
- Évitez le spamming.

D'après le site web: www.afa-france.com.

---

[1]conduct; [2]Be; [3]proper nouns; [4]capital letters

L'Internet: Un moyen de perfectionner votre français

ALTHOUGH LORI BECKER is far from home, she has several technological tools she can use to stay in touch with her friends. The two she would most likely use every day are a social networking site, such as Facebook (available in French as well as many other of the world's languages) and Skype, a software application that allows users to make voice and video phone calls over the Internet. Skype also allows users to text each other, send photos, and have conference calls. These and other electronic tools provide a wonderful way to build French vocabulary. Simply switch the "language" function of your Facebook page, your Skype account, or your cellphone menu from English into French!

Vocabulaire

Petit lexique de l'Internet

cliquer sur	*to click on*
le courrier électronique	*e-mail*
l'e-mail (le courriel [Canada])	*e-mail*
envoyer	*to send*
le mot de passe	*password*
naviguer sur Internet	*to surf the Internet*
le portable	*laptop; cell phone*
le réseau social	*social network*
le site web	*website*
télécharger	*to download*

ENTRE AMIS **J'aime beaucoup vos chaussures. Elles sont très belles.**

Role-play the following conversation with a partner.

1. Compliment your partner on some article of clothing s/he is wearing.
2. S/he should respond in a culturally appropriate manner.
3. Ask your partner what s/he usually wears to class.
4. S/he should respond and ask the same of you.

PRONONCIATION

🔊 **LES VOYELLES NASALES: [ɛ̃], [ɑ̃] ET [ɔ̃]**

Track 1-30

► Note the pronunciation of the following words:

[ɛ̃]
- **im**possible, **im**probable, **in**telligent, **cin**quante, v**in**, v**in**gt, m**in**ce
- **sym**pathique, **sym**phonie, **syn**thèse
- f**aim**, améric**ain**, maroc**ain**, mexic**ain**, tr**ain**
- h**ein**
- canad**ien**, ital**ien**, b**ien**, je v**iens**, ch**ien**, comb**ien**, t**iens**

[ɑ̃]
- ch**am**bre, **an**, fr**an**çais, ch**an**ter, m**an**ger, gr**an**d, p**en**dant, étudi**an**te, t**an**te, dem**an**dent
- **en**semble, m**em**bre, par ex**em**ple, **en**, **en**core, comm**en**t, souv**en**t

EXCEPTION exam**en** [ɛgzamɛ̃]

[ɔ̃]
- t**om**ber, c**om**bien, n**om**, prén**om**, **on**, **on**t, c**on**versation, n**on**, **on**cle, **on**ze

► Now go back and look at how these sounds are spelled and in what kinds of letter combinations they appear. What patterns do you notice?

💬 When **-m-** or **-n-** is followed by a consonant or is at the end of a word, it is usually not pronounced. It serves instead to indicate that the preceding vowel is nasal.

cinquante   **en**sem**ble**   **com**bien   **im**possible

💬 When **-m-** or **-n-** is followed by a written vowel (pronounced or not pronounced), the preceding vowel is not nasal.

ca**n**adien   crè**m**e   télép**h**one
bru**n**e   i**n**évitable   i**m**aginaire

NOTE The vowel preceding a written **-mm-** or **-nn-** is also not nasal.

i**nn**ocent   i**mm**obile   co**mm**e   perso**nn**e

► Practice saying the following words after your instructor, paying particular attention to the highlighted vowel sound. In these words, the highlighted vowel sound is *not* nasal.

américain   mê**m**e   li**m**onade   co**mm**e   **u**ne
Mad**a**me   **ai**me   cous**i**ne   co**mm**ent   l**u**nettes
exam**e**n   améric**ai**ne   i**n**actif   perso**nn**e   f**u**me

► In each of the following pairs of words, one of the words contains a nasal vowel and one does not. Pronounce each word correctly.

1. impossible / immobile
2. minuit / mince
3. faim / aime
4. marocain / marocaine
5. canadienne / canadien
6. une / un

7. ambulance / ami
8. anglaise / année
9. crème / membre
10. dentiste / Denise
11. combien / comment
12. bonne / bon

Buts communicatifs

I. DESCRIBING PERSONAL ATTRIBUTES

Track 1-31

Comment est votre meilleur(e) ami(e)? Est-il (elle) …

calme	ou	nerveux (nerveuse)?	
charmant(e)	ou	désagréable?	
compréhensif (compréhensive)°	ou	intolérant(e)°?	*understanding / intolerant*
discret (discrète)	ou	bavard(e)°?	*talkative*
généreux (généreuse)	ou	avare°?	*stingy*
gentil(le)	ou	méchant(e)°?	*mean*
heureux (heureuse)	ou	triste°?	*sad*
intelligent(e)	ou	stupide?	
intéressant(e)	ou	ennuyeux (ennuyeuse)°?	*boring*
optimiste	ou	pessimiste?	
patient(e)	ou	impatient(e)?	
travailleur (travailleuse)°	ou	paresseux (paresseuse)°?	*hard-working / lazy*

Et vous? Comment êtes-vous? Comment sont vos professeurs?

Il y a un geste

Paresseux. The thumb and index finger of one hand "caress" an imaginary hair in the palm of the other hand. This gesture signifies that someone is so lazy that a hair could grow in his/her palm.

© Cengage Learning

Ennuyeux. The gesture for **ennuyeux** is made by rubbing the knuckles back and forth on the side of the jaw. This rubbing of the "beard" is used to indicate that something is so boring that one could grow a beard while it is happening.

© Cengage Learning

I **La famille de Sandrine.** Correct the following false impressions. Begin with **Mais pas du tout!** and use the opposite adjective. Make sure each adjective agrees with the noun it modifies.

MODÈLE: Le frère de Sandrine est désagréable.
Mais pas du tout! Il est charmant.

1. Sandrine est paresseuse.
2. Ses parents sont ennuyeux.
3. Leurs enfants sont très stupides.
4. La mère de Sandrine est triste et pessimiste.
5. Ses frères sont désagréables.
6. La sœur de Sandrine est méchante.
7. Son père est impatient.
8. Sa famille est bavarde.

A. Quelques groupes d'adjectifs

Grammar
Tutorials

FÉMININ	MASCULIN
active(s)	actif(s)
compréhensive(s)	compréhensif(s)
discrète(s)	discret(s)
ennuyeuse(s)	ennuyeux
généreuse(s)	généreux
gentille(s)	gentil(s)
heureuse(s)	heureux
intellectuelle(s)	intellectuel(s)
naïve(s)	naïf(s)
nerveuse(s)	nerveux
paresseuse(s)	paresseux
sportive(s)	sportif(s)
travailleuse(s)	travailleur(s)
veuve(s)	veuf(s)

► The **-l** in the masculine form **gentil** is not pronounced. The final consonant sound of the feminine form **gentille** is [j], like the English **y** in *yes*.

gentil   [ʒɑ̃ti]   gentille   [ʒɑ̃tij]

► Many feminine adjectives in written French follow the pattern **-è-** + consonant + **-e**. Their masculine forms omit the final **-e** and the accent on the initial **e**. This may or may not affect pronunciation.

chère   cher *(no change in pronunciation)*
discrète   discret *(pronunciation varies)*

► Some French adjectives are invariable. There is no change to indicate gender or number.

deux femmes **snob**   des chaussures **chic**

2 Qui est comme ça? Answer the following questions. Make sure each adjective agrees with the subject.

MODÈLE: Qui est patient dans votre famille?
Ma mère est patiente.
Mes sœurs sont patientes aussi.

1. Qui est travailleur dans votre famille?
2. Qui est bavard dans votre cours de français?
3. Qui est quelquefois triste?
4. Qui est généreux et optimiste?
5. Qui est sportif?
6. Qui est discret?
7. Qui est snob?
8. Comment sont vos parents?
9. Avez-vous des amis qui sont naïfs?
10. Et vous? Comment êtes-vous?

B. Ne ... *jamais*

Mon amie **n'**est **jamais** méchante. *My friend is never mean.*
Mon petit ami **ne** porte **jamais** de chaussettes. *My boyfriend never wears socks.*

Review the formation of the negative in Ch. 1, p. 21.

▶ **Ne ... jamais** *(never)* is placed around the conjugated verb just like **ne ... pas.** It is one of the possible answers to the question **Quand?** *(When?)*.

Quand est-ce que tu étudies? *When do you study?*
Je **n'**étudie **jamais!** *I never study.*

NOTE

Jamais can be used alone to answer a question.
Quand est-ce que tu pleures? *When do you cry?*
Jamais! *Never!*

Vocabulaire

Quand? *(Adverbes de fréquence)*

toujours	*always*	quelquefois	*sometimes*
d'habitude	*usually*	rarement	*rarely*
généralement	*generally*	(ne ...) jamais	*never*
souvent	*often*		

—Quand est-ce que vous regardez la télévision?
—D'habitude, je regarde la télévision le soir.

3 **Comment sont-ils?** Describe the following people with as many true sentences as you can create. Use an item from each list below (or their opposites). Make all necessary changes, paying special attention to adjective agreement.

MODÈLE: **Mes parents ne sont jamais impatients.**
Ils sont toujours patients.

		intolérant
mes parents		méchant
je	ne ... jamais	triste
mon petit ami	rarement	paresseux
ma petite amie	quelquefois	bavard
mes amis	souvent	impatient
mon professeur	d'habitude	pessimiste
nous (les étudiants)	toujours	ennuyeux
le (la) président(e)		désagréable
de l'université		avare

4 Un test de personnalité. Complete the questionnaire by answering **oui** or **non.** Then read the analysis that follows and write a paragraph to describe yourself.

	oui	non
1. Vous parlez beaucoup avec certaines personnes, mais vous refusez de parler avec tout le monde.	_____	_____
2. Vous aimez beaucoup le sport, mais vous détestez étudier et travailler.	_____	_____
3. Vous détestez jouer, danser ou chanter avec les autres, mais vous aimez bien étudier.	_____	_____
4. Vous avez beaucoup d'argent *(money),* mais vous donnez rarement de l'argent à vos amis.	_____	_____
5. Vous n'avez pas d'argent, mais vous n'êtes jamais triste.	_____	_____
6. Votre conversation est toujours agréable et vous parlez avec tout le monde.	_____	_____
7. Vous étudiez beaucoup, vous aimez parler français et vous êtes certain(e) que votre professeur de français est charmant.	_____	_____

Une analyse de vos réponses

1. Si vous répondez **oui** au numéro 1, vous êtes extraverti(e) et bavard(e), mais vous êtes aussi un peu snob.
2. Si vous répondez **oui** au numéro 2, vous êtes sportif (sportive), mais aussi paresseux (paresseuse). Vous n'avez probablement pas de bonnes notes *(good grades).*
3. Un **oui** au numéro 3, et vous êtes introverti(e), mais aussi travailleur (travailleuse). Vous avez probablement des notes excellentes.
4. Un **oui** au numéro 4, et vous êtes avare et pessimiste. Vous n'avez probablement pas beaucoup d'amis.
5. Si vous répondez **oui** au numéro 5, vous êtes d'habitude optimiste et heureux (heureuse), mais peut-être aussi un peu naïf (naïve).
6. Si vous répondez **oui** au numéro 6, vous n'êtes pas du tout ennuyeux (ennuyeuse). Vos amis sont contents d'être avec vous.
7. Enfin *(finally),* si votre réponse est **oui** au numéro 7, vous êtes certainement très intelligent(e), charmant(e) et intéressant(e). Les professeurs de français adorent les étudiant(e)s comme vous.

5 Cinq personnes que j'aime. Write a description of five people you like. How much can you tell about each one?

MODÈLE: **Charles Thomas est mon ami.**
Charles est petit et un peu gros.
Il est très gentil et intelligent.
Mais il est aussi un peu paresseux.
Voilà pourquoi il n'est pas du tout sportif.

ENTRE AMIS **Qui est la personne sur la photo?**

Follow the steps below to describe someone to your partner.

1. Show your partner a picture (real or imaginary) of someone.
2. Identify that person (name, age, where s/he lives).
3. Describe his/her personality.
4. Give a physical description as well.
5. Your partner will try to recall what you have shared.

🔊 **2. DESCRIBING CLOTHING**

Track 1-32

une cravate — une chemise
— une montre
— une ceinture
— un complet / un costume
des lunettes (f. pl.) — un chapeau
— un foulard
— des gants (m.)
un imperméable
des chaussettes (f.)
— des chaussures (f.)
— des bottes (f.)

The plural of **chapeau** *is* **chapeaux.**

Voilà Jean-Pierre.

Qu'est-ce qu'il porte?

Il porte un costume, une chemise, une cravate, une montre, une ceinture, des chaussettes et des chaussures.

Voilà Marie-Claire.

Qu'est-ce qu'elle porte?

Elle porte un chapeau, un foulard, un imperméable, des gants et des bottes. Elle porte aussi des lunettes.

🌐 **Et vous?** Qu'est-ce que vous portez aujourd'hui?

6 Qu'est-ce que c'est? (*What is it?*) Identify the following items.

MODÈLES:

—Qu'est-ce que c'est?
—C'est une ceinture.

—Qu'est-ce que c'est?
—Ce sont des chaussures.

1.

2.

3.

4.

5.

6.

7.

8.

9.

7 Qu'est-ce qu'ils portent? Describe the clothing tastes of several people you know. What items of clothing do they wear often, rarely, never?

MODÈLES: **Mon professeur de français ne porte jamais de jean.**
Je porte souvent un tee-shirt, mais je porte rarement un chapeau.

1. mon professeur de français
2. les étudiants de mon cours de français
3. un acteur/une actrice de Hollywood
4. mon/ma meilleur(e) ami(e)
5. les musiciens d'un groupe rock
6. les membres de ma famille
7. moi

Réalités culturelles
Les vêtements traditionnels au Sénégal

PEOPLE IN ALL SOCIETIES use fashion and dress to express their identity. This is certainly true in Senegal where one sees both traditional and western clothing worn, reflecting the country's blending the old with the new. The traditional garments of the Wolof, the primary ethnic group in Senegal, have even become associated with the country's national identity due to the inspiration they've provided to internationally known Senegalese fashion designers, such as Oumou Sy. Traditional garments for men include **boubous,** loose robes with long sleeves worn over baggy trousers, and **pagnes,** a length of cloth wrapped around the hips and waist like a skirt and worn with a shirt. Younger women in Senegal may also wear a **pagne** or skirt, accompanied by a close-fitting tunic, and headscarf while older women often wear a type of **boubou.** The fabrics used for traditional attire range from brightly colored cottons, batiks, and tie-dyed cloth to heavily embroidered brocades.

Horizon International Images Limited/Alamy

C. Les adjectifs de couleur

De quelle couleur est le pantalon de Jean-Pierre?
Il est **gris.** C'est un pantalon **gris.**

De quelle couleur est sa chemise?
Elle est **bleue.** C'est une chemise **bleue.**

De quelle couleur sont ses chaussures?
Elles sont **noires.** Ce sont des chaussures **noires.**

◉ **Et vous?** De quelle couleur sont vos vêtements?

Vocabulaire

Quelques couleurs

Féminin (s)	Masculin (s)	Féminin	Masculin
blanche	blanc	marron	marron
grise	gris	jaune	jaune
verte	vert	orange	orange
violette	violet	rose	rose
bleue	bleu	rouge	rouge
noire	noir	beige	beige

NOTE
Plurals of colors are formed by adding **-s.** Exceptions in this list are **gris,** (which already ends in **-s**) and **marron** and **orange,** which are invariable: **des cheveux *marron,* des chaussettes *orange.***

8 De quelle couleur sont leurs vêtements? *their* Ask your partner about the color of the following articles of clothing.

MODÈLES: les chaussures de Jérôme (noir)   *his*

> VOUS: **De quelle couleur sont *ses* chaussures?**
> VOTRE PARTENAIRE: **Elles sont noires. Ce sont des chaussures noires.**

le pull de Martine (bleu)

> VOUS: **De quelle couleur est son pull?**
> VOTRE PARTENAIRE: **Il est bleu. C'est un pull bleu.**

1. la cravate de Denis (jaune et bleu)
2. la robe de Françoise (vert)
3. la veste de Jean (gris)
4. l'imperméable d'Annette (blanc)
5. les chaussettes d'un(e) autre étudiant(e)
6. la chemise d'une autre personne
7. les chaussures de votre partenaire
8. les vêtements du professeur
9. les collants ou les bas d'une autre étudiante

Vocabulaire

Pour décrire *(to describe)* les vêtements

bon marché	*inexpensive*	ou	cher (chère)	*expensive*
chic	*stylish*	ou	confortable	*comfortable*
élégant(e)	*elegant*	ou	ordinaire	*ordinary, everyday*
propre	*clean*	ou	sale	*dirty*

Il y a un geste

C'est cher! Similar to its English equivalent, the gesture for **C'est cher!** is made by rubbing the thumb, index, and middle fingers together.

© Cengage Learning

NOTE
Chic and **bon marché** are invariable. They do not change in the feminine or in the plural: **Ce sont des chaussures *chic,* mais elles sont *bon marché.***

Confortable *is not used to describe how a person feels. It is used to describe a thing:* **une chemise confortable, une vie confortable.**

Synthèse: les adjectifs invariables				
bon marché	chic	marron	orange	snob

9 Au contraire! Your partner will make a series of statements. Disagree with your partner and state that the opposite is true. Follow the model.

MODÈLE: la robe de Simone (cher)

VOTRE PARTENAIRE: **La robe de Simone est chère.**

VOUS: **Non, elle n'est pas chère. C'est une robe bon marché.**

1. la veste de Martin (élégant)
2. le sweat-shirt de Monsieur Dupont (propre)
3. la robe de Pascale (chic)
4. les chaussettes du professeur (?)
5. les chaussures d'un(e) autre étudiant(e) (?)
6. les vêtements de deux autres étudiants (?)

Supply the adjectives for #4-6.

10 À vous. Answer the following questions.

1. Qu'est-ce que vous portez aujourd'hui?
2. De quelle couleur sont vos vêtements?
3. Décrivez les vêtements que vous portez.
4. Décrivez les vêtements d'un(e) autre étudiant(e).
5. Qu'est-ce que le professeur porte d'habitude?
6. De quelle couleur sont ses vêtements?
7. Qui ne porte jamais de jean dans votre classe de français?
8. Qui porte rarement des chaussures bon marché?
9. Qu'est-ce qu'on porte quand il fait froid?

D. L'adjectif démonstratif

Grammar
Tutorials

Cette femme est très intelligente.	*That (this) woman is very intelligent.*
Ce vin est excellent!	*This (that) wine is excellent!*
Vous aimez **cet** appartement?	*Do you like this (that) apartment?*
Qui sont **ces** deux personnes?	*Who are those (these) two people?*

	SINGULIER	PLURIEL
masculin:	ce (cet)	ces
féminin:	cette	ces

▶ The demonstrative adjectives are the equivalent of the English adjectives *this (that)* and *these (those)*.

ce garçon	*this boy*	or	*that boy*
cet ami	*this (male) friend*	or	*that (male) friend*
cette amie	*this (female) friend*	or	*that (female) friend*
ces amis	*these friends*	or	*those friends*
ces amies	*these (female) friends*	or	*those (female) friends*

▶ **Cet** is used before masculine singular words that begin with a vowel sound. It is pronounced exactly like **cette.**

cet homme	*this man*	or	*that man*
cet autre professeur	*this other teacher*	or	*that other teacher*

▶ If the context does not distinguish between the meanings *this* and *that* or *these* and *those,* it is possible to make the distinction by adding **-ci** (for *this/these*) or **-là** (for *that/those*) to the noun.

J'aime beaucoup cette chemise-**ci.**	*I like this shirt a lot.*
Ces femmes-**là** sont françaises.	*Those women are French.*

⑪ Au grand magasin (*At the department store*). While shopping, you overhear a number of comments but are unable to make out all the words. Try to complete the following sentences using one of the demonstrative adjectives **ce, cet, cette,** or **ces,** as appropriate.

1. Vous aimez _ces_ chaussures? Oui, mais je déteste _cette_ chemise.
2. _Ce_ pantalon est beau. Mais _ces_ jupes sont très chères.
3. _Ce_ jean est trop petit pour _cet_ homme-là.
4. Je ne sais pas comment s'appelle _cet_ vêtement-là.
5. _Ces_ robes sont jolies, mais _ce_ sweat-shirt est laid.
6. J'aime beaucoup _ce_ pull-là, mais je trouve _cette_ veste trop longue.

⑫ Non, je n'aime pas ça. Your shopping has made you tired and grouchy. Respond to your friend's questions or comments by saying that you dislike the item(s) in question. Use a demonstrative adjective in each response and invent a reason for your disapproval.

MODÈLE: Voilà une robe rouge.
Je n'aime pas beaucoup cette robe; elle est bizarre.

1. Voilà une belle cravate.
2. Voilà un ordinateur!
3. Oh! la petite calculatrice!
4. C'est un beau chapeau!
5. Tu aimes les chaussures vertes?
6. Voilà des chaussettes blanches intéressantes.
7. J'adore le chemisier bleu.
8. Tu aimes la veste de ce monsieur?

⑬ Qui est-ce? Describe as completely as possible the clothing of a fellow classmate.

MODÈLE: **Cette personne porte un pull jaune et un pantalon vert. Elle porte des chaussures marron. Elle ne porte pas de chaussettes. Ses vêtements ne sont pas très élégants mais ils sont confortables.**

*The French answer
the phone by saying
«Allô!».*

ENTRE AMIS **Au téléphone**

You are meeting a friend for dinner in twenty minutes. Role-
play the following situation.

1. Call to find out what s/he is wearing.
2. Find out the colors of his/her clothing.
3. Describe what you are wearing as completely as possible.

◀)) 3. DESCRIBING PEOPLE AND THINGS

Track 1-33

De quelle couleur sont les yeux° et les cheveux°   *eyes / hair*
  de Michèle?

Elle a les yeux bleus.

Elle a les cheveux blonds.

De quelle couleur sont les yeux et les cheveux de
  Thierry?

Il a les yeux verts et les cheveux roux°.   *red*

De quelle couleur sont les yeux et les cheveux de
  Monsieur Monot?

Il a les yeux noirs, mais il n'a pas de cheveux.

Il est chauve°.   *bald*

◉ **Et vous?** De quelle couleur sont vos yeux et vos cheveux?

1. Use the definite article **les** with the verb **avoir** to describe the color of a person's hair and eyes.

   Thierry **a les** yeux verts et **les** cheveux roux.

2. The word **cheveu** is almost always used in the plural, which is formed by adding **-x.**

   Michèle a **les cheveux** blonds.

3. Note that the adjective used to describe red hair is **roux (rousse)**, never **rouge.**

   Il a les cheveux **roux.**

   Notre petite-fille est **rousse.**

4. Use the adjective **brun(e)** to describe brown hair, never **marron.**

   Alissa a les cheveux **bruns.**

   Elle est **brune.**

> Remember that the masculine plural adjective is used with the words **yeux** and **cheveux: les yeux bleus, les cheveux noirs.**

14 **Leurs yeux et leurs cheveux.** Complete the following sentences with a form of the verb **être** or **avoir,** as appropriate.

1. Mon père _____ les yeux bleus. Il _____ chauve.
2. Brigitte et Virginie _____ les cheveux roux.
3. Vous _____ les yeux noirs.
4. De quelle couleur _____ les yeux de votre mère?
5. Elle _____ les yeux verts.
6. Mes oncles _____ les cheveux blonds, mais ils _____ aussi un peu chauves.

15 **De quelle couleur ... ?** Ask and answer questions with a partner based on the list below. If you don't know the answer, guess.

MODÈLES: vos yeux

> VOUS: **De quelle couleur sont vos yeux?**
> VOTRE PARTENAIRE: **J'ai les yeux verts.**

les cheveux de votre oncle

> VOUS: **De quelle couleur sont ses cheveux?**
> VOTRE PARTENAIRE: **Il n'a pas de cheveux. Il est chauve.**

1. vos yeux
2. vos cheveux
3. les yeux de votre meilleur(e) ami(e)
4. les cheveux de votre meilleur(e) ami(e)
5. les yeux et les cheveux d'un(e) autre étudiant(e)
6. les cheveux de vos grands-parents
7. les yeux et les cheveux de vos frères et sœurs (ou de vos amis)

Grammar
Tutorials

un livre **intéressant**	*an interesting book*
une femme **charmante**	*a charming woman*
un **bon** livre	*a good book*
l'**autre** professeur	*the other teacher*

► Most adjectives (including colors and nationalities) follow the noun they modify.

un homme **charmant**	un garçon **bavard**
une femme **intelligente**	une fille **sportive**
une robe **bleue**	une voiture **française**

► Certain very common adjectives, however, normally precede the noun.

1. Some that you already know are:

autre	grand	joli
beau	gros	petit
bon	jeune	vieux

2. Two others that usually precede the noun are:

MASCULIN SINGULIER	FÉMININ SINGULIER	MASCULIN PLURIEL	FÉMININ PLURIEL	ÉQUIVALENT ANGLAIS
mauvais	mauvaise	mauvais	mauvaises	*bad*
nouveau	nouvelle	nouveaux	nouvelles	*new*

Remember that **nouveau,** *like* **beau** *and* **chapeau,** *forms the plural by adding* **-x.**

✳ 3. **Beau, vieux,** and **nouveau** each have a special masculine singular form (**bel, vieil, nouvel**) for use when they precede a noun beginning with a vowel sound. These special forms are pronounced exactly like the feminine forms.

   un **bel** homme   un **vieil** ami   un **nouvel** appartement

4. Adjectives ending in a silent consonant are linked by liaison to words beginning with a vowel sound. When linked, a final **-s** or **-x** is pronounced [z] and a final **-d** is pronounced [t].

   un mauvais [z]hôtel   deux vieux [z]amis   un grand [t]hôtel

5. A few adjectives can be used either before or after the noun. Their position determines the exact meaning of the adjective.

un **ancien** professeur	*a former teacher*
un château **ancien**	*an ancient castle*
le **pauvre** garçon	*the unfortunate boy*
le garçon **pauvre**	*the boy who has no money*

In formal spoken and written French, **des** is replaced by **de** if a plural adjective comes *before* the noun:

	des professeurs intelligents	**des** voitures françaises
Mais:	**de** bons professeurs intelligents	**d**'autres voitures françaises

16 C'est vrai. Restate the following sentences by describing what Monsieur Masselot has. Follow the model.

MODÈLES: Les chaussures de Monsieur Masselot sont sales.
C'est vrai. Il a des chaussures sales.

L'appartement de Monsieur Masselot est vieux.
C'est vrai. Il a un vieil appartement.

1. L'appartement de Monsieur Masselot est beau.
2. Les enfants de Monsieur Masselot sont jeunes.
3. La femme de Monsieur Masselot est intelligente.
4. Les parents de Monsieur Masselot sont charmants.
5. Le chat de Monsieur Masselot est gros.
6. Le chien de Monsieur Masselot est méchant.
7. La voiture de Monsieur Masselot est mauvaise.
8. L'ordinateur de Monsieur Masselot est nouveau.
9. L'appartement de Monsieur Masselot est grand.
10. Le réfrigérateur de Monsieur Masselot est petit.
11. La cravate de Monsieur Masselot est bleue.
12. Les chaussettes de Monsieur Masselot sont bizarres.

17 Quelques compliments. Select items from each of the lists to pay a few compliments. How many compliments can you give? Make all necessary changes.

MODÈLES: **C'est une jolie robe.**
Tu as des chaussures chic.

		robe	joli
		maison	élégant
		appartement	bon
tu as	un	vêtements	magnifique
c'est	une	chemise	intéressant
ce sont	des	chemisier	superbe
		chaussettes	beau
		chaussures	chic
		jean	

18 **Une identité secrète.** Choose the name of someone famous that everyone will recognize. The other students will attempt to guess the identity of this person by asking questions. Answer only **oui** or **non**.

Review adjectives from this chapter and Ch. 1.

MODÈLE: **C'est une femme?**
   Est-ce qu'elle est belle?
   A-t-elle les cheveux roux?
   Est-ce qu'elle porte souvent des vêtements élégants? etc.

ENTRE AMIS   Mon ami(e)

Follow these steps to interview your partner.

1. Find out the name and age of your partner's best friend.
2. Find out the friend's hair and eye color.
3. Inquire about the clothing the friend usually wears.
4. What else can you find out about that friend?
5. Repeat the information you obtained in order to verify it.

4. DESCRIBING WHAT YOU DO AT HOME

Track 1-34

Que fais°-tu chez toi°, Catherine?	*do / at home*
Je regarde la télé ou j'écoute la radio.	
J'étudie et je fais mes devoirs°.	*homework*
Je fais souvent la cuisine°.	*the cooking*
Je parle avec mes parents.	
Je fais quelquefois la vaisselle°.	*the dishes*
Je fais rarement le ménage°.	*housework*

Et vous? Que faites-vous chez vous?

Vocabulaire

Des choses (*things*) qu'on fait

les courses	*errands; shopping*	une promenade	*walk; ride*
la cuisine	*cooking; food*	les provisions	*groceries*
les devoirs	*homework*	la sieste	*nap*
la lessive	*wash; laundry*	la vaisselle	*dishes*

Grammar
Tutorials

Je déteste **faire** les courses, mais j'aime **faire** la liste.	*I hate doing the shopping, but I like making the list.*
Ma mère **fait** les provisions pour le pique-nique.	*My mother is doing the grocery shopping for the picnic.*
Mes sœurs **font** la cuisine.	*My sisters do the cooking.*
Et c'est moi qui **fais** la vaisselle.	*And I'm the one who does the dishes.*
Nous **faisons** tous la lessive.	*We all do the wash.*

faire *(to do; to make)*			
je	**fais**	nous	**faisons**
tu	**fais**	vous	**faites**
il/elle/on	**fait**	ils/elles	**font**

▶ The **-ai-** in **nous faisons** is pronounced [ə] as in **le, de,** etc.

▶ The plural **les devoirs** means *homework*. The singular **la vaisselle** means *the dishes*. The plural **les courses** means *the shopping*.

Je fais **mes devoirs.**	*I do my homework.*
Qui aime faire **la vaisselle?**	*Who likes to do the dishes?*
Nous faisons **nos courses** ensemble.	*We do our shopping together.*

▶ There are a number of idiomatic uses of the verb **faire.**

Je ne **fais** jamais **la sieste.**	*I never take a nap.*
Veux-tu **faire une promenade?**	*Would you like to take a walk?*
Quel temps fait-il?	*What is the weather like?*
Il fait chaud.	*It's hot out.*
Faites attention!	*Pay attention!* or *Watch out!*

▶ A question using **faire** does not necessarily require the verb **faire** in the response.

Que **faites**-vous?
Je *patine,* je *chante,* je *regarde* la télé, j' *écoute* la radio, etc.

19 **Nous faisons beaucoup de choses.** Use the list below to create as many factual sentences as you can.

MODÈLES: **Mon petit ami ne fait jamais de promenade.**
Ma mère ne fait jamais la sieste.
Nous faisons souvent les courses.

mes amis			la lessive
mon petit ami		toujours	la vaisselle
ma petite amie		d'habitude	la sieste
ma mère	faire	souvent	les courses
mon père		quelquefois	la cuisine
nous (ma famille)		rarement	une promenade
je		ne … jamais	le ménage
			des provisions
			attention

20 **À vous.** Answer the following questions.

1. Faites-vous toujours vos devoirs?
2. Faites-vous la sieste l'après-midi?
3. Faites-vous souvent des promenades?
4. Faites-vous quelquefois la cuisine pour vos amis?
5. Est-ce que vous aimez la cuisine italienne?
6. Qui fait le ménage d'habitude dans votre famille?
7. Qui fait généralement la lessive?

ENTRE AMIS **Chez toi**

Interview your partner.

1. Find out where your partner lives.
2. Find out who does the grocery shopping and who does the cooking at his/her house.
3. How much can you find out about what your partner does or does not do at home?

En France, on aime faire ses courses au marché.

5. IDENTIFYING SOMEONE'S PROFESSION

—Chantal, qu'est-ce que tu veux faire dans la vie?°

what do you want to do in life?

—Je voudrais être journaliste. Et toi?

—Je ne sais pas encore.°

I don't know yet.

A more extensive list of professions can be found in App. B at the end of this book.

Et vous? Qu'est-ce que vous voulez faire dans la vie?

Vocabulaire

Quelques professions

agriculteur (agricultrice)	*farmer*	interprète		
architecte		journaliste		
artiste		*médecin	*doctor*	
assistant(e) social(e)	*social worker*	*militaire	*serviceman (-woman)*	
athlète		pharmacien(ne)		
avocat(e)	*lawyer*	*professeur		
comptable	*accountant*	informaticien (informaticienne)	*programmer*	
cuisinier (cuisinière)	*cook*	secrétaire		
*écrivain	*writer*	vendeur (vendeuse)	*salesperson*	
femme au foyer	*housewife*			
fonctionnaire	*civil servant*	**Quelques statuts dans le monde du travail**		
homme (femme) d'affaires	*businessman (-woman)*	*cadre	*executive*	
homme (femme) politique	*politician*	employé(e)	*employee*	
infirmier (infirmière)	*nurse*	ouvrier (ouvrière)	*laborer*	
*ingénieur	*engineer*	patron(ne)	*boss*	

*Certain professions are used only with masculine articles and adjectives (**un, mon, ce**) for a woman, as well as a man: **Elle est médecin.**
C'est un médecin.

1. There are two ways to identify someone's profession:
   - One can use a name or a subject pronoun **+ être +** profession/position, without any article.

Céline **est artiste.**	*Céline is an artist.*
Je **suis pharmacienne.**	*I am a pharmacist.*
Il **est ouvrier.**	*He is a factory worker.*

   Nouns of profession, nationality, and religion all act like adjectives when used this way.

   - For *he, she,* and *they,* one can also say **c'est (ce sont) +** indefinite article **+** profession.

C'est un professeur.	*He (she) is a teacher.*
Ce n'est pas un employé; c'est le patron.	*He isn't an employee; he's the boss.*
Ce sont des fonctionnaires.	*They are civil servants.*

2. To give more detail, one can use a possessive adjective or an article with an adjective. **C'est (ce sont),** not **il/elle est (ils/elles sont),** is used.

C'est ton secrétaire?	*Is he your secretary?*
Monique est une athlète **excellente.**	*Monique is an excellent athlete.*
Ce sont des cuisiniers **français.**	*They are French cooks.*

21 Que voulez-vous faire? Use the vocabulary list above to select professions that you would like and professions that you would not like.

MODÈLE: **Je voudrais être journaliste, mais je ne voudrais pas être écrivain.**

22 Qu'est-ce qu'il faut faire? *(What do you have to do?)*
The following sentences tell what preparation is needed for different careers. Complete the sentences with the name of the appropriate career(s).

MODÈLE: Il faut étudier la biologie pour être **médecin, dentiste** ou **infirmier.**

    1. Il faut étudier la pédagogie pour être ...
    2. Il faut étudier la comptabilité pour être ...
    3. Il faut étudier le commerce pour être ...
    4. Il faut étudier le journalisme pour être ...
    5. Il faut étudier l'agriculture pour être ...
    6. Il faut parler deux ou trois langues pour être ...
    7. Il faut désirer aider les autres pour être ...
    8. Il faut avoir une personnalité agréable pour être ...
    9. Il faut faire très bien la cuisine pour être ...

 Premium Website

Réalités culturelles

L'économie française et la population active

FRANCE HAS the fifth largest economy in the world. The country has a strong industrial base, is the second-largest agricultural producer (after the United States), and has a highly skilled labor force, nearly half of it made up of women. Most of the labor force works in the service sector, with three out of four workers holding a job in such areas as trade, finance, real estate, transportation, service, education, administration, and health and human services. Even in times of economic difficulty, this sector of the economy continues to grow. Perhaps the most coveted jobs by the French, however, are those held by **les fonctionnaires** (*civil servants*). Many young people aspire to such jobs, which are perceived as providing good income and a certain degree of economic stability.

Sources: http://www.state.gov/r/pa/ei/bgn/3842.htm,
Francoscopie 2010

G. Les mots interrogatifs qui, que et quel

Qui fait la cuisine dans votre famille?	*Who does the cooking in your family?*
Que faites-vous après le dîner?	*What do you do after dinner?*
À **quelle** heure dînez-vous?	*At what time do you eat dinner?*

▶ **Qui** *(who, whom)* is a pronoun. Use it in questions as the subject of a verb or as the object of a verb or preposition.

Qui est-ce?	*Who is it?*
Qui regardez-vous?	*At whom are you looking?*
Avec **qui** parlez-vous?	*With whom are you talking?*

▶ **Que** *(what)* is also a pronoun. Use it in questions as the object of a verb. It will be followed either by inversion of the verb and subject or by **est-ce que.** There are therefore two forms of this question: **Que ... ?** and **Qu'est-ce que ... ?**

Que font-ils?	*What do they do?*
Qu est-ce qu'ils font?	

▶ Don't confuse **Est-ce que ... ?** (simple question) and **Qu'est-ce que ... ?** *(What?).*

Est-ce que vous voulez danser?	*Do you want to dance?*
Qu'est-ce que vous voulez faire?	*What do you want to do?*
Qu'est-ce qu'il y a?	*What is it? What's the matter?*

▶ **Quel** *(which, what)* is an adjective. It is always used with a noun and agrees with the noun.

Quel temps fait-il?	*What is the weather like?*
Quelles actrices aimez-vous?	*Which actresses do you like?*

	singulier	pluriel
masculine	quel	quels
féminin	quelle	quelles

NOTE

The noun may either follow **quel** or be separated from it by the verb **être.**

Quels vêtements portez-vous?	*Which clothes are you wearing?*
Quelle est votre **adresse?**	*What is your address?*

23 Quelles questions! Ask questions using the appropriate form of **quel** with the words provided below.

MODÈLE: votre profession
Quelle est votre profession?

1. heure/il est
2. à/heure/vous mangez
3. temps/il fait
4. votre nationalité
5. âge/vous avez
6. vêtements/vous portez/quand il fait chaud
7. votre numéro (m.) de téléphone
8. de/couleur/vos yeux

24 Qui, que ou quel? Complete the following sentences.

1. _____ fait le ménage chez toi?
2. _____ font tes parents?
3. _____ âge ont tes amis?
4. De _____ couleur sont les cheveux du professeur?
5. Avec _____ parles-tu français?
6. À _____ heure dînes-tu d'habitude?
7. _____ désires-tu faire dans la vie?
8. _____ fais-tu après le dîner?

25 À vous. Answer the following questions.

1. Avez-vous des frères ou des sœurs? Si oui, que font-ils à la maison? Qu'est-ce qu'ils désirent faire dans la vie?
2. Que voulez-vous faire dans la vie?
3. Qu'est-ce que vous étudiez ce semestre?
4. Qu'est-ce que votre meilleur(e) ami(e) désire faire dans la vie?
5. Qui fait la cuisine chez vous?
6. À quelle heure faites-vous vos devoirs d'habitude?
7. Que font vos amis après le dîner?
8. Qui ne fait jamais la vaisselle?

iLrn
Self Test

ENTRE AMIS **Sondage (Survey)**

Imagine you are conducting a survey regarding people's professions. Follow the steps below to conduct your interview.

1. Greet your partner.
2. Find out his/her name and address.
3. Find out what s/he does.
4. What can you find out about his/her family?
5. Find out what the family members do.

Intégration

RÉVISION

A **Portraits personnels.** Provide the information requested below.

1. Décrivez les membres de votre famille.
2. Décrivez votre meilleur(e) ami(e).
3. Décrivez une personne dans la salle de classe. Demandez à votre partenaire de deviner *(guess)* l'identité de cette personne.

B **Trouvez quelqu'un qui ...** Interview your classmates in French to find someone who ...

MODÈLE: wants to be a doctor
Est-ce que tu désires être médecin?

1. likes to wear jeans and a sweatshirt
2. is wearing white socks
3. never wears a hat
4. has green eyes
5. likes to cook
6. likes French food
7. hates to do housework
8. wants to be a teacher
9. takes a nap in the afternoon

C **À l'écoute.** Listen to the following descriptions of different people and decide whether they are **a) logique** or **b) illogique**.

Track 1-36

D **À vous.** Answer the following questions.

1. De quelle couleur sont les vêtements que vous portez aujourd'hui?
2. Qu'est-ce que vos amis portent en cours d'habitude?
3. Quels vêtements aimez-vous porter quand il fait chaud? De quelle couleur sont les yeux de votre meilleur(e) ami(e)?
4. De quelle couleur sont les cheveux de votre meilleur(e) ami(e)?
5. Que faites-vous à la maison?
6. Que font les autres membres de votre famille chez vous?
7. Que voulez-vous faire dans la vie?
8. Qu'est-ce que votre meilleur(e) ami(e) désire faire?

Communication and Communities. To learn more about the culture presented in this chapter, go to the *Premium Website* and click on the Web Search Activities.

Also see the *Entre amis* Video Program and Video Worksheet in the *Cahier.*

NÉGOCIATIONS

 Nos amis. Work with your partner to complete the forms. Your partner's form is in Appendix D. Ask questions to determine the information that is missing.

MODÈLE: **Est-ce que Marie a les yeux bleus?**

A

nom	yeux	cheveux	description	à la maison	dans la vie	vêtement
Marie	verts			vaisselle	avocate	
Alain		bruns	calme		professeur	cravate
Chantal	marron		extravertie			lunettes
Éric		chauve		cuisine		veste
Karine		blonds				
Pierre	bleus		sportif	ménage	vendeur	
Sylvie	gris					chaussures
Jean		noirs	travailleur	sieste	ingénieur	

LECTURE 1

LA MÉTHODO When you scan for information, you read to find a particular fact or piece of information. You do not have to understand every word if that is your purpose. You need only scan the text until you find what you are looking for.

A **Parcourez les petites annonces.** Glance at the classified ads on the next page to find out what kind of job each one is advertising. Guess which one would pay the most. Which ones require a car? Which ones do not require experience? Which ones are for summer employment only?

B **Cela vous intéresse? (Does this interest you?)** Read classified ads that follow, then reorder them according to how much they appeal to you (which ones you would apply for and in what order). Be prepared to explain your reasons.

Offres d'emploi

1 _____
Bébé, un an et demi, cherche fille au pair de nationalité américaine ou canadienne, expérience avec enfants. Appelez Cunin en fin de matinée 02.43.07.47.26.

2 _____
Nous recherchons des secrétaires bilingues anglais pour aider les responsables de l'entreprise. Appelez l'Agence Paul Grassin au 02.42.76.10.14.

3 _____
Professeurs anglophones pour enseigner l'anglais aux lycéens étrangers en France, école internationale. Deux sessions: du 30 juin au 21 juillet; du 25 juillet au 14 août. Tél. 02.41.93.21.62.

4 _____
Famille offre logement et repas en échange de baby-sitting le soir et certains week-ends. Les journées sont libres. Écrivez BP 749, 49000 Angers.

5 _____
Opportunité de carrière. Compagnie internationale, établie depuis 71 ans, est à la recherche de jeunes personnes ambitieuses pour compléter son équipe commerciale. Si vous avez une apparence soignée, si vous êtes positif(ve), si vous possédez une voiture, appelez-nous au 02.41.43.00.22.

6 _____
Vous cherchez un job d'été (juillet et août) bien rémunéré, vous aimez discuter et vous possédez une voiture: venez rejoindre notre équipe de commerciaux. Formation assurée. Débutants acceptés. Tél. 02.41.43.15.80.

C **Votre petite annonce.** Write a classified ad to say you are looking for work in France. Describe yourself and your experience and include the fact that you speak French. Be sure to tell how you can be contacted.

LECTURE II

A **Parcourez le texte.** Scan the poem that follows, looking for words you recognize. Based on the words you found, what do you think the poem is about?

B **Étude du vocabulaire.** Study the following sentences and choose the English words that correspond to the French words in bold print: *knits, killed, no more, war, nothing.*

1. Cet étudiant paresseux **ne** travaille **plus.**
2. Oui, il **ne** fait **rien.**
3. Ma grand-mère **tricote** souvent des vêtements. Elle **fait du tricot** quand elle regarde la télévision.
4. Il y a des militaires qui sont **tués** pendant la **guerre.**

Track 1-37

Familiale

La mère fait du tricot
Le fils fait la guerre
Elle trouve ça tout naturel la mère
Et le père qu'est-ce qu'il fait le père?
Il fait des affaires
Sa femme fait du tricot
Son fils la guerre
Lui[1] des affaires
Il trouve ça tout naturel le père
Et le fils et le fils
Qu'est-ce qu'il trouve le fils?
Il ne trouve rien absolument rien le fils
Le fils sa mère fait du tricot son père des affaires lui la guerre
Quand il aura fini[2] la guerre
Il fera[3] des affaires avec son père
La guerre continue la mère continue elle tricote
Le père continue il fait des affaires
Le fils est tué il ne continue plus
Le père et la mère vont au cimetière
Ils trouvent ça naturel le père et la mère
La vie continue la vie avec le tricot la guerre les affaires
Les affaires la guerre le tricot la guerre
Les affaires les affaires et les affaires
La vie avec le cimetière.

Jacques Prévert, "Familiale", from *Paroles*.
© Éditions Gallimard. Reprinted with permission.

1. *him* / 2. *is over (lit. will have finished)* / 3. *will do*

C Correspondances. The poet associates each of the family members with specific activities. Read the poem and then identify the person(s) that the poet associates with the activities in the right-hand column.

© Bernard Annebicque/Corbis Sygma

_____ fait la guerre
_____ fait des affaires
a. le fils   _____ fait du tricot
b. la mère   _____ est tué
c. le père   _____ est femme au foyer
                 _____ est homme d'affaires
                 _____ est militaire
                 _____ va au cimetière

D **Familles de mots.** Can you guess the meaning of the following words? At least one member of each word family is found in the reading.

1. tricoter, le tricot, un tricoteur, une tricoteuse
2. vivre, vivant(e), la vie
3. la nature, naturel, naturelle, naturellement

E **Questions.** Read the poem again and answer the following questions in French.

1. Qui sont les personnages du poème?
2. Quel est le rôle de chaque personnage?
3. Qu'est-ce que le père et la mère trouvent naturel?

F **Discussion.**

1. Prévert wrote this poem shortly after the Second World War. What does the poem reveal about his experience of war?
2. What words are repeated in the poem? How does the poet use repetition to reinforce his message?

RÉDACTION

LA MÉTHODO Using a graphic organizer can help you brainstorm and remember details you would like to use in your writing. To create a simple graphic organizer, draw a square containing the object or person you wish to describe. Then draw lines extending from the square to its characteristics. You might even draw more lines extending from each characteristic to its details. See the example.

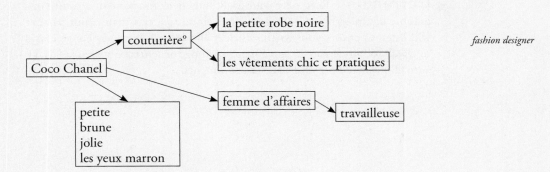

fashion designer

PORTRAIT

Think of someone you admire, a man or a woman. Write a short descriptive essay in which you create his or her "portrait." In your essay:

- describe this person's physical appearance, personality, and taste in clothing
- indicate his or her profession
- indicate what this person does and doesn't do (and how often)
- explain why you like or admire this person
- include any other details you think are important

Vocabulaire utile

j'admire	I admire
parce que	because
que	that

A **Avant d'écrire.** After reading the instructions for the writing assignment, create a graphic organizer like the one in **La méthodo.** In your primary square, write the name of the person you admire. In the radiating squares, include details about this person's physical appearance, personality, clothing, and profession.

B **Écrire.** Draft your essay, using the details listed in your graphic organizer. Include one or two reasons that you admire this person. You might begin or conclude the essay with this statement. If you are writing about someone you know, you might also state your relationship.

C **Correction.** Read over your draft and check the content against your graphic organizer. Now read your draft aloud to a classmate. Your partner will listen to ensure your writing is clear and logical. Next, exchange essays to check for any errors in agreement, spelling, or sentence structure. Make corrections based on your partner's comments.

Vocabulaire Actif

Practice this vocabulary with the flashcards on iLrn.

Quelques professions et statuts dans le monde du travail

un agriculteur/une agricultrice *farmer*
un(e) assistant(e) social(e) *social worker*
un(e) avocat(e) *lawyer*
un cadre *executive*
un(e) comptable *accountant*
un cuisinier/une cuisinière *cook*
un écrivain *writer*
un(e) employé(e) *employee*
une femme au foyer *housewife*
un(e) fonctionnaire *civil servant*
un homme d'affaires/une femme d'affaires *businessman/businesswoman*
un homme politique/une femme politique *politician*
un infirmier/une infirmière *nurse*
un informaticien/une informaticienne *programmer*
un ingénieur *engineer*
un médecin *doctor*
un(e) militaire *serviceman (-woman)*
un ouvrier/une ouvrière *laborer*
un(e) patron(ne) *boss*
un(e) pharmacien(ne) *pharmacist*
un(e) secrétaire *secretary*
un vendeur/une vendeuse *salesman/ saleswoman*

Description personnelle

ancien(ne) *old; former*
avare *miserly; stingy*
bavard(e) *talkative*
calme *calm*
chauve *bald*
compréhensif (compréhensive) *understanding*
désagréable *disagreeable*
discret (discrète) *discreet; reserved*
ennuyeux (ennuyeuse) *boring*
extraverti(e) *outgoing*
généreux (généreuse) *generous*
gentil (gentille) *nice*
heureux (heureuse) *happy*
impatient(e) *impatient*
intellectuel (intellectuelle) *intellectual*
intelligent(e) *intelligent*
intéressant(e) *interesting*
intolérant(e) *intolerant*
méchant(e) *nasty; mean*
naïf (naïve) *naive*
nerveux (nerveuse) *nervous*
optimiste *optimistic*

paresseux (paresseuse) *lazy*
patient(e) *patient*
pauvre *poor*
pessimiste *pessimistic*
sportif (sportive) *athletic*
stupide *stupid*
travailleur (travailleuse) *hard-working*
triste *sad*

Des choses qu'on fait

les courses *(f. pl.) errands; shopping*
la cuisine *cooking; food*
les devoirs *(m. pl.) homework*
la lessive *wash; laundry*
le ménage *housework*
une promenade *walk; ride*
les provisions *(f. pl.) groceries*
la sieste *nap*
la vaisselle *dishes*

D'autres noms

une adresse *address*
les cheveux *(m.) hair*
une chose *thing*
une couleur *color*
le dîner *dinner*
les gens *(m. pl.) people*
une note *note; grade, mark*
un numéro de téléphone *telephone number*
le temps *weather*
la vie *life*
une ville *city*
les yeux *(m. pl.) eyes*

Adjectifs de couleur

beige *beige*
blanc (blanche) *white*
bleu(e) *blue*
gris(e) *grey*
jaune *yellow*
marron *brown*
noir(e) *black*
orange *orange*
rose *pink*
rouge *red*
vert(e) *green*
violet(te) *purple*

Pour décrire les vêtements

bizarre *weird, funny-looking*
bon marché *inexpensive*
cher (chère) *dear; expensive*
chic *chic; stylish*

confortable *comfortable*
élégant(e) *elegant*
ordinaire *ordinary, everyday*
propre *clean*
sale *dirty*
simple *simple, plain*

Vêtements

des bas (m.) *(panty)hose*
des baskets (f.) *high-top sneakers*
un blouson *windbreaker, jacket*
des bottes (f.) *boots*
une ceinture *belt*
un chapeau *hat*
des chaussettes (f.) *socks*
des chaussures (f.) *shoes*
une chemise *shirt*
un chemisier *blouse*
des collants (m.) *tights*
un costume *suit*
une cravate *tie*
un foulard *scarf*
des gants (m.) *gloves*
un imperméable *raincoat*
un jean *(pair of) jeans*
une jupe *skirt*
des lunettes (f. pl.) *eyeglasses*
un manteau *coat*
une montre *watch*
un pantalon *(pair of) pants*
un pull-over (un pull) *sweater*
une robe *dress*
un short *(pair of) shorts*
un sweat-shirt *sweatshirt*
un tee-shirt *tee-shirt*
des tennis (f.) *tennis shoes*
une veste *sportscoat*
un vêtement *an article of clothing*

D'autres adjectifs

blond(e) *blond*
brun(e) *brown(-haired)*
ce/cet (cette) *this; that*
ces *these; those*
mauvais(e) *bad*
nouveau/nouvel (nouvelle) *new*
roux (rousse) *red(-haired)*

Pronoms

cela (ça) *that*
toi *you*
tous *(m. pl.) all*

Verbes

aller en cours *to go to class*
dîner *to eat dinner*
donner *to give*
envoie (envoyer) *send (to send)*
faire *to do; to make*
garder *to keep; to look after*
porter *to wear; to carry*

Adverbes de fréquence: Quand?

aujourd'hui *today*
d'habitude *usually*
généralement *generally*

jamais (ne ... jamais) *never*
quand *when*
quelquefois *sometimes*
rarement *rarely*
toujours *always*

Mots invariables

ici *here*
puis *then; next*

Mots interrogatifs

que ... ? *what ... ?*
qu'est-ce que ... ? *what ... ?*
quel(le) ... ? *which ... ? what ... ?*

Expressions utiles

chaleureusement *warmly*
Comment est (sont) ... ? *What is (are) ... like?*
De quelle couleur est (sont) ... ? *What color is (are) ... ?*
en cours *in class; to class*
faire attention (à) *to pay attention (to)*
Il fait chaud. *It's hot out.*
Il faut ... *It is necessary ...*
Quel temps fait-il? *What is the weather like?*
Quel(le) ... ! *What ... !*
Qu'est-ce que c'est? *What is this?*

La vie universitaire

Oberhaeuser/Caro/Ullstein Bild/The Image Works

BUTS COMMUNICATIFS

- Expressing future time
- Telling time
- Explaining your schedule
- Telling where to find places

STRUCTURES UTILES

- **À** + article défini
- Le verbe **aller** (suite)
- L'heure
- Les jours de la semaine
- Le verbe **devoir**
- Quelques prépositions de lieu
- L'impératif
- Les prépositions de lieu avec une ville ou un pays
- Les mots interrogatifs **où** et **quand**

CULTURE

Zoom sur la vie universitaire

- **Vidéo buzz:** Les campus universitaires
- **Vu sur le web:** Aller au cinéma
- **Repères:** Angers souhaite la bienvenue aux étudiants
- **Insolite:** Je t'invite.
- **Article:** Les invitations: Des différences culturelles

Il y a un geste

- **Au revoir/Salut**

Lectures

- **L'université d'Angers:** Infos
- «Village natal»

RESSOURCES

Audio

iLrn Heinle Learning Center

Premium Website

Pair Work

Group Work

Entre amis Video Program

Coup d'envoi

🔊 PRISE DE CONTACT: **QU'EST-CE QUE VOUS ALLEZ FAIRE?**

Track 2-1

Qu'est-ce que tu vas faire le week-end prochain°, Sylvie?

    Je vais sortir vendredi° soir.

    Je vais danser parce que j'adore danser.

    Je vais déjeuner dimanche° avec mes amis.

    Je vais aller à la bibliothèque.°

    Je vais étudier et faire mes devoirs.

    Mais je ne vais pas rester° dans ma chambre tout le week-end°.

What are you going to do next weekend

I'm going to go out on Friday

I'm going to have lunch on Sunday
I'm going to go to the library.

to stay
the whole weekend

💬 **Et vous?** Qu'est-ce que vous allez faire le week-end prochain? Où allez-vous étudier?

ack 2-2

C'est vendredi après-midi. Lori rencontre° son amie　　meets
Denise après° son cours de littérature française.　　after

LORI:　Salut, Denise. Comment vas-tu?

DENISE:　Bien, Lori. Quoi de neuf?°　　What's new?
　　(Elles s'embrassent° trois fois°.)　　kiss / times

LORI:　Pas grand-chose°, mais c'est vendredi et je n'ai　　Not much
　　pas l'habitude de passer° tout le week-end dans　　I'm not used to spending
　　ma chambre. Tu as envie d'aller au cinéma?°　　Do you feel like going to
　　　　the movies?

DENISE:　Quand ça?

LORI:　Ce soir ou demain° soir?　　tomorrow

DENISE:　Ce soir je ne suis pas libre°. Mais demain peut-　　free
　　être. Tu vas voir° quel film?　　to see

LORI:　Ça m'est égal.° Il y a toujours un bon film au　　I don't care.
　　cinéma Variétés.

DENISE:　D'accord°, très bien. À quelle heure?　　Okay

LORI:　Vers 7 heures et demie°. Ça va?° Rendez-vous　　Around 7:30 / Okay?
　　devant° le cinéma?　　in front of

DENISE:　C'est parfait°.　　perfect

LORI:　Au revoir, Denise. Bonne soirée, et à
　　demain soir.

ⓒ Jouez ces rôles. Répétez la conversation avec votre partenaire. Utilisez vos noms et le nom d'un cinéma près de chez vous.

© Cengage Learning

Il y a un geste

Au revoir/Salut. When waving goodbye, the open palm, held at about ear level, is normally turned toward the person to whom one is waving. It is often moved toward the other person.

Vocabulaire

Pour dire *au revoir*

à bientôt	*see you soon*
à demain	*see you tomorrow*
à la prochaine	*until next time, be seeing you*
à tout à l'heure	*see you in a little while*
au plaisir (de vous revoir)	*(I hope to) see you again*
au revoir	*goodbye, see you again*
bon après-midi	*have a good afternoon*
bonne journée	*have a good day*
bonne nuit	*pleasant dreams (lit. good night)*
bonne soirée	*have a good evening*
bonsoir	*good evening, good night*
salut	*bye(-bye) (fam.)*
tchao	*bye (fam.)*

Zoom sur la vie universitaire

Premium Website

VU SUR LE WEB

Aller au cinéma

GOING TO THE MOVIES is a popular activity among university students in France. A movie ticket can be quite expensive, however, averaging between 8€ and 10€ in big cities like Paris. To make movies more affordable, most theaters offer discounts to students, seniors, and the unemployed. Movie theater chains also extend several other discount plans to customers, such as unlimited single-entry tickets for a monthly fee and five-ticket packages for a lower price than individual tickets purchased separately. In addition, many moviegoers now reserve their tickets online and pick them up at automated kiosks in front of the theater. To learn more about going to the movies in France, browse the links on the *Premium Website*.

Denkou City Life/Denkou Images/Alamy

INSOLITE

Je t'invite

IN THE CONVERSATION **Une sortie,** Lori asks her classmate Denise if she wants to go to the movies. Such an invitation implies that each girl will pay her own way. If Lori had used the verb **inviter,** Denise would have understood that Lori was paying her way. The verb **inviter** means "to treat" someone; therefore, if someone tells you **Je t'invite,** they are saying "My treat" or "It's on me."

Les invitations: Des différences culturelles

A COMMON cultural misunderstanding between North Americans and the French is the way each culture views invitations. North Americans sometimes complain about not being invited to French homes right away. Typically, the French are more hesitant to extend an invitation to their home or chat with strangers. However, once they do, they take it seriously. North Americans, on the other hand, may readily and casually extend invitations to "come and see us" and are surprised when French acquaintances write to say they are actually coming.

Angers souhaite la bienvenue aux étudiants

Lori Becker is going to college in Angers. Each year the city welcomes thousands of students to its two universities: **l'Université d'Angers** *and* **l'Université Catholique de l'Ouest.** *Take a look at this poster welcoming students. What kinds of activities have been planned for them?*

Étudiants Bievenue à Angers

Forum d'accueil
5 & 6 octobre
• 14h–19h
Greniers Saint-Jean Jobs,
Activités loisirs, Aides et démarches,
engagement, transports,
international,
santé & bien-être

Soirée étudiants au quai
7 octobre
• 19h
Le Quai

Concert étudiants 1ère anneé
14 octobre
• 21h
Le Chabada

Soirée étudiants étrangers
6 octobre
• 18h30
Greniers Saint Jean

VIDÉO BUZZ

Les campus universitaires

UNIVERSITY CAMPUSES in the Francophone world vary from place to place, just as they do in the United States. Some are virtual, some have buildings all in one location, while others have buildings spread out over a city or are composed of several campuses in multiple locations. Browse the links on the *Premium Website* to see what university campuses look like in the Francophone world.

À vous. Répondez aux questions.

1. Comment allez-vous?
2. Allez-vous rester dans votre chambre ce soir?
3. À quelle heure allez-vous faire vos devoirs?
4. Qu'est-ce que vous allez faire demain soir?
5. Avez-vous envie d'aller au cinéma?

ENTRE AMIS **Le week-end prochain**

Role-play the following situation in which you invite a friend to go to the movies.

1. Greet your partner.
2. Find out how s/he is doing.
3. Find out what s/he is going to do this weekend.
4. Find out if s/he wants to go to a movie.
5. If so, agree on a time.
6. Be sure to vary the way you say goodbye.

PRONONCIATION

 LES SYLLABES OUVERTES

Track 2-3

▶ There is a strong tendency in French to end spoken syllables with a vowel sound. It is therefore important to learn to link a pronounced consonant to the vowel that follows it.

| il a | [i la] | votre ami | [vɔ tʀa mi] |
| elle a | [ɛ la] | femme américaine | [fa ma me ʀi kɛn] |

▶ The above is also true in the case of liaison. Liaison must occur in the following situations.

Synthèse: les liaisons obligatoires

	ALONE	WITH LIAISON
1. when a pronoun is followed by a verb	nous vous	nous [z]a vons vous [z]êtes
2. when a verb and pronoun are inverted	est ont sont	est-[t]elle ont-[t]ils sont-[t]ils
3. when an article or adjective is followed by a noun	un des deux trois mon petit	un [n]homme des [z]en fants deux [z]heures trois [z]ans mon [n]a mi petit [t]a mi
4. after one-syllable adverbs or prepositions	très en dans	très [z]im por tant en [n]A mé rique dans [z]une fa mille

Buts communicatifs

Track 2-4

I. EXPRESSING FUTURE TIME

Qu'est-ce que tu vas faire samedi° prochain, Julien?   *Saturday*
    D'abord° je vais jouer au tennis avec mes amis.   *First (of all)*
    Ensuite° nous allons étudier° à la bibliothèque.   *Next / we're going to study*
    Je n'aime pas manger seul°, alors après°, nous   *alone / so after(wards)*
        allons dîner ensemble au restaurant
        universitaire.
    Enfin°, nous allons regarder la télé.   *Finally*

Et vous? Qu'est-ce que vous allez faire?

Note culturelle

Le restaurant universitaire, qu'on appelle d'habitude le Resto U,
est très bon marché. C'est parce qu'en France on subventionne
(subsidizes) en partie les repas *(meals)* des étudiants. Si on a une
carte d'étudiant, on bénéficie d'une réduction sur le prix des repas.

A. À + *article défini*

Grammar
Tutorials

Céline ne travaille pas **à la**   *Céline doesn't work at the*
    bibliothèque.   *library.*
Elle travaille **au** restaurant universitaire.   *She works in the dining hall.*

> The preposition **à** can mean *to, at,* or *in,* depending on the context. When
> used with the articles **la** and **l',** it does not change, but when used with the
> articles **le** and **les,** it is contracted to **au** and **aux.**

> *Remember to consult App. C, the Glossary of Grammatical Terms, at the end of the book to review any terms with which you are not familiar.*

à	+	le	**au**	au restaurant
à	+	les	**aux**	aux toilettes
à	+	la	**à la**	à la maison
à	+	l'	**à l'**	à l'hôtel

> Liaison occurs when **aux** precedes a vowel sound: **aux [z]États-Unis**.

Quelques endroits (A few places)

Sur le campus

latin grek (handwritten)

un bâtiment	*building*	une librairie	*bookstore*
une bibliothèque	*library*	un parking	*parking lot, garage*
une cafétéria	*cafeteria*	une piscine	*swimming pool*
un campus	*campus*	une résidence	
un couloir	*hall, corridor*	(universitaire)	*dormitory*
un cours	*course, class*	une salle de classe	*classroom*
un gymnase	*gymnasium*	les toilettes *(f. pl.)*	*restroom*

En ville

un aéroport	*airport*	une école	*school*
une banque	*bank*	une église	*church*
un bistro	*bar and café*	une épicerie	*grocery store*
une boulangerie	*bakery*	une gare	*railroad station*
un bureau de poste	*post office*	un hôtel	*hotel*
un bureau de tabac	*tobacco shop*	un musée	*museum*
un centre	*shopping center,*	une pharmacie	*pharmacy*
commercial	*mall*	un restaurant	*restaurant*
un château	*chateau, castle*	une ville	*city*
un cinéma	*movie theater*		

*Do not pronounce the **c** in the word **tabac.***

❶ Qu'est-ce que c'est? Identifiez les endroits suivants.

MODÈLE: **C'est une église.**

1.

2.

3.

4.

5.

6.

2 Où vas-tu? Demandez à votre partenaire s'il/elle va à l'endroit indiqué. Votre partenaire va répondre non et dire où il/elle va. Suivez (*Follow*) le modèle.

MODÈLE: restaurant (bibliothèque)
> —**Tu vas au restaurant?**
> —**Non, je ne vais pas au restaurant; je vais à la bibliothèque.**

1. bureau de poste (pharmacie)
2. église (centre commercial)
3. restaurant (cinéma)
4. librairie (bibliothèque)
5. hôtel (appartement de ma sœur)
6. gare (aéroport)

3 Qu'est-ce que vous allez faire? Indiquez vos projets avec **Je vais à** + article défini et les mots donnés (*given*). Utilisez aussi les mots **d'abord, ensuite** et **après**.

MODÈLE: banque, centre commercial, épicerie
> **D'abord je vais à la banque, ensuite je vais au centre commercial et après je vais à l'épicerie.**

1. école, bibliothèque, librairie
2. banque, restaurant, aéroport
3. bureau de poste, pharmacie, cinéma
4. église, campus, résidence

ENTRE AMIS D'abord, ensuite, après

You and your partner are talking about your plans. Follow the steps below for your conversation.

1. Tell your partner that you are going to go out.
2. S/he will try to guess three places where you are going.
3. S/he will try to guess in what order you are going to the three places.
4. Switch roles.

B. Le verbe aller (suite)

Grammar Tutorials

Je vais en classe à 8 h.	*I go to class at 8:00 a.m..*
Allez-vous en ville ce soir?	*Are you going into town this evening?*
Où **allons-nous** dîner?	*Where are we going to eat dinner?*
Les petits Français ne **vont** pas à l'école le mercredi.	*French children don't go to school on Wednesday.*

> Review the conjugation of **aller** on p. 38.

▶ The fundamental meaning of **aller** is *to go*.

Où **vas-tu?**   *Where are you going?*

▶ As you have already learned, the verb **aller** is also used to discuss health and well-being.

Comment allez-vous?	*How are you?*
Je vais bien, merci.	*I'm fine, thanks.*
Ça va, merci.	*Fine, thanks.*

> The verb **aller** is also very often used with an infinitive to indicate the future, especially the near future.

Qu'est-ce que **tu vas faire** ce soir?   *What are you going to do this evening?*
Je vais étudier, comme d'habitude.   *I'm going to study, as usual.*
Nous allons passer un test demain.   *We are going to take a test tomorrow.*
Thierry **ne va pas déjeuner** demain.   *Thierry won't eat lunch tomorrow.*

4 Comment vont-ils? Utilisez le verbe **aller** pour poser des questions. Votre partenaire va répondre.

MODÈLE: ton frère

> VOUS: **Comment va ton frère?**
> VOTRE PARTENAIRE: **Il va très bien, merci.** ou
> **Quel frère? Je n'ai pas de frère.**

1. tes amis du cours de français
2. tu
3. ton professeur de français
4. ta sœur
5. ton ami(e) qui s'appelle …
6. tes grands-parents
7. ta nièce
8. tes neveux

Vocabulaire

Quelques expressions de temps (futur)

tout à l'heure	*in a little while*
dans une heure	*one hour from now*
ce soir	*tonight*
avant (après) le dîner	*before (after) dinner*
demain (matin, soir)	*tomorrow (morning, evening)*
dans trois jours	*three days from now*
le week-end prochain	*next weekend*
la semaine prochaine	*next week*
la semaine suivante	*the following week*

*Several of these expressions can be preceded by à to mean "See you …" or "Until …," e.g., **à ce soir, au week-end prochain.***

5 Que vont-ils faire ce soir? Qu'est-ce que les personnes suivantes vont faire et qu'est-ce qu'ils ne vont pas faire? Si vous ne savez pas, imaginez. *(If you don't know, guess.)*

MODÈLE: mes parents / jouer au tennis ou regarder la télévision
Ce soir, ils vont regarder la télévision; ils ne vont pas jouer au tennis.

1. je / sortir ou rester dans ma chambre
2. le professeur / dîner au restaurant ou dîner à la maison
3. mes amis / étudier à la bibliothèque ou étudier dans leur chambre
4. je / regarder la télévision ou faire mes devoirs
5. mon ami(e) _____ / travailler sur ordinateur ou aller au centre commercial
6. les étudiants / rester sur le campus ou aller au bistro

6 **À vous.** Répondez aux questions.

1. Qu'est-ce que vous allez faire ce soir?
2. Qu'est-ce que vos amis vont faire?
3. Qui va passer un test cette semaine?
4. Où allez-vous déjeuner demain midi?
5. Où et à quelle heure allez-vous dîner demain soir?
6. Quand allez-vous étudier? Avec qui?
7. Qu'est-ce que vous allez faire samedi prochain?
8. Qu'est-ce que vous allez faire dimanche après-midi?

 **ENTRE AMIS** **Est-ce que tu vas jouer au tennis?**

Role-play the following conversation with a partner.

1. Tell your partner that you are not going to stay in your room this weekend.
2. S/he will try to guess three things you are going to do.
3. S/he will try to guess in what order you will do them.

2. TELLING TIME

Track 2-5

Quelle heure est-il maintenant?°   *What time is it now?*
     Il est 10 heures et demie.°   *It's half past ten.*
     Je vais au cours de français à 11 heures.
     Je déjeune à midi.°   *I eat lunch at noon.*
     Je vais à la bibliothèque à une heure.
     Je vais au gymnase à 4 heures.
     J'étudie de 7 heures à 10 heures du soir.
     J'étudie au moins° trois heures par jour.°   *at least / per day*

> -- cours de français 11 h
> -- déjeuner 12 h avec Étienne
> -- bibliothèque 13 h
> -- gymnase 16 h

Et vous? À quelle heure déjeunez-vous?
     À quelle heure allez-vous à la bibliothèque?
     À quelle heure allez-vous au gymnase?
     À quelle heure allez-vous au cours de français?
     Quelle heure est-il maintenant?

REMARQUE

The word **heure** has more than one meaning.

J'étudie trois **heures** par jour.	*I study three hours a day.*
De quelle **heure** à quelle **heure**?	*From what time to what time?*
De 15 **heures** à 18 **heures**.	*From three until six o'clock.*

C. L'heure

> You have already learned to tell time in a general way. Now that you know how to count to 60, you can be more precise. There are two methods of telling time. The first is an official 24-hour system, which can be thought of as a digital watch on which the hour is always followed by the minutes. The other is an informal 12-hour system that includes the expressions **et quart** *(quarter past, quarter after)*, **et demi(e)** *(half past)*, **moins le quart** *(quarter to, quarter till)*, **midi,** and **minuit** *(midnight)*.

Review Understanding Basic Expressions of Time, *p. 3, and numbers, pp. 3, 68.*

The word **heure(s)** is usually represented as **h** (without a period) on schedules, e.g., **5 h 30.**

	Système officiel	*Système ordinaire*
9 h 01	neuf heures une	neuf heures une
9 h 15	neuf heures quinze	neuf heures et quart
9 h 30	neuf heures trente	neuf heures et demie
9 h 45	neuf heures quarante-cinq	dix heures moins le quart
12 h 30	douze heures trente	midi et demi
13 h 30	treize heures trente	une heure et demie
18 h 51	dix-huit heures cinquante et une	sept heures moins neuf
23 h 45	vingt-trois heures quarante-cinq	minuit moins le quart

> In both systems, the feminine number **une** is used to refer to hours and minutes because both **heure** and **minute** are feminine.

1 h 21   **une** heure vingt et **une**

> In the 12-hour system, **moins** is used to give the time from 1 to 29 minutes *before* the hour. For 15 minutes *before* or *after* the hour, the expressions **moins le quart** and **et quart,** respectively, are used. For 30 minutes past the hour, one says **et demie.**

9 h 40   dix heures **moins** vingt

9 h 45   dix heures **moins le quart**

10 h 15   dix heures **et quart**

10 h 30   dix heures **et demie**

NOTE

After **midi** and **minuit,** which are both masculine, **et demi** is spelled without a final **-e: midi et demi.**

> The phrases **du matin, de l'après-midi,** and **du soir** are commonly used in the 12-hour system to specify A.M. or P.M. when it is not otherwise clear from the context.

trois heures **du matin** (3 h)

trois heures **de l'après-midi** (15 h)

dix heures **du matin** (10 h)

dix heures **du soir** (22 h)

7 Quelle heure est-il? Donnez les heures suivantes. Indiquez l'heure officielle et l'heure ordinaire s'il y a une différence.

MODÈLE: 13 h 35

> *système officiel:* **Il est treize heures trente-cinq.**
> *système ordinaire:* **Il est deux heures moins vingt-cinq de l'après-midi.**

1. 2 h 20
2. 4 h 10
3. 15 h 41
4. 1 h 17
5. 6 h 55

6. 1 h 33
7. 22 h 05
8. 3 h 45
9. 11 h 15
10. 10 h 30

Remember that these numbers are based on a 24-hour system.

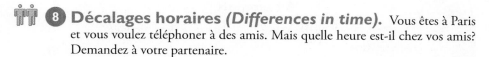

8 Décalages horaires (*Differences in time*). Vous êtes à Paris et vous voulez téléphoner à des amis. Mais quelle heure est-il chez vos amis? Demandez à votre partenaire.

Décalages horaires
(calculés par rapport à l'heure de Paris)

Anchorage (USA)	− 10	Montréal (CDN)	− 6
Athènes (Grèce)	+ 1	Mexico (MEX)	− 7
Bangkok (Thaïlande)	+ 6	Nouméa	
Casablanca (MA)	− 1	(Nouvelle-Calédonie)	+ 10
Chicago (USA)	− 7	New York (USA)	− 6
Dakar (SN)	− 1	Papeete (Polynésie)	− 11
Denver (USA)	− 8	Saint–Denis (Réunion)	+ 3
Fort–de–France		San Francisco (USA)	− 9
(Martinique)	− 5	Sydney (Australie)	+ 9
Halifax (CDN)	− 5	Tokyo (J)	+ 8
Le Caire (Égypte)	+ 1	Tunis (Tunisie)	0
Londres (GB)	− 1		

Use the maps on the inside covers of this book to locate as many of these places as possible.

MODÈLE: 3 h à Paris/Bangkok?

> VOUS: **S'il est trois heures à Paris, quelle heure est-il à Bangkok?**
> VOTRE PARTENAIRE: **Il est neuf heures à Bangkok**

1. 23 h à Paris/Anchorage?
2. 6 h à Paris/Montréal?
3. 14 h à Paris/Londres?
4. 18 h 30 à Paris/Fort-de-France?
5. 12 h à Paris/Mexico?
6. 3 h 20 à Paris/Chicago?
7. 15 h 45 à Paris/Saint-Denis?
8. 11 h à Paris/Tokyo?

Track 2-6

9 **À vous.** Répondez aux questions.

1. Quelle heure est-il maintenant?
2. À quelle heure déjeunez-vous d'habitude?
3. Allez-vous faire vos devoirs ce soir? Si oui, de quelle heure à quelle heure?
4. Combien d'heures étudiez-vous par jour?
5. À quelle heure allez-vous dîner ce soir?
6. Allez-vous sortir ce soir? Si oui, à quelle heure? Avec qui?
7. Allez-vous regarder la télévision ce soir? Si oui, de quelle heure à quelle heure? Qu'est-ce que vous allez regarder?

ENTRE AMIS À l'aéroport

Imagine you are at the airport and role-play the following conversation.

1. Ask your partner what time it is.
2. Ask if s/he is going to Paris. (S/he is.)
3. Ask what time it is in Paris now.
4. Ask at what time s/he is going to arrive in Paris.
5. Find out what s/he is going to do in Paris.

3. EXPLAINING YOUR SCHEDULE

Quel jour est-ce aujourd'hui?
C'est ...

> lundi°
> mardi°
> mercredi
> jeudi°
> vendredi
> samedi
> dimanche

Quel jour est-ce demain?
Quel est votre jour préféré°?

Monday
Tuesday
Thursday

favorite

D. Les jours de la semaine

➤ Days of the week are not capitalized in French.

▶ The calendar week begins on Monday and ends on Sunday.

janvier January

lundi	mardi	mercredi	jeudi	vendredi	samedi	dimanche
		1	2	3	4	5
6	7	8	9	10	11	12
13	14	15	16	17	18	19
20	21	22	23	24	25	26
27	28	29	30	31		

▶ When referring to a specific day, neither an article nor a preposition is used.

Demain, c'est **vendredi.**	*Tomorrow is Friday.*
C'est **vendredi** demain.	*Tomorrow is Friday.*
J'ai envie de sortir **vendredi** soir.	*I feel like going out Friday evening.*
J'ai l'intention d'étudier **samedi.**	*I plan to study Saturday.*

▶ To express the meaning *Saturdays, every Saturday, on Saturdays,* etc., the article **le** is used with the name of the day.

Je n'ai pas de cours **le samedi.**	*I don't have class on Saturdays.*
Le mardi, mon premier cours est à 10 heures.	*On Tuesdays, my first class is at ten o'clock.*
Le vendredi soir, j'ai l'habitude de sortir avec mes amis.	*On Friday nights, I usually go out with my friends.*

> Review the verb **avoir,** p. 66. It is used with **envie, l'intention,** and **l'habitude.** Remember to use **de** + infinitive after these expressions.

▶ Similarly, to express the meaning *mornings, every morning, in the morning,* etc., with parts of the day, **le** or **la** is used before the noun.

Le matin, je vais au cours de français.	*Every morning, I go to French class.*
L'après-midi, je vais à la bibliothèque.	*Afternoons, I go to the library.*
Le soir, je fais mes devoirs.	*In the evening, I do my homework.*
La nuit, je suis au lit.	*At night, I'm in bed.*

10 Le samedi soir. Dites ce que (*what*) ces personnes ont et n'ont pas envie de faire ou ce qu'elles ont l'habitude ou n'ont pas l'habitude de faire samedi soir. Suivez les modèles.

MODÈLES: les étudiants / envie / sortir ou rester dans leur chambre

Le samedi soir, ils ont envie de sortir; ils n'ont pas envie de rester dans leur chambre.

ma sœur / l'habitude / aller au cinéma ou faire ses devoirs

Le samedi soir, elle a l'habitude d'aller au cinéma; elle n'a pas l'habitude de faire ses devoirs.

1. les étudiants / envie / rester sur le campus ou aller au cinéma
2. je / l'habitude / voir un film ou faire mes devoirs
3. le professeur / l'habitude / préparer ses cours ou regarder la télévision
4. mes amis et moi, nous / envie / dîner entre amis ou dîner seuls
5. mon ami(e) _____ / l'habitude / sortir avec moi ou rester dans sa chambre

11 À vous. Répondez aux questions.

1. Quels sont les jours où vous allez au cours de français?
2. À quelle heure est votre cours?
3. Quels sont les jours où vous n'avez pas de cours?
4. Qu'est-ce que vous avez l'intention de faire le week-end prochain?
5. Avez-vous l'habitude d'aller au gymnase? Si oui, quels jours et à quelle heure?
6. À quelle heure avez-vous votre premier cours le mardi?
7. Quand est-ce que vous allez à la bibliothèque?
8. Quand écoutez-vous la radio?
9. Quand avez-vous envie de regarder la télévision?

Vocabulaire

Quelques cours

l'art *(m.)*	art	la musique	*music*
la chimie	*chemistry*	la pédagogie	*education, teacher preparation*
le commerce	*business*		
la comptabilité	*accounting*	la philosophie	*philosophy*
la gestion	*management*	la psychologie	*psychology*
la gymnastique	*gymnastics*	les sciences *(f. pl.)*	*science*
l'histoire *(f.)*	*history*	les sciences économiques *(f. pl.)*	*economics*
l'informatique *(f.)*	*computer science*		
la littérature	*literature*	les sciences politiques *(f. pl.)*	political science
les mathématiques *(f. pl.)*	*math*		

12 Mon emploi du temps (My schedule). Indiquez votre emploi du temps pour ce semestre. Indiquez le jour, l'heure et le cours.

MODÈLE: **Le lundi à dix heures, j'ai un cours de français.**
Le lundi à onze heures, j'ai un cours de mathématiques.
Le lundi à une heure, j'ai un cours d'histoire.

13 As-tu un cours de ... ? Essayez de deviner *(try to guess)* deux des cours de votre partenaire. Demandez ensuite quels jours et à quelle heure votre partenaire va à ces cours. Votre partenaire va répondre à vos questions.

MODÈLE: **As-tu un cours d'histoire?**
Quels jours vas-tu à ce cours?
À quelle heure vas-tu à ce cours?

Réalités culturelles
L'enseignement supérieur

Directphoto.org/Alamy

EACH YEAR over 2 million students are enrolled in institutions of higher learning in France. Some enroll in two-year programs that will prepare them to directly enter the workforce. These offer two types of diplomas: **le diplôme universitaire de technologie (DUT)** and **le brevet de technicien supérieur (BTS).** The **DUT** prepares students for careers in industry and technology while the **BTS** prepares them for work in such industries as hospitality, agriculture, health, and applied arts. Others enroll in **les universités,** public universities open to all students, or **les écoles supérieures,** public or private universities where admission is through a competitive examination and interview process. There are three levels of study with corresponding diplomas offered in **les universités: la licence,** which takes six semesters to complete, **le master,** which requires four more semesters after the **licence,** and **le doctorat,** which takes six more semesters after **le master. Les écoles supérieures** provide highly specialized studies in such areas as engineering, architecture, business, translation and interpretation, and journalism. Among **les écoles supérieures** are a group of institutions called **les grandes écoles.** These highly selective and often quite expensive institutions train students to enter the highest levels of a particular field. Students wishing to enter a **grande école** usually take a two-year preparatory course just to prepare for the entrance exam. Studies generally take five years to complete (the two years of preparation count toward this) and students finish with **le master.**

Cultural Activities

The **Université d'Angers** that Lori from this chapter attends is a public university. Like many public French universities, it is multidisciplinary and tuition costs are low. To find out more about this typical French university, go to www.univ-angers.fr.

E. Le verbe devoir

Grammar
Tutorials

Les étudiants doivent beaucoup travailler.

Students have to work a lot.

Vous devez être fatigués.

You must be tired.

devoir *(to have to, must; to owe)*	
je	**dois**
tu	**dois**
il/elle/on	**doit**
vous	**devez**
nous	**devons**
ils/elles	**doivent**

▶ **Devoir** is often used with the infinitive to express an obligation or a probability.

Vous **devez faire** attention! *(obligation)*   *You must pay attention!*

Lori **doit avoir** 20 ans. *(probability)*   *Lori must be 20.*

▶ **Devoir** plus a noun means *to owe.*

Je dois vingt dollars à mes parents.   *I owe my parents twenty dollars.*

Synthèse: révision des verbes

	PARLER	ÊTRE	AVOIR	FAIRE	ALLER	DEVOIR
je	parle	suis	ai	fais	vais	dois
tu	parles	es	as	fais	vas	dois
il/elle/on	parle	est	a	fait	va	doit
nous	parlons	sommes	avons	faisons	allons	devons
vous	parlez	êtes	avez	faites	allez	devez
ils/elles	parlent	sont	ont	font	vont	doivent

14 **Mais qu'est-ce qu'on doit faire?** Utilisez l'expression entre parenthèses pour indiquer ce que chaque personne doit faire.

MODÈLE: Guillaume a envie d'aller au cinéma. (étudier)
                Guillaume **a envie d'aller au cinéma mais il doit étudier.**

1. Nous avons envie de sortir ce soir. (préparer un examen)
2. Les étudiants ont envie de regarder la télévision. (étudier)
3. Tu as envie de danser ce soir. (faire tes devoirs)
4. J'ai envie de rester au lit. (aller aux cours)
5. Le professeur a envie de faire un voyage. (enseigner)
6. Tes amis ont envie d'aller en ville. (faire la lessive)

15 **Je dois faire ça cette semaine.** Faites une liste de sept choses que vous devez faire cette semaine (une chose pour chaque jour).

MODÈLE: **Samedi, je dois faire le ménage.**

16 **Et alors?** Pour chaque phrase, inventez une ou deux conclusions logiques.

MODÈLE: Lori n'a pas envie de passer le week-end dans sa chambre.
Qu'est-ce qu'elle va faire?
Elle va sortir. ou **Elle a l'intention d'aller au cinéma.**

1. Lori a envie de sortir ce soir. Où va-t-elle? Que fait-elle?
2. Mais son amie Denise n'est pas libre. Qu'est-ce qu'elle doit faire?
3. Lori et Denise font souvent les courses ensemble. Où vont-elles?
4. Aujourd'hui Denise reste dans sa chambre. Pourquoi? Comment va-t-elle?
5. Lori téléphone à Denise. Pourquoi? De quoi parle-t-elle?

ENTRE AMIS **Ton emploi du temps**

You and a classmate are discussing your schedules to see when you might do something together. Role-play the following conversation.

1. Find out what classes your partner has this week.
2. Find out when your partner goes to the library.
3. Find out if your partner has to work and, if so, on what days.
4. Find out if your partner feels like going to the movies on a night you are both free.

Je dois aller à la librairie.

🔊 4. TELLING WHERE TO FIND PLACES

Où se trouve° la souris?

where is the mouse?

is located

La souris est loin du fromage.

cheese

de=e

M's

La souris est près du fromage.

near

La souris est devant le fromage.

in front of

La souris est derrière le fromage.

behind

La souris est sur le fromage.

on the

La souris est sous le fromage.

under

La souris est dans le fromage.

inside

Où se trouve le fromage? Le fromage est dans la souris.

inside

F. Quelques prépositions de lieu (place)

🌐 Grammar Tutorials

Les toilettes se trouvent **dans** le couloir.
Les toilettes sont **à côté de** la salle de classe.
Le cinéma se trouve **au** centre commercial.
La banque est **à droite** ou **à gauche** du parking?
Allez **tout droit** et ensuite tournez **à droite.**

The restroom is in the hall.
The restroom is next to the classroom.
The movie theater is at the mall.
Is the bank on the right or on the left of the parking lot?
Go straight ahead and then turn to the right.

complete prepositions texts

à	at; in; to		dans	in (inside)
à côté de	next to, beside		entre	between; among
à droite de	to (on) the right of	≠	à gauche de	to (on) the left of
derrière	behind	≠	devant	in front of
loin de	far from	≠	près de	near
sous	under	≠	sur	on

opposites

Remember that **à droite** means *to (on) the right,* while **tout droit** means *straight ahead.*

▶ **À côté, à droite, à gauche, loin,** and **près** can all drop the **de** and stand alone.

Nous habitons **à côté d'**une église.

But: **L'église est à côté.**

We live next to a church.
The church is next door.

17 Où se trouvent ces endroits? Votre partenaire veut savoir (*wants to know*) où se trouvent les endroits suivants. Répondez à ses questions.

Review contractions with **de**, p. 78.

MODÈLE: La bibliothèque (près / bâtiment des sciences)
VOTRE PARTENAIRE: **Où se trouve la bibliothèque?**
VOUS: **Elle est près du bâtiment des sciences.**

1. le bâtiment administratif (près / bibliothèque) *Il est près de la*
2. la pharmacie (à côté / église) *Elle est à côté de l'église*
3. les résidences universitaires (sur / campus) *Elles sont sur le campus*
4. le restaurant universitaire (dans / résidence) *Il est dans la résidence*
5. le cinéma (à / centre commercial) *Elle est ôte au centre commercial*
6. le bureau de poste (derrière / pharmacie) *Il est derri*
7. le centre commercial (loin / campus) *Il est loin du campus*
8. les toilettes (devant / salle de classe) *Elles sont devant la salle de classe*
9. le parking (à gauche / banque) *Il est à gauche de la banque*

18 Votre campus. Faites rapidement le plan (*Draw a map*) de votre campus. Expliquez où se trouvent cinq endroits différents.

MODÈLE: **Voilà la résidence qui s'appelle Brown Hall. Elle est près de la bibliothèque.**

G. L'impératif

Grammar Tutorials

Regarde!	Look!
Regardez!	Look!
Regardons!	Let's look!
Tourne à gauche!	Turn to the left!
Tournez à gauche!	Turn to the left!
Tournons à gauche!	Let's turn to the left!

You already learned a number of imperatives in the Preliminary Chapter, p. 2.

▶ The imperative is used to give commands and to make suggestions. The forms are usually the same as the present tense for **tu, vous,** and **nous**.

▶ If the infinitive ends in **-er**, the final **-s** is omitted from the form that corresponds to **tu**.

parler français

tu parle**s** français   But: **Parle** français!

aller aux cours

tu va**s** aux cours   But: **Va** aux cours!

▶ For negative commands, **ne** precedes the verb and **pas** follows it.
Ne regardez **pas** la télévision!
Ne fais **pas** attention à Papa!

19 **En ville.** Regardez le plan *(map)* de la ville. Demandez où se trouvent les endroits suivants. Votre partenaire va expliquer où ils se trouvent.

MODÈLE: cinéma

VOUS: **Où se trouve le cinéma, s'il vous plaît?**

VOTRE PARTENAIRE: **Il est à côté du café. Allez tout droit et tournez à gauche. Il est à droite.**

1. café
2. épicerie
3. église
4. boulangerie
5. bureau de poste

6. bureau de tabac
7. banque
8. cinéma
9. pharmacie
10. hôtel

20 **Qu'est-ce que les bons étudiants doivent faire?** Utilisez l'impératif pour répondre à la question. Décidez ce qu'un bon étudiant doit ou ne doit pas faire.

MODÈLE: Est-ce que je dois passer tout le week-end dans ma chambre?

Ne passez pas tout le week-end dans votre chambre! ou

Oui, passez tout le week-end dans votre chambre!

1. Est-ce que je dois habiter dans une résidence universitaire?
2. Est-ce que je dois manger à la cafétéria?
3. Est-ce que je dois faire mes devoirs dans ma chambre?
4. Est-ce que je dois étudier à la bibliothèque?
5. Est-ce que je ne dois pas aller au bistro?
6. Est-ce que je ne dois pas parler anglais en cours de français?

H. Les prépositions de lieu avec une ville ou un pays

Review the contractions in this chapter on p. 133.

Grammar Tutorials

NOTE

▶ Use **à** to say that you are in a city or are going to a city.

In cases where the name of a city contains the definite article (**Le Mans, Le Caire, La Nouvelle-Orléans**), the article is retained and the normal contractions occur where necessary.

Emmanuelle habite **à La Nouvelle-Orléans.** Nous allons **au Mans.** Je suis **à Paris.** Je vais **à New York.**

▶ Most countries, states, and provinces ending in **-e** are feminine. An exception is **le Mexique.**

la Belgiqu**e**   *But:*   **le Mexique**

la Virgini**e**

la Colombi**e**-Britannique

la Californi**e**

▶ To say you are in or going to a *country,* the preposition varies. Use **en** before feminine countries or those that begin with a vowel sound. Use **au** before masculine countries which begin with a consonant. Use **aux** when the name of the country is plural.

en France   **au** Canada   **aux** États-Unis

en Israël   **au** Mexique   **aux** Pays-Bas

▶ To say you are in or going to an American *state* or a Canadian *province,* **en** is normally used before those that are feminine or that begin with a vowel sound. The preposition **au** is often used with masculine provinces that begin with a consonant and with the states of Texas and New Mexico.

en Virginie   **au** Manitoba

en Nouvelle-Écosse   **au** Nouveau-Mexique

en Ontario

en Ohio

▶ **Dans l'état de** or **dans la province de** can be used with any state or province, masculine or feminine.

dans l'État de New York

dans la province d'Alberta

dans l'État de Californie

Review the adjectives of nationality in Ch. 1, p. 19. The adjective corresponding to **Irak** is **irakien(ne)**.

See how many of the countries listed you can find on the maps on the inside covers of your text.

Quelques langues et quelques pays

On parle ...		en ...	
	allemand		Allemagne
	anglais		Angleterre
	français et flamand		Belgique
	chinois		Chine
	espagnol		Espagne
	français		France
	arabe		Irak
	anglais et irlandais		Irlande
	italien		Italie
	russe		Russie
	suédois		Suède
	français, allemand et italien		Suisse
On parle ...	français et anglais	au ...	Canada
	japonais		Japon
	français et arabe		Maroc
	espagnol		Mexique
	portugais		Portugal
	français et wolof		Sénégal
On parle ...	anglais, espagnol et français	aux ...	États-Unis
	hollandais		Pays-Bas

▶ When talking about more than one country, use a preposition before each one.

On parle français **en** France, **en** Belgique, **au** Canada, **au** Maroc, **au** Sénégal, etc.

▶ When there is no preposition with a country, state, or province, the definite article must be used.

La France est un beau pays.

J'adore **le Canada.**

NOTE

Israël is an exception.

Israël est à côté de la Syrie.

21 **Où habitent-ils?** Dans quel pays les personnes suivantes habitent-elles?

MODÈLE: Vous êtes français.

Vous habitez en France.

1. Lucie est canadienne.
2. Les Dewonck sont belges.
3. Phoebe est anglaise.
4. Pepe et María sont mexicains.
5. Yuko est japonaise.

6. Yolande est sénégalaise.
7. Sean et Deirdre sont irlandais.
8. Caterina est italienne.
9. Hassan est marocain.
10. Nous sommes américains.

22 Qui sont ces personnes? Où habitent-elles? Vous êtes à l'aéroport de Roissy-Charles-de-Gaulle et vous écoutez des touristes de divers pays. Devinez leur nationalité et où ils vont.

MODÈLE: Il y a deux hommes qui parlent espagnol.
Ils doivent être espagnols ou mexicains.
Ils vont probablement en Espagne ou au Mexique.

1. Il y a un homme et une femme qui parlent français.
2. Il y a deux enfants qui parlent anglais.
3. Il y a une jeune fille qui parle russe.
4. Il y a trois garçons qui parlent arabe.
5. Il y a une personne qui parle suédois.
6. Il y a un homme qui parle allemand.
7. Il y a deux couples qui parlent flamand.
8. Il y a deux jeunes filles qui parlent italien.
9. Il y a un homme et une femme qui parlent japonais.

I. Les mots interrogatifs où et quand

Grammar Tutorials

► A question using **quand** or **où** is formed like any other question, using inversion or **est-ce que**.

Où habitent-ils?   Quand arrive-t-elle?
Où est-ce qu'ils habitent?   Quand est-ce qu'elle arrive?

NOTE ⌐ In **Quand est-ce que,** the **-d** is pronounced [t]. When **quand** is followed by inversion, there is no liaison.

► With a *noun* subject, the inversion order is *noun + verb + subject pronoun.*

Où **tes parents habitent-ils?**   Quand **ta sœur arrive-t-elle?**

Review interrogative forms, pp. 50–51.

► In addition, if there is only one verb and no object, the noun subject and the verb may be inverted.

Où **habitent tes parents?**   Quand **arrive ta sœur?**

23 Où et quand? Pour chaque phrase, posez une question avec **où.** Votre partenaire va inventer une réponse. Ensuite, posez une question avec **quand.** Votre partenaire va inventer une réponse à cette question aussi.

MODÈLE: Mon frère fait un voyage.
                VOUS: **Où est-ce qu'il fait un voyage?**
    VOTRE PARTENAIRE: **Il fait un voyage en France.**
                VOUS: **Quand est-ce qu'il fait ce voyage?**
    VOTRE PARTENAIRE: **Il fait ce voyage la semaine prochaine.**

1. Mon amie a envie de faire des courses.
2. Nous avons l'intention de déjeuner ensemble.
3. Je vais au cinéma.
4. Mon cousin travaille.
5. Mes amis étudient.

24 À **vous.** Répondez aux questions.

1. Où les étudiants de votre université habitent-ils?
2. Où se trouve la bibliothèque sur votre campus?
3. Quels bâtiments se trouvent près de la bibliothèque?
4. Où se trouve la salle de classe pour la biologie?
5. Quand avez-vous votre cours de français?
6. Où les étudiants dînent-ils d'habitude le dimanche soir?
7. Où allez-vous vendredi prochain? Pourquoi?

ENTRE AMIS Vous êtes un(e) nouvel(le) étudiant(e).

Choose a new name and a new country of origin from among the French-speaking countries, and role-play the following conversation between two students.

1. Greet your partner and find out if s/he speaks French. (S/he does.)
2. State your new name and tell where you live.
3. Say that you are a new student.
4. Find out where the library is.
5. Get directions to a shopping center.
6. Thank your partner and say goodbye.

Cultural Activities

Réalités culturelles
Les étudiants étrangers en France

FRANCE WELCOMES over 265,000 international students each year to its institutions of higher learning. The United States and the United Kingdom are the only other two countries that have more foreign students attending their universities. The majority of France's international students, nearly 50%, come from French-speaking Africa, primarily Morocco, Algeria, and Tunisia. The next largest group comes from other European countries, followed by Asian students, and Americans.

Monkey Business Images/
Shutterstock.com

For students wishing to study in France, students must register with CampusFrance, a service provided by the French government. This organization helps them choose a course and place of study, plan academic projects, navigate administrative paperwork such as visa applications and registration at an institution of higher learning, and it helps them find financial aid.

Intégration

RÉVISION

A **Au revoir.** Quels sont cinq synonymes de l'expression **au revoir**?

B **Les pays.** Répondez.

1. Mentionnez cinq pays où on parle français.
2. Nommez deux pays en Europe, deux pays en Asie et deux pays en Afrique.
3. Dans quels pays se trouvent ces villes? Dakar, Genève, Trois-Rivières, Lyon, Montréal, Prairie du Chien, Rabat, Bruxelles, Des Moines, Bâton Rouge.

C **Trouvez quelqu'un qui …** Interviewez les autres étudiants pour trouver quelqu'un qui …

MODÈLE: joue au tennis
Est-ce que tu joues au tennis?

1. étudie l'informatique
2. va rarement à la bibliothèque
3. a envie d'aller au Sénégal, au Maroc ou en Suisse
4. doit travailler ce soir
5. va au cinéma vendredi soir prochain
6. a l'habitude d'étudier dans sa chambre
7. n'a pas de cours le mardi matin
8. aime manger seul
9. étudie au moins trois heures par jour

D **À l'écoute.** Deux étudiants, Amélie et Sébastien, se rencontrent à l'université. Écoutez leur conversation et répondez aux questions.

Track 2-8

1. Où Amélie va-t-elle?
2. Quand est-ce qu'elle y va?
3. Quel cours est-ce qu'Amélie a aujourd'hui?
4. À quelle heure est son cours?
5. Qu'est-ce que Sébastien et Amélie vont faire ensemble?
6. Où est-ce qu'ils vont? Pourquoi? (*Why?*)
7. Où va Sébastien cet après-midi?

E **À vous.** Répondez.

1. Qu'est-ce que vous avez envie de faire ce week-end?
2. Qu'est-ce que vous devez faire?
3. Qu'est-ce que vos amis aiment faire le samedi soir?
4. Qu'est-ce que vous faites le lundi? (trois choses)
5. Quels sont les jours où vous allez à votre cours de français?
6. À quelle heure allez-vous à ce cours?
7. Dans quel bâtiment avez-vous ce cours? Où se trouve ce bâtiment?
8. Quel est votre jour préféré? Pourquoi?

Communication and Communities. To learn more about the culture presented in this chapter, go to the *Premium Website* and click on the Web Search Activities.

Also see the *Entre amis* Video Program and Video Worksheet in the *Cahier*.

NÉGOCIATIONS

L'emploi du temps de Sahibou. Interviewez votre partenaire pour trouver les renseignements qui manquent *(missing information)*. La copie de votre partenaire est dans l'Appendice D.

MODÈLE: **Est-ce qu'il a un cours le mercredi à 11 heures?**
Est-ce que c'est un cours de mathématiques?

A

	lundi	mardi	mercredi	jeudi	vendredi	samedi	dimanche
9h	histoire		histoire		histoire		
10h						gymnase	
11h		sciences économiques		sciences économiques		gymnase	
12h		philosophie		philosophie			
13h	chimie		chimie		chimie		
14h	travail	travail	travail	travail	banque		sieste
19h						restaurant	
20h						chez des amis	

LECTURE I

LA MÉTHODO When you encounter a word you don't know in your native language, you use the context of the sentence or paragraph to deduce what it means. You can use this same skill when reading French. Specifically, you might look at headings to tell you what a paragraph is about, or you might analyze sentence structure to determine what part of speech (noun, adjective, verb, etc.) the unknown word is. Your guesses will most likely give you the gist of what you are trying to read.

A **Étude du vocabulaire.** Utilisez les pistes de contexte pour trouver le sens *(meaning)* des mots en caractères gras dans les phrases suivantes. Ensuite, choisissez le mot correspondant en anglais pour chacun *(each one)*: *close, choice, means, training, turned, eager, heritage, field of study.*

1. **Soucieuse** d'avoir du succès à l'université, Valentine étudie beaucoup.
2. Nos cours dans **la filière** des sciences humaines sont la sociologie, l'anthropologie, etc.
3. Le train et le bus sont des **moyens** de transport.
4. Anne **a eu** 30 ans en 2001.
5. La ville a un **patrimoine** riche en histoire, architecture et beaux-arts.
6. La relation entre les amis est d'habitude très **étroite.**
7. Le restaurant propose un large **choix** de boissons, plus de 25!
8. Paul étudie à l'Institut d'hôtellerie; il fait **une formation** en gestion hôtelière.

Parcourez la page web. Lisez rapidement la page web et dites en anglais quatre choses que vous avez apprises (*you learned*) sur l'université d'Angers.

L'UNIVERSITÉ D'ANGERS: INFOS

UN PEU D'HISTOIRE

Fondée au Moyen-Âge, l'Université d'Angers a été recréée sous sa forme actuelle en 1971. Elle a eu 40 ans en 2011.

Atouts[1]

- Au centre du Val de Loire, à une heure trente de Paris, l'Université d'Angers, à vocation pluridisciplinaire, offre un large choix de formations traditionnelles et novatrices.
- Plus de 19 000 étudiants et 4 000 stagiaires[2] en formation continue bénéficient de filières de formations diversifiées et à finalité professionnelle.
- Soucieuse de renforcer[3] son potentiel de recherche[4], l'Université d'Angers concentre ses moyens autour[5] d'axes privilégiés de développement, en liaison étroite avec les collectivités et les entreprises.

Une vocation pluridisciplinaire

L'Université d'Angers propose un large choix de formations, dans tous les grands secteurs fondamentaux. Caractérisée par une grande capacité à évoluer et à s'adapter aux attentes[6] nouvelles, elle offre des formations universitaires traditionnelles et des formations professionnalisées originales.

L'Université et sa région

Angers offre un patrimoine historique et artistique unique:

- Tapisseries[7] de l'Apocalypse et du Chant du Monde
- Château du Roi[8] René
- Musées
- Une Cité médiévale

Source: http://www.univ-angers.fr by permission of the University of Angers

---

[1]*assets* / [2]*interns* / [3]*to reinforce* / [4]*research* / [5]*around* / [6]*expectations* / [7]*tapestries* / [8]*King*

C **Familles de mots.** Essayez de deviner le sens *(try to guess the meaning)* des mots suivants.

1. recréer, créer, une création, créatif (créative)
2. discipliner, une discipline, disciplinaire
3. privilégier, un privilège, privilégié(e)
4. innover, une innovation, novateur (novatrice)
5. bénéficier, un bénéfice, bénéfique
6. finir, une finalité, final(e)

D **Vrai ou faux.** Relisez toute la lecture et ensuite décidez si les phrases suivantes sont **vraies** ou **fausses.** Corrigez les phrases fausses.

1. L'Université d'Angers est très vieille, mais sa forme actuelle est assez récente.
2. Angers est très loin de Paris.
3. L'université offre beaucoup de formations différentes dans plusieurs disciplines.
4. L'université est très traditionnelle.
5. Il y a plus de 17 000 personnes qui étudient à l'université.
6. L'université travaille souvent avec les entreprises pour faire de la recherche *(research)*.
7. Il est probable que très peu de personnes étudient les sciences et la technologie à l'Université d'Angers.
8. La ville d'Angers offre plusieurs activités culturelles.

LECTURE II

Les étudiants d'Angers ont des liens avec les gens du Cameroun grâce aux projets bénévoles *(charitable)* et aux collaborations entre les universités. Cependant *(However)* la vie urbaine d'Angers est très différente de la vie rurale de beaucoup de Camerounais. Le poème que vous allez lire parle de cette différence.

A **Trouvez le Cameroun.** Cherchez le Cameroun sur la carte à l'intérieur de la couverture de ce livre. Sur quel continent se trouve ce pays? Quelle est la capitale du Cameroun? Quels sont les pays qui se trouvent près du Cameroun?

B **Étude du vocabulaire.** Étudiez les phrases suivantes. Utilisez les pistes de contexte pour choisir les mots anglais qui correspondent aux mots français en caractères gras: *birds, against, a cooking utensil, I see, each one, I hear, people, a popular African food, mine, peace, bark, roof.*

1. **J'entends** quelquefois des chiens qui **aboient** quand une voiture passe.
2. Il y a des **oiseaux** sur le **toit** de la maison.
3. **Je vois** des **gens** qui portent des vêtements africains.
4. **Chacun** porte des sandales.
5. Dans leur village on mange du **taro.**
6. On prépare la cuisine avec un **pilon.**
7. Êtes-vous pour ou **contre** la **paix** dans ce pauvre pays?
8. Voilà ton livre; où est **le mien?**

Track 2-9

Village natal

Ici je suis chez moi,
Je suis vraiment chez moi.
Les hommes que je vois,
Les femmes que je croise[1]
M'appellent leur fils
Et les enfants leur frère.
Le patois qu'on parle est le mien,
Les chants que j'entends expriment[2]
Des joies et des peines qui sont
    miennes.
L'herbe que je foule reconnaît mes
    pas[3].
Les chiens n'aboient pas contre moi,
Mais ils remuent la queue[4]
En signe de reconnaissance.
Les oiseaux me saluent au passage
Par des chants affectueux.
Des coups de pilon m'invitent

À me régaler de[5] taro
Si mon ventre est creux[6].
Sous chacun de ces toits qui
    fument
Lentement dans la paix du soir
On voudra m'accueillir[7].
Bientôt c'est la fête, la fête de
chaque soir:
    Chants et danses autour du feu[8],
Au rythme du tam-tam, du
    tambour, du balafon[9].
Nos gens sont pauvres
Mais très simples, très heureux;
Je suis simple comme eux[10]
Content comme eux,
Heureux comme eux.
Ici je suis chez moi,
Je suis vraiment chez moi.

Jean-Louis Dongmo, "Village natal". Reprinted with permission of Jean-Louis Dongmo from *Neaf Camerounai: Anthologie par Lilyan Kesteloot,* deuxième edition, (Yaoundé: Editions Clé, 1971).

---

1. *that I meet* / 2. *express* / 3. *the grass I walk on recognizes my steps* / 4. *wag their tails* / 5. *have a delicious meal of* / 6. *stomach is empty* / 7. *people will welcome me* / 8. *around the fire* / 9. *musical instruments* / 10. *them*

C Discussion. Lisez le poème et répondez aux questions en anglais ou en français.

1. Cherchez les exemples dans le poème qui prouvent que le poète est heureux d'être dans son village.
2. Quelles ressemblances et quelles différences y a-t-il entre le poète et vous?

Réalités culturelles
Le Cameroun

LOCATED IN CENTRAL AFRICA along the continent's western coast, **le Cameroun** is composed of sweltering rain forests, isolated beaches, and densely populated cities like Yaoundé, the capital. Cameroon also includes stretches of savannah and arid desert regions in the north, volcanoes, wildlife parks, and mountain ranges. The Waza national park is one of Central Africa's best, hosting several wildlife and bird species.

Stephanie Meng/Bios/PhotoLibrary

Cameroon's population is ethnically diverse, speaking twenty-four different African languages. English and French, reminiscent of Cameroon's colonial past, are its official languages. Christianity, Islam, and several indigenous religions are practiced. The cuisine of Cameroon is considered among the best in Central Africa, and its **macossa** music is popular in other African countries.

RÉDACTION

LA MÉTHODO To write accurate and clear directions, use a map, either one you draw yourself or one from the Internet. A map will help you identify each direction to give and the order in which to give it.

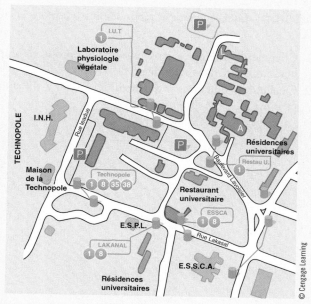

© Cengage Learning

QUEL EST LE CHEMIN POUR ALLER ...?

Vous allez aider un nouvel étudiant francophone de votre université à s'orienter. Écrivez-lui un e-mail dans lequel:

- vous vous présentez
- vous lui donnez rendez-vous à un endroit sur votre campus (donnez le jour et l'heure)
- vous expliquez où cet endroit se trouve et comment y arriver avec des indications précises
- vous expliquez que vous allez parler de son emploi du temps, du campus, de la ville
- vous lui donnez vos coordonnées (numéro de portable, adresse e-mail)

A **Avant d'écrire.** Trouvez un plan d'accès de votre campus et un bon endroit pour un rendez-vous. Notez les bâtiments autour de cet endroit et tracez le chemin depuis un parking ou un arrêt d'autobus (*bus stop*) près de cet endroit.

B **Écrire.** Écrivez une ébauche de votre e-mail. Suivez les indications ci-dessus (*above*). Utilisez le plan pour être sûr que vous avez mentionné tous les détails nécessaires. Cet étudiant vient d'un autre pays, alors votre e-mail doit être simple et clair.

C **Correction.** Donnez votre plan à un(e) camarade de classe. Lisez-lui votre e-mail, et il/elle va tracer le chemin. Est-ce qu'il/elle arrive au bon endroit? Si non, faites les corrections nécessaires.

Vocabulaire Actif

Practice some of this vocabulary with the flashcards on **iLrn**.

Pour dire au revoir
à bientôt *see you soon*
à demain *see you tomorrow*
à la prochaine *until next time, be seeing you*
à tout à l'heure *see you in a little while*
au plaisir (de vous revoir) *(I hope to) see you again*
au revoir *goodbye, see you again*
bon après-midi *have a good afternoon*
bonne journée *have a good day*
bonne nuit *pleasant dreams (lit. good night)*
bonne soirée *have a good evening*

bonsoir *good evening, good night*
salut *bye(-bye) (fam.)*

Adverbes
après *after*
au moins *at least*
avant *before*
d'abord *at first*
demain *tomorrow*
enfin *finally*
ensuite *next, then*
maintenant *now*

Jours de la semaine
lundi *(m.) Monday*
mardi *(m.) Tuesday*
mercredi *(m.) Wednesday*
jeudi *(m.) Thursday*
vendredi *(m.) Friday*
samedi *(m.) Saturday*
dimanche *(m.) Sunday*

Adjectifs
libre *free*
parfait(e) *perfect*

Vocabulaire Actif (continued)

préféré(e) *favorite*
premier (première) *first*
prochain(e) *next*
seul(e) *alone; only*
suivant(e) *following*

Expressions de lieu
à côté *next door; to the side*
à côté de *next to, beside*
derrière *behind*
devant *in front of*
à droite *on (to) the right*
à gauche *on (to) the left*
entre *between, among*
loin *far — away from (loin de)*
sous *under*
tout droit *straight ahead*

Pays
l'Allemagne *(f.) Germany*
l'Angleterre *(f.) England*
la Belgique *Belgium*
le Canada *Canada*
la Chine *China*
l'Espagne *(f.) Spain*
les États-Unis *(m. pl.) United States*
la France *France*
l'Irlande *(f.) Ireland*
Israël *(m.) Israel*
l'Italie *(f.) Italy*
le Japon *Japan*
le Maroc *Morocco*
le Mexique *Mexico*
les Pays-Bas *(m. pl.) Netherlands*
le Portugal *Portugal*
la Russie *Russia*
le Sénégal *Senegal*
la Suède *Sweden*
la Suisse *Switzerland*

Verbes
aller *to go*
aller en ville *to go into town*
avoir envie de *to want to, to feel like*
avoir l'habitude de *to usually; to be in the habit of*
avoir l'intention de *to plan to*
déjeuner *to have lunch*
devoir *to have to, must, to owe*
s'embrasser *to kiss*
faire un voyage *to take a trip*

passer un test *to take a test*
rester *to stay*
tourner *to turn*

Cours
l'art *(m.) art*
la chimie *chemistry*
le commerce *business*
la comptabilité *accounting*
la gestion *management*
la gymnastique *gymnastics*
l'histoire *(f.) history*
l'informatique *(f.) computer science*
la littérature *literature*
la pédagogie *education, teacher preparation*
la philosophie *philosophy*
la psychologie *psychology*
les sciences *(f.) sciences*
les sciences économiques *(f.) economics*

Autres prépositions
par *per; by; through*
vers (8 heures) *approximately, around (8 o'clock)*

Expressions de temps
Quelle heure est-il? *What time is it?*
Quel jour est-ce? *What day is it?*
Il est ... heure(s). *It is ... o'clock.*
Il est midi (minuit). *It is noon (midnight).*
et demi(e) *half past*
et quart *quarter past, quarter after*
moins le quart *quarter to, quarter till*
ce soir *tonight*
dans une heure (trois jours, etc.) *one hour (three days, etc.) from now*
une minute *minute*
une semaine *week*
tout à l'heure *in a little while*
tout le week-end *all weekend (long)*

D'autres expressions utiles
Cela (ça) m'est égal. *I don't care.*
D'accord. *Okay.*
Je vais sortir. *I'm going to go out.*
Où se trouve (se trouvent) ... ? *Where is (are) ... ?*
pas grand-chose *not much*
Quoi de neuf? *What's new?*
Ça va? *Okay?*
Tu vas voir. *You are going to see.*

D'autres noms
une bise *kiss*
un emploi du temps *schedule*
une fois *(one) time*
un film *film, movie*
le fromage *cheese*
un rendez-vous *appointment; date*
une souris *mouse*
un voyage *trip, voyage*
l'arabe *Arabic*
le flamand *Flemish*
le portugais *Portuguese*
le wolof *Wolof*

Endroits
un aéroport *airport*
une banque *bank*
un bâtiment *building*
une bibliothèque *library*
un bistro *bar and café; bistro*
une boulangerie *bakery*
un bureau de poste *post office*
un bureau de tabac *tobacco shop*
une cafétéria *cafeteria*
un campus *campus*
un centre commercial *shopping center, mall*
un château *chateau; castle*
un cinéma *movie theater*
un couloir *hall; corridor*
un cours *course; class*
une école *school*
une église *church*
un endroit *place*
une épicerie *grocery store*
un état *state*
une gare *train station*
un gymnase *gymnasium*
un hôtel *hotel*
une librairie *bookstore*
un musée *museum*
un parking *parking lot, garage*
un pays *country*
une pharmacie *pharmacy*
une piscine *swimming pool*
une province *province*
une résidence (universitaire) *dormitory*
un restaurant *restaurant*
une salle de classe *classroom*
les toilettes *(f. pl.) restroom*
une ville *city*

Vos activités

BUTS COMMUNICATIFS
- Relating past events
- Describing your study habits
- Describing your weekend activities

STRUCTURES UTILES
- Le **passé composé** avec **avoir**
- Les verbes **écrire** et **lire**
- **Ne ... rien**
- **Temps, heure** et **fois**
- Les verbes pronominaux
- **Jouer de** et **jouer à**
- Les pronoms accentués
- Les verbes **dormir, partir** et **sortir**
- Les verbes **nettoyer** et **envoyer**

CULTURE
Zoom sur le logement
- **Article:** La maison
- **Insolite:** Relativité culturelle: La maison
- **Repères:** Le riad
- **Vidéo buzz:** Le logement social
- **Vu sur le web:** Les maisons traditionnelles du monde francophone

Il y a un geste
- C'est la vie.
- J'ai oublié!

Lectures
- Tunisie: L'offre de loisirs pour la jeunesse
- «Les droits imprescriptibles du lecteur»

RESOURCES

Audio   iLrn Heinle Learning Center   Premium Website

Pair Work   Group Work   *Entre amis* Video Program

David A. Barnes/Alamy

🔊 PRISE DE CONTACT: QU'EST-CE QUE TU AS FAIT HIER?

Track 2-10

Sébastien, qu'est-ce que tu as fait hier?°

What did you do yesterday?

    J'ai téléphoné à deux amis.

    J'ai envoyé des textos et des e-mails°.

sent text messages and e-mails

    J'ai fait mes devoirs.

    J'ai étudié pendant° trois heures.

for

    J'ai déjeuné à midi et j'ai dîné à
        7 heures du soir.

    J'ai regardé un peu la télévision.

    Mais je n'ai pas fait le ménage.

    Et je n'ai pas passé d'examen°.

didn't take a test

  Et vous? Qu'est-ce que vous avez fait?

Lori a écrit un e-mail à deux de ses camarades du cours de français aux États-Unis.

To:
CC:
BCC:
Sub:

Chers John et Cathy,   *Angers, le 15 décembre*

Merci beaucoup pour vos e-mails. Que le temps passe vite![1] Je suis en France depuis déjà trois mois.[2] Vous avez demandé si j'ai le temps de voyager. Oui, mais la plupart[3] du temps je suis très active et très occupée parce qu[4]'il y a toujours tant de[5] choses à faire chaque[6] jour. C'est la vie, n'est-ce pas?

 Dimanche dernier[7], j'ai accompagné ma famille française au Mans chez les parents de Mme Martin. Nous avons passé trois heures à table! Cette semaine, j'ai lu une pièce[8] de Molière pour mon cours de littérature et j'ai écrit une dissertation[9]. J'ai aussi fait le ménage et j'ai gardé[10] les enfants pour Mme Martin.

 Heureusement, je ne me lève pas tôt[11] le samedi.

 Vous avez demandé si j'ai remarqué[12] des différences entre la France et les États-Unis. Eh bien, oui. Chez les Martin, par exemple, les portes à l'intérieur de la maison sont toujours fermées[13], les toilettes ne sont pas dans la salle de bain et les robinets[14] sont marqués «C» et «F». J'ai déjà oublié[15] deux fois[16] que «C» ne veut pas dire «cold». Aïe![17]

 Passez le bonjour[18] à Madame Walter pour moi, s.v.p. Écrivez-moi à lbecker@wanadoo.fr

 Bonnes vacances!

Votre amie «française»,
Lori

---

1. *How time flies!* / 2. *I've already been in France for three months.* / 3. *most* / 4. *because* / 5. *so many* / 6. *each; every* / 7. *last* / 8. *I read a play* / 9. *I wrote a (term) paper* / 10. *watched, looked after* / 11. *Fortunately, I don't get up early* / 12. *I noticed* / 13. *closed* / 14. *faucets* / 15. *I already forgot* / 16. *times* / 17. *Ouch!* / 18. *Say hello*

Compréhension. Décidez si les phrases suivantes sont vraies ou fausses. Si une phrase est fausse, corrigez-la.

1. Lori a déjà passé trois mois en France.
2. En France on passe beaucoup de temps à table.
3. Lori n'a pas passé d'examen.
4. Lori a beaucoup de temps libre.
5. On ferme les portes dans une maison française.
6. «C» sur un robinet veut dire «chaud».
7. «F» sur un robinet veut dire «français».

Zoom sur le logement

Premium Website

La maison

LIVING IN FRANCE has meant more to Lori than just learning the French language. She has also had the opportunity to become part of a French family and has had to learn to cope with a number of cultural differences. For example, there is no need in French for a separate word to distinguish between *house* and *home*. Both are **la maison,** and **la maison** is seen as a refuge from the storm of the world outside, a place to find comfort and solace and to put order into one's existence. Given the French attitude about **la maison,** it is not surprising to find social and architectural indications of that need for order. There is a set time for meals, and family members are expected to be there. There is an order to a French meal that is quite different from the everything-on-one-plate-at-one-time eating style prevalent in English-speaking North America. The walls around French houses, the shutters on the windows, and the closing of the doors inside the home are other examples of the French desire for order, clearly established boundaries, and privacy.

Mark Burnett/David R. Frazier Photolibrary, Inc.

INSOLITE

Relativité culturelle: La maison

THE HOME is undoubtedly the scene of the greatest number of cultural contrasts. There are, therefore, some adjustments to make. Some of them are described below.

In France	In North America
Doors are closed, especially the bathroom door, even when no one is in the room. In winter, this maintains warmth. Also, the French tend to not like drafts **(des courants d'air)** in a room.	Doors inside a house are often left open.
In many homes, the bathtub, shower, and sink, are in one room, **la salle de bain,** while the toilet (and often a sink) are in another, **les toilettes.** Therefore, one should be specific about which room one is looking for.	The toilet, bathtub, shower, and sink are usually all in one room, the bathroom. Some houses may also have half-bathrooms which consist of a toilet and sink.
There are no screens on windows to keep out insects, but most houses have shutters.	Most windows have screens. Houses in some regions may also have storm windows and shutters.
There are almost always walls or a hedge to ensure privacy and clearly mark the limits of one's property.	In many neighborhoods there are no walls or fences to separate houses, or if there are fences, they may be made of chain-link or wooden pickets, thus making them "see-through."

Le riad

A riad is a type of traditional house found in the old quarter, or **medina,** *in North African cities. Closed off to the outside world and built around an interior courtyard,* **Riads** *have in general two or three stories. The kitchen, salons for entertaining and family gatherings, a garden, and the courtyard are on the ground floor. Bedrooms and rooms where women gather together are on the next floor, and the top floor usually consists of a terrace and sleeping areas for when the weather is hot. Many* **Riads** *have today been converted into bed and breakfasts, like the one whose ground floor appears in the plan below.*

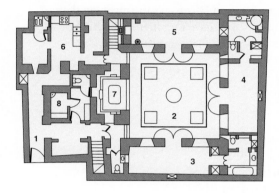

1. Entrée
2. Jardin/Cour
3. Chambre avec salle de bain
4. Chambre avec douche
5. Salon et salle à manger
6. Cuisine et garde-manger
7. Jacuzzi-fontaine
8. Hammam *(Steamroom)*

Le logement social

HOUSING COSTS IN FRANCE continue to rise. People with modest incomes find assistance in three different ways. They can apply for money to subsidize their housing expenses; they can apply for special loans to buy a home; or, they can apply to live in public housing, or **les logements sociaux.** By law, towns with more than 3,500 inhabitants have to provide some form of public housing. The people given highest priority are single-parent families, people with very low incomes, or those whose housing situation is perilous. To learn more about public housing in France, watch the videos linked to the *Premium Website*.

French Polynesia

Les maisons traditionnelles du monde francophone

THE ARCHITECTURE of traditional homes in France and the Francophone world are not only influenced by the climate and geography of where they are built, but also reflect cultural beliefs and practices. Explore the links on the *Premium Website* to learn more about:

► how French colonial architecture was adapted in Louisiana
► the **Riad** and **Dar,** traditional homes of North Africa
► the thatched roof homes of French Polynesia
► contemporary homes and apartments in Paris
► the traditional farm house of Provence called **un mas**

What does the style of each type of house tell you about the beliefs and social practices of the people who live in it?

Il y a un geste

C'est la vie. A gesture often accompanies the expression **C'est la vie:** the shoulders are shrugged, and the head is slightly tilted to one side. Sometimes the lips are pursed as well, and the palms are upturned. The idea is *That's life and I can't do anything about it.*

J'ai oublié! The palm of the hand is raised against the temple. This gesture conveys the meaning that you have forgotten something or have made a mistake.

À vous. Donnez une réponse personnelle.

1. Où avez-vous dîné hier soir?
2. Combien de temps avez-vous passé à table?
3. Qu'est-ce que vous avez fait après le dîner?

ENTRE AMIS   Hier

Follow these steps to find out what your partner did yesterday.

1. Ask what your partner did yesterday.
2. S/he will tell you at least two things.
3. Choose one of the things s/he did and find out as much as you can about it (at what time, where, etc.).

PRONONCIATION

LES SONS [u] et [y]

Track 2-12

▶ Because of differences in meaning in words such as **tout** and **tu,** it is very important to distinguish between the vowel sounds [u] and [y]. The following words contain these two important vowel sounds. Practice saying these words after your teacher, paying particular attention to the highlighted vowel sound.

[u] • bon**jou**r, **rou**ge, **cou**rs, éc**ou**ter, **jou**er, tr**ou**ver, v**ou**lez, je v**ou**drais, t**ou**jours, beauc**ou**p, p**ou**rquoi, s**ou**vent, **cou**sin, d**ou**te, **ou**vrier, bl**ou**son, **cou**leur, **cou**rse, n**ou**veau, auj**ou**rd'hui, **cou**loir, s**ou**s, t**ou**t, **ou**blié

• **où**

[y] • **ju**s, **u**ne, ét**u**dier, ét**u**diants, **tu,** b**u**reau, calc**u**latrice, voit**u**re, s**u**r, **ju**pe, l**u**nettes, p**u**ll-over, n**u**méro, diffic**u**lté, br**u**ne, st**u**pide, camp**u**s, **u**niversitaire, m**u**sique, R**u**ssie, min**u**te, d**u,** occ**u**pé, j'ai l**u,** littérat**u**re

► The [u] sound, represented by written **ou** or **où,** is close to the sound in the English word *tooth*.

n**ou**s   r**ou**ge   **où**

► The [y] sound is represented by a single written **-u-.** There is, however, no English "equivalent" for this French sound. To produce it, round your lips as if drinking through a straw; then, without moving your lips, pronounce the vowel in the word **ici.**

d**u**   **u**ne   sal**u**t   v**u**e

In each of the following pairs of words, one of the words contains the [u] sound, the other the [y] sound. Pronounce each word correctly.

1. sur / sous
2. jour / jupe
3. vous / vu
4. pure / pour
5. cours / cure

6. russe / rousse
7. roux / rue
8. ou / eu
9. tout / tu

Buts communicatifs

I. RELATING PAST EVENTS

Track 2-13

Avez-vous déjà[1] nettoyé[2] votre chambre cette semaine?

Oui, j'ai déjà nettoyé ma chambre.
Non, je n'ai pas encore nettoyé ma chambre.

	oui	non
Avez-vous déjà étudié pour votre cours de français?	_____	_____
Avez-vous déjà envoyé des textos aujourd'hui?	_____	_____
Avez-vous déjà déjeuné?	_____	_____
Avez-vous déjà regardé la télé cette semaine?	_____	_____
Avez-vous déjà travaillé beaucoup ce semestre?	_____	_____
Avez-vous déjà fumé[3] un cigare ou une cigarette aujourd'hui?	_____	_____
Avez-vous déjà été absent(e) ce semestre?	_____	_____
Avez-vous déjà eu d'autres cours aujourd'hui?	_____	_____
Avez-vous déjà fait vos devoirs pour demain?	_____	_____
Avez-vous déjà eu la grippe[4] ce semestre?	_____	_____

1. *already* / 2. *cleaned* / 3. *smoked* / 4. *flu*

A. Le passé composé *avec* avoir

Grammar
Tutorial

Hier soir, **Michel a regardé**
la télévision.
Et puis **il a fait** ses devoirs.
Pendant combien de temps **a-t-il étudié**?
Il a étudié pendant deux heures.

*Last night, Michel watched
television.
And then he did his homework.
How long did he study?
He studied for two hours.*

> *Remember to consult
> App. C at the end of
> the book to review
> any grammatical
> terms with which you
> are not familiar.*

► The **passé composé** *(compound past)* is used to tell about or narrate specific events that have already taken place. Depending on the context, its English translation may be any one of several possibilities.

J'ai mangé une pomme.
{ *I ate an apple.*
I did eat an apple.
I have eaten an apple.

► The **passé composé** is formed with the present tense of an auxiliary verb (normally **avoir**) and a past participle.

manger *(au passé composé)*

j'	ai mangé	nous	avons mangé
tu	as mangé	vous	avez mangé
il/elle/on	a mangé	ils/elles	ont mangé

► The past participles of all **-er** verbs are pronounced the same as the infinitive. They are spelled by replacing the **-er** ending of the infinitive with **-é.**

étudi~~er~~	+	-é	⟶	**étudié**
mang~~er~~	+	-é	⟶	**mangé**
jou~~er~~	+	-é	⟶	**joué**

> *In the expression **j'ai
> eu** (I had) the word
> **eu** is pronounced [y].*

► The past participles of many verbs that *don't* end in **-er** must be memorized.

eu (avoir)   **été** (être)   **fait** (faire)   **dû** (devoir)

J'**ai eu** la grippe pendant trois jours!
Anne et Guy **ont fait** la cuisine
ensemble.
Ils **ont dû** dîner à la maison.

*I had the flu for three days!
Anne and Guy did the cooking
together.
They must have eaten at home.
They had to eat at home.*

▶ In the negative, **ne ... pas (ne ... jamais)** is placed around the auxiliary verb.

> **ne (n')** + auxiliary verb + **pas (jamais)** + past participle

Il **n'**a **pas** écouté la radio.	*He didn't listen to the radio.*
Nous **n'**avons **pas** fait de promenade.	*We didn't take a walk.*
La plupart des étudiants **n'**ont **jamais** fumé de cigare.	*Most students have never smoked a cigar.*

▶ Questions in the **passé composé** are formed the way they are in the present tense. Note, however, that in all cases of inversion, only the auxiliary verb and the subject pronoun are involved. The past participle follows the inverted pronoun.

Review the formation of questions in Ch. 2, pp. 50–51.

Il a fait ses devoirs?	
Est-ce qu'il a fait ses devoirs?	*Has he (Marc) done his homework?*
A-t-il fait ses devoirs?	
Marc a-t-il fait ses devoirs?	

 ❶ Mais il a fait ça hier. Demandez si David fait les choses suivantes aujourd'hui. Votre partenaire va répondre que David a fait ces choses hier.

MODÈLE: travailler

> VOUS: **Est-ce que David travaille aujourd'hui?**
> VOTRE PARTENAIRE: **Non, mais il a travaillé hier.**

1. jouer au tennis
2. être absent
3. avoir une lettre de ses grands-parents
4. dîner avec Véronique
5. manger une pizza
6. faire la vaisselle
7. regarder la télé

❷ Véronique. Pierre aime Véronique et il vous pose des questions parce qu'elle a dîné avec David hier soir. Répondez à ses questions d'après le modèle.

MODÈLE: Véronique a-t-elle dîné seule? (avec David)
> **Non, elle n'a pas dîné seule; elle a dîné avec David.**

1. Ont-ils dîné au restaurant? (chez David)
2. David a-t-il fait la cuisine? (la vaisselle)
3. Ont-ils mangé un sandwich? (une pizza)
4. Véronique a-t-elle détesté la pizza? (aimé)
5. Ont-ils dansé après le dîner? (regardé la télévision)

3 La plupart des étudiants. Qu'est-ce que la plupart des étudiants ont fait hier? Décidez.

Be sure to use plural verb forms with **la plupart des.**

MODÈLE: fumer une cigarette

VOTRE PARTENAIRE: **Est-ce que la plupart des étudiants ont fumé une cigarette hier?**

VOUS: **Non, la plupart des étudiants n'ont pas fumé de cigarette.**

1. étudier à la bibliothèque
2. faire leurs devoirs
3. passer un test
4. avoir une bonne note
5. déjeuner avec leurs professeurs
6. travailler après les cours

Remember that **tout à l'heure** *can also refer to the future:* in a little while. *The expression* **à tout à l'heure** *means* see you soon.

Vocabulaire

Expressions de temps (passé)

tout à l'heure	*a little while ago*
ce matin	*this morning*
hier	*yesterday*
hier matin	*yesterday morning*
hier soir	*last night*
lundi dernier	*last Monday*
le week-end dernier	*last weekend*
la semaine dernière	*last week*
le mois dernier	*last month*
l'année dernière	*last year*
récemment	*recently*
il y a deux (trois, etc.) ans	*two (three, etc.) years ago*
il y a longtemps	*a long time ago*
la dernière fois	*the last time*
pendant les vacances	*during vacation*

NOTES

1. **Il y a,** used with an expression of time, means *ago:* **il y a deux mois** *(two months ago);* **il y a trois ans** *(three years ago).*

2. In general, the word **an** is used when counting the number of years: **un an, deux ans,** etc. The word **année** is normally used when referring to a specific year: **cette année, l'année dernière,** etc. The same distinction is made between **jour** and **journée: Il y a trois jours; une belle journée.**

4 Il y a combien de temps? Qu'avons-nous fait? Que n'avons-nous pas fait? Composez des phrases avec un élément de chaque colonne.

MODÈLES: **Mes parents ont fait un voyage il y a deux ans.**
Mes parents n'ont jamais parlé français.

	faire un voyage	ne ... jamais
je	avoir des vacances	il y a ...
mes parents	dîner au restaurant	... dernier (dernière)
mon meilleur ami	avoir un e-mail	pendant les vacances
ma meilleure amie	envoyer des textos	hier (...)
nous	être absent(e)(s)	ce matin
	faire la vaisselle	tout à l'heure
	parler français	récemment
	étudier pendant trois heures	

5 La dernière fois. Demandez à votre partenaire quand il (elle) a fait ces choses pour la dernière fois. Il (elle) va répondre.

MODÈLE: être absent(e)

VOUS: **Quelle est la dernière fois que vous avez été absent(e) ce semestre?**
VOTRE PARTENAIRE: **J'ai été absent(e) la semaine dernière.** ou
Je n'ai jamais été absent(e).

1. étudier seul(e)
2. fumer
3. devoir passer un examen
4. être malade
5. téléphoner à un ami
6. avoir «A» à l'examen
7. passer trois heures à table
8. nager à la piscine
9. manger une pizza
10. envoyer un e-mail

6 À vous. Répondez aux questions.

1. Pendant combien de temps avez-vous étudié hier soir?
2. Pendant combien de temps avez-vous regardé la télévision?
3. Quelle est la dernière fois que vous avez téléphoné à un(e) ami(e)? Pendant combien de temps avez-vous parlé au téléphone?
4. Quelle est la dernière fois que vous avez eu la grippe? Pendant combien de temps avez-vous été malade?
5. Quelle est la dernière fois que vous avez été absent(e)?
6. Pendant combien de jours avez-vous été absent(e) ce semestre?

ENTRE AMIS Hier soir

Talk about what you and your partner did last night.

1. Find out where your partner ate last night.
2. Find out if s/he watched TV or listened to the radio.
3. If so, find out what s/he watched or listened to.
4. Find out if s/he did his/her homework.
5. If so, find out where.
6. If so, find out how long s/he studied.

	vrai	faux
J'aime étudier seul(e).	_____	_____
Je fais mes devoirs à la bibliothèque.	_____	_____
J'écris[1] souvent des dissertations.	_____	_____
Je ne passe pas beaucoup de temps à faire mes devoirs.	_____	_____
Je passe au moins[2] trois heures par jour à étudier.	_____	_____
Je lis[3] au moins un livre par semaine.	_____	_____
J'écoute la radio pendant que[4] j'étudie.	_____	_____
Je regarde la télé pendant que j'étudie.	_____	_____

1. write / 2. at least / 3. read / 4. while

REMARQUE

Use **passer** + unit(s) of time + **à** + infinitive to express how long you spend doing something.

Nous **avons passé deux heures à manger.**

We spent two hours eating.

D'habitude, Marc **passe quatre heures à faire** ses devoirs.

Marc usually spends four hours doing his homework.

B. Les verbes écrire et lire

J'aime **lire** des romans policiers.	*I like to read detective stories.*
J'ai passé trois heures à **lire** hier soir.	*I spent three hours reading last night.*
Quelles langues **lisez-vous**?	*What languages do you read?*
Éric lit le journal pendant qu'il mange.	*Éric reads the newspaper while he eats.*
Mes parents n'**écrivent** pas souvent.	*My parents don't write often.*
À qui **écrivez-vous**?	*Who are you writing to?*
Comment est-ce qu'**on écrit** le mot «lisent»?	*How do you spell the word "lisent"?*

écrire (to write)	
j'	**écris**
tu	**écris**
il/elle/on	**écrit**
nous	**écrivons**
vous	**écrivez**
ils/elles	**écrivent**
passé composé:	**j'ai écrit**

lire (to read)	
je	**lis**
tu	**lis**
il/elle/on	**lit**
nous	**lisons**
vous	**lisez**
ils/elles	**lisent**
passé composé:	**j'ai lu**

▶ Note the pronunciation distinction between the third person singular and plural forms.

il écri~~t~~ [ekRi]   ils [z]écriv~~ent~~ [ekRiv]   elle li~~t~~ [li]   elles lis~~ent~~ [liz]

▶ The verb **décrire** *(to describe)* is conjugated like **écrire.**

Nous **décrivons** nos familles au professeur.

Vocabulaire

The plural of **journal** is **journaux**.

Des choses à lire ou à écrire

une bande dessinée	*comic strip*	un magazine	*magazine*
un blog	*blog*	un message (instantané)	*(instant) message*
une carte postale	*postcard*	une pièce	*play*
une dissertation	*(term) paper*	un poème	*poem*
un e-mail	*e-mail*	un roman	*novel*
un journal	*newspaper*	un roman policier	*detective story*
une lettre	*letter*	un texto (SMS)	*text message*
un livre	*book*		

7 Qu'est-ce qu'ils lisent? Qu'est-ce qu'ils écrivent?

Répondez aux questions. Si vous ne savez pas la réponse, devinez.

1. Combien de livres lisez-vous par semestre?
2. Vos parents écrivent-ils beaucoup d'e-mails?
3. À qui écrivez-vous des SMS ou des messages instantanés?
4. Qui, dans votre famille, lit des bandes dessinées?
5. Combien de dissertations un étudiant écrit-il par an?
6. Avez-vous déjà écrit une dissertation ce semestre? Si oui, pour quel(s) cours?
7. Avez-vous lu un blog, un journal ou un magazine cette semaine? Si non, pourquoi pas?
8. Combien d'heures passez-vous à lire par semaine? par mois?

C. Ne ... *rien*

▶ The opposite of **quelque chose** is **ne ... rien** *(nothing, not anything)*.

Mangez-vous **quelque chose**?	*Are you eating something?*
Non, je **ne** mange **rien**.	*No, I am not eating anything.*

▶ **Ne ... rien** works like **ne ... pas** and **ne ... jamais**; that is, **ne** and **rien** are placed around the conjugated verb. This means that in the **passé composé**, **ne** and **rien** surround the auxiliary verb and the past participle follows **rien**.

Je **ne** vais **rien** écrire.	*I'm not going to write anything.*
Je **n'ai rien** écrit hier soir.	*I didn't write anything last night.*

▶ **Rien** can follow a preposition.

Je **ne** parle **de rien**.	*I'm not talking about anything.*
Je **n'ai** parlé **de rien**.	*I didn't talk about anything.*

Review the use of **ne ... jamais**, p. 99.

▶ Unlike English, French allows the use of more than one negative word in a sentence.

Il **ne** fait **jamais rien**!	*He never does anything!*

▶ Like **jamais**, **rien** can be used alone to answer a question.

Qu'est-ce que tu as lu? **Rien**.

> **Quelque chose** and **rien** can be made slightly more specific by the addition of **de** + *masculine adjective* or of **à** + *infinitive*. The two constructions can even be combined.
>
> Jean lit **quelque chose** *d'intéressant.*   Éric **ne** lit **rien** *d'intéressant.*
> Il a **quelque chose** *à lire.*   Il **n'**a **rien** *à lire.*
> Il a **quelque chose** *d'intéressant à lire.*   Il **n'**a **rien** *d'intéressant à lire.*

8 Une personne paresseuse. Éric ne fait rien. Répondez aux questions suivantes en utilisant **ne... rien.**

MODÈLES: Qu'est-ce qu'il fait le vendredi soir?   **Il ne fait rien.**
Qu'est-ce qu'il a fait vendredi dernier?   **Il n'a rien fait.**
Qu'est-ce qu'il va faire vendredi prochain?   **Il ne va rien faire.**

1. Qu'est-ce qu'il étudie à la bibliothèque?
2. Qu'est-ce qu'il lit pendant le week-end?
3. Qu'est-ce qu'il va faire cet après-midi?
4. Qu'est-ce qu'il va lire pour ses cours?
5. Qu'est-ce qu'il a écrit pendant les vacances?
6. Qu'est-ce qu'il a lu l'année dernière?

9 Ces travailleurs. Sylvie et David sont très travailleurs et la semaine dernière, ils n'ont pas eu le temps de faire des choses amusantes. Demandez à votre partenaire s'ils ont fait les activités suivantes. Il/Elle va utiliser **ne ... rien** dans sa réponse. Suivez le modèle.

MODÈLE: regarder quelque chose à la télé
VOUS: **Est-ce qu'ils ont regardé quelque chose à la télé?**
VOTRE PARTENAIRE: **Non, ils n'ont rien regardé.**

1. écouter quelque chose à la radio
2. écrire des poèmes
3. manger dans un bistro
4. lire un roman policier
5. faire quelque chose en ville

10 À vous. Répondez aux questions.

1. D'habitude qu'est-ce que vous lisez le matin?
2. À qui avez-vous écrit la semaine dernière?
3. Qu'avez-vous lu hier soir?
4. Avez-vous écouté la radio ce matin? Si oui, qu'est-ce que vous avez écouté?
5. Avez-vous des amis qui regardent la télé pendant qu'ils étudient?
6. Qu'est-ce que vous regardez à la télévision pendant que vous étudiez?
7. Combien de temps passez-vous d'habitude à préparer vos cours?
8. Lisez-vous souvent des blogs ou des magazines? Si oui, quels blogs ou magazines?
9. Combien de dissertations écrivez-vous par semestre?

➤ Depending on the context, the French use different words to express what, in English, could always be expressed by the word *time*.

• **L'heure,** as you already know, means *clock time*.

Quelle **heure** est-il?	*What time is it?*

REMINDER

> **Heure** can also mean *hour* or *o'clock*.
>
> J'ai étudié pendant trois **heures.** *I studied for three hours.*
>
> Il est deux **heures.** *It is two o'clock.*

• **La fois** means *time* in a countable or repeated sense.

Combien de **fois** par an?	*How many times per year?*
la dernière **fois**	*the last time*
chaque **fois**	*each time*

• **Le temps** means *time* in a general sense.

Je n'ai pas **le temps** d'étudier.	*I don't have time to study.*
Avez-vous **le temps** de voyager?	*Do you have time to travel?*
Combien de **temps** avez-vous?	*How much time do you have?*

> *Remember that* **temps** *can also mean* weather: **Quel temps fait-il aujourd'hui?**

⓫ Hier soir. Utilisez **temps, heure** ou **fois** pour compléter ce dialogue.

1. Hier soir j'ai étudié pendant quatre _____.
2. Avez-vous eu assez de (d')_____ pour regarder la télévision?
3. Non, parce que mes parents ont téléphoné trois _____.
4. À quelle _____ ont-ils téléphoné la première _____?
5. À six _____.
6. Combien de (d') _____ par mois allez-vous chez vos parents?
7. Trois ou quatre _____.
8. Quand avez-vous dîné hier soir? À sept _____.
9. Combien de (d') _____ avez-vous passé à table?
10. Une _____.

⓬ À vous. Répondez aux questions.

1. D'habitude combien de temps passez-vous à faire vos devoirs?
2. Pendant combien d'heures avez-vous étudié hier soir? Combien de temps avez-vous passé à faire vos devoirs pour le cours de français?
3. À quelle heure avez-vous dîné? Combien de temps avez-vous passé à table?
4. Combien de temps par semaine passez-vous avec votre meilleur(e) ami(e)?
5. Combien de fois par mois allez-vous au cinéma?
6. Combien de temps avez-vous passé à la bibliothèque la semaine dernière?
7. Combien de fois par jour envoyez-vous des textos?

ENTRE AMIS **Es-tu un(e) bon(ne) étudiant(e)?**

Interview your partner to find out what kind of student s/he is.

1. Find out if your partner spends a lot of time studying.
2. Ask if s/he watches TV while s/he studies.
3. Find out how long s/he studied last night.
4. Ask what s/he read for your French course.
5. Ask your partner how to spell some word in French.
6. Compliment your partner on his/her French.

3. DESCRIBING YOUR WEEKEND ACTIVITIES

Track 2-15

Qu'est-ce que vous faites pendant le week-end?

	oui	non
Je pars[1] du campus chaque week-end.	_____	_____
Je sors[2] avec mes amis.	_____	_____
Je m'amuse[3] bien.	_____	_____
Je vais au cinema.	_____	_____
Je joue du piano.	_____	_____
Je joue au golf.	_____	_____
Je fais du vélo.	_____	_____
Je fais beaucoup de sport.	_____	_____
Je dors[4] beaucoup.	_____	_____
Je me lève tard[5].	_____	_____
Je ne me couche[6] pas tôt.	_____	_____
Je nettoie[7] ma chambre.	_____	_____

1. *leave* / 2. *go out* / 3. *have fun* / 4. *sleep* / 5. *late* / 6. *go to bed* / 7. *clean*

E. Les verbes pronominaux

Grammar Tutorials

► Reflexive verbs **(les verbes pronominaux)** are those whose subject and object are the same. English examples of reflexive verbs are *he cut himself* or *she bought herself a dress.*

► You have already learned a number of expressions that use reflexive verbs in French.

Comment vous appelez-vous?	*What is your name?*
Je m'appelle ...	*My name is ...*
Comment s'appellent vos amis?	*What are your friends' names?*
Asseyez-vous là!	*Sit there!*

► Reflexive verbs use an object pronoun **(me, te, se, nous, vous)** in addition to the subject. With the exception of affirmative commands, this pronoun is always placed directly in front of the verb.

s'amuser	
je	**m'**amuse
tu	**t'**amuses
il/elle/on	**s'**amuse
nous	**nous** amusons
vous	**vous** amusez
ils/elles	**s'**amusent

se lever	
je	**me** lève
tu	**te** lèves
il/elle/on	**se** lève
nous	**nous** levons
vous	**vous** levez
ils/elles	**se** lèvent

▶ Use **est-ce que** or a rising intonation to ask a yes/no question.

Est-ce que tu te lèves tôt le matin?   *Do you get up early in the morning?*

Tu t'amuses au cours de français?   *Do you have fun in French class?*

▶ In the negative, **ne** is placed before the object pronoun and **pas** after the verb.

Je **ne** me lève **pas** tôt.   *I don't get up early.*

Mes professeurs **ne** s'amusent **pas**.   *My teachers don't have fun.*

Vous **ne** vous couchez **pas** avant minuit?   *Don't you go to bed before midnight?*

▶ When the reflexive verb is used in the infinitive form after another verb, the reflexive pronoun agrees with the subject of the sentence.

À quelle heure vas-**tu te** coucher?   *At what time are you going to go to bed?*

Je n'aime pas **me** lever tôt.   *I don't like to get up early.*

Les étudiants ont l'habitude de **s'**amuser le samedi soir.   *Students are used to having fun on Saturday night.*

⑬ Identifications. Identifiez, si possible, des personnes qui correspondent aux descriptions suivantes.

MODÈLE: une personne qui se lève très tôt le dimanche matin
          Mon père se lève très tôt le dimanche matin.

1. une personne qui se couche tôt le dimanche soir
2. une personne qui ne se couche pas s'il y a quelque chose d'intéressant à la télévision
3. deux étudiants qui se couchent tard s'ils ont un examen
4. deux personnes qui s'amusent beaucoup au cours de français
5. deux de vos amis qui ne se lèvent pas tôt le samedi matin
6. une personne qui ne va pas s'amuser pendant les vacances
7. une personne qui se lève quelquefois trop tard pour le cours de français

14 **À vous.** Répondez aux questions.

1. Comment vous appelez-vous et comment s'appelle votre meilleur(e) ami(e)?
2. Quel jour est-ce que vous vous couchez tard?
3. Est-ce que vous vous levez tôt ou tard le samedi matin? Expliquez votre réponse.
4. Avez-vous des amis qui ne s'amusent pas beaucoup? Si oui, comment s'appellent-ils?
5. Est-ce que vos professeurs aiment s'amuser en classe?
6. Est-ce que vous vous amusez au cours de français? Pourquoi ou pourquoi pas?
7. À quelle heure est-ce que vous vous levez le lundi matin? Pourquoi?
8. À quelle heure est-ce que vous allez vous coucher ce soir? Expliquez votre réponse.

F. Jouer de et jouer à

Grammar Tutorials

> *To play a musical instrument* is expressed by **jouer de** + definite article + musical instrument. The definite article is retained in the negative before the name of the instrument.

Mon frère **joue du** saxophone, mais il ne **joue** pas **de la** guitare.	*My brother plays the saxophone but he doesn't play the guitar.*
De quoi **jouez**-vous?	*What (instrument) do you play?*
Moi, je ne **joue de** rien.	*I don't play any (instrument).*

Review **de** *+ article, p. 78, and* **à** *+ article, p. 133.*

Vocabulaire

Quelques instruments de musique

un accordéon	*accordion*	un piano	*piano*
une batterie	*drums*	un saxophone	*saxophone*
une flûte	*flute*	une trompette	*trumpet*
une guitare	*guitar*	un violon	*violin*

Howard Harrison/Alamy

> *To play a game* is expressed by **jouer à** + definite article + game.

— Mon amie **joue au** golf le lundi, elle **joue à la** pétanque le mercredi et elle **joue aux** cartes le vendredi soir. Mais elle ne **joue** jamais **aux** échecs.

— **À** quoi **jouez**-vous?

— Moi, je ne **joue à** rien.

Vocabulaire

Quelques jeux *(Several games)*

le basket-ball (le basket)	*basketball*	le football américain	*football*
le bridge	*bridge*	le golf	*golf*
les cartes *(f. pl.)*	*cards*	le hockey	*hockey*
les dames *(f. pl.)*	*checkers*	la pétanque	*lawn bowling*
les échecs *(m. pl.)*	*chess*	le rugby	*rugby*
le football (le foot)	*soccer*	le tennis	*tennis*

Note culturelle

La pétanque est un jeu de boules très populaire en France. On joue à la pétanque à l'extérieur. Pour marquer des points, il faut placer les boules le plus près possible du cochonnet *(small wooden ball)*.

15 Tout le monde joue. À quoi jouent-ils? De quoi jouent-ils? Faites des phrases complètes avec les éléments donnés.

MODÈLES: **Les Canadiens jouent au hockey.**
Ma sœur ne joue pas de l'accordéon.

les Français			la pétanque
Tiger Woods			l'accordéon
Shaquille O'Neal			le piano
ma sœur			les cartes
mon frère		de	le saxophone
les violonistes	(ne ... pas) jouer	à	le basket-ball
les Américains			la guitare
les Canadiens			les échecs
les sœurs Williams			le violon
je			le golf
mon ami(e) ...			le hockey
...			le tennis

objetsforall/Shutterstock.com

16 À vous. Répondez aux questions.

1. Quel est votre instrument de musique préféré?
2. Quel est votre sport préféré?
3. Jouez-vous d'un instrument de musique? De quoi jouez-vous?
4. Êtes-vous sportif (sportive)? Si oui, à quoi jouez-vous?
5. Avez-vous des amis qui jouent d'un instrument de musique? Si oui, de quoi jouent-ils?

▶ *Stress pronouns* (**les pronoms accentués**) are used in certain circumstances where a subject pronoun cannot be used. Each stress pronoun has a corresponding subject pronoun.

je	→	**moi**	nous	→	**nous**
tu	→	**toi**	vous	→	**vous**
il	→	**lui**	ils	→	**eux**
elle	→	**elle**	elles	→	**elles**
on	→	**soi**			

▶ Stress pronouns are used in the following circumstances:

• to stress the subject of a sentence

Moi, je n'aime pas le café.   ***I** don't like coffee.*
Ils aiment le thé, **eux.**   ***They** like tea.*

• in a compound subject

Mes parents et **moi,** nous habitons ici.   *My parents and I live here.*
Monsieur Martin a des enfants?
Oui, sa femme et **lui** ont six enfants.   *Yes, he and his wife have six children.*

• after a preposition

chez **soi**   *at one's house*   pour **lui**   *for him*
entre **nous**   *between us*   sans **elles**   *without them*

NOTE
A stress pronoun after the expression **être à** indicates possession.
Ce livre est **à moi.**   *This book belongs to me.*
Il est **à toi,** ce pull?   *Is this sweater yours?*

• after **c'est** and **ce sont**

C'est **moi.**   *It is I (me).*   Ce n'est pas **elle.**   *It is not she (her).*

NOTE
C'est is used with **nous** and **vous**. **Ce sont** is used only with **eux** and **elles**.
C'est nous.   *It is we (us).*   **Ce sont** eux.   *It is they (them).*

• alone or in phrases without a verb

Lui!   *Him!*
Et **toi**?   *And you?*
Elle aussi.   *So does she. So has she. So is she. She too.*
Moi non plus.   *Me neither. Nor I.*

• with the suffix **-même(s)**

toi-même   *yourself*   **eux**-mêmes   *themselves*

17 **Eux aussi.** La famille de Paul et lui font les mêmes choses. Utilisez un pronom accentué pour répondre à chaque question. Si la phrase est affirmative, répondez affirmativement. Si elle est négative, répondez négativement.

MODÈLES: Paul a fait le ménage. Et sa sœur?   **Elle aussi.**

Paul n'a pas regardé la télévision. Et son frère?   **Lui non plus.**

1. Paul n'a pas lu le journal ce matin. Et ses sœurs?
2. Paul écrit des lettres. Et ses parents?
3. Paul ne se lève jamais tard. Et sa sœur?
4. Il a déjà mangé. Et son frère?
5. Paul n'aime pas les cigares. Et ses parents?
6. Il va souvent au cinéma le vendredi soir. Et sa sœur?

18 **À vous.** Répondez aux questions suivantes. Utilisez un pronom accentué dans chaque réponse.

1. Faites-vous la cuisine vous-même?
2. Déjeunez-vous d'habitude avec votre meilleur(e) ami(e)?
3. Avez-vous passé les dernières vacances chez vos parents?
4. Vos amis et vous, allez-vous souvent au cinéma?
5. Faites-vous vos devoirs avec vos amis?

Réalités culturelles

Les loisirs préférés des Français

COMMENT LES Français ont-ils passé leur temps libre au cours des derniers douze mois. Voici quelques pourcentages:

87%	ont regardé la télé tous les jours
70%	ont lu un livre
17%	ont lu 20 livres ou plus
69%	ont lu un journal quotidien
29%	ont lu un journal quotidien tous les jours
67%	ont écouté la radio tous les jours
63%	ont regardé des DVD toutes les semaines
57%	sont allés (*went*) au cinéma au moins une fois
50%	ont utilisé l'Internet régulièrement
30%	ont visité un musée

Et les jeunes Français? Voici quelques pourcentages:

Âge 15–24 ans	Âge 25–34 ans	
58%	57%	ont utilisé l'Internet tous les jours
56%	69%	ont écouté la radio tous les jours
58%	66%	ont lu un journal quotidien régulièrement
78%	73%	ont lu un livre l'année dernière
15%	15%	ont lu 20 livres ou plus
29%	15%	sont allés au cinéma une fois par mois

CandyBoxPhoto/Shutterstock.com

H. Les verbes dormir, partir et sortir

Grammar
Tutorials

Je ne **dors** pas bien.   *I don't sleep well.*
Quand **partez-vous** en vacances?   *When are you leaving on vacation?*
Avec qui Annie **sort-elle** vendredi?   *With whom is Annie going out on Friday?*

dormir *(to sleep)*	
je	**dors**
tu	**dors**
il/elle/on	**dort**
nous	**dormons**
vous	**dormez**
ils/elles	**dorment**

partir *(to leave)*	
je	**pars**
tu	**pars**
il/elle/on	**part**
nous	**partons**
vous	**partez**
ils/elles	**partent**

sortir *(to go out)*	
je	**sors**
tu	**sors**
il/elle/on	**sort**
nous	**sortons**
vous	**sortez**
ils/elles	**sortent**

Partir and **sortir** use **être** as the auxiliary in the **passé composé** and will be studied in the past tense in Ch. 7.

▶ Note the pronunciation distinction between the third person singular and plural forms.

elle dor*t* [dɔʀ]   il par*t* [paʀ]   elle sor*t* [sɔʀ]
elles dor**m**e*nt* [dɔʀm]   ils par*tent* [paʀt]   elles sor*tent* [sɔʀt]

▶ The past participle of **dormir** is **dormi.**

J'ai **dormi** pendant huit heures.

19 **Notre vie à l'université.** Complétez les phrases suivantes avec les verbes **dormir**, **partir** et **sortir.** Faites attention au choix du verbe et au choix entre le présent et l'infinitif.

1. Les étudiants de notre université _____ du campus chaque week-end pour aller chez leurs parents.
2. Mais ils ont envie de s'amuser et c'est pourquoi ils _____ avec leurs amis le jeudi soir.
3. Si on _____ le jeudi soir, on est naturellement fatigué le vendredi matin.
4. Si on ne _____ pas pendant huit heures, on ne se lève pas tôt.
5. Quelquefois, si on est très fatigué, on a envie de _____ en classe!
6. Si vous _____ en classe, les professeurs ne vont pas être très contents.
7. Alors, si vous allez _____ le jeudi soir, il faut faire la sieste le jeudi après-midi.

20 **La vie des étudiants.** Répondez aux questions suivantes.

1. Combien d'heures dormez-vous d'habitude par nuit?
2. Pendant combien de temps avez-vous dormi la nuit dernière?
3. Y a-t-il des étudiants qui ne dorment pas le samedi matin? Si oui, pourquoi?
4. Qui dort mal avant un examen important? Pourquoi?
5. Les étudiants sortent-ils quelquefois pendant la semaine? Si oui, où vont-ils? Si non, pourquoi pas?
6. Est-ce que la plupart des étudiants partent le week-end ou est-ce qu'ils restent sur le campus?
7. Quand allez-vous partir en vacances cette année?

Tu nettoies ta chambre ce matin?　*Are you cleaning your room this morning?*

Oui, mais d'abord **j'envoie** un e-mail.　*Yes, but first I'm sending an e-mail.*

nettoyer (to clean)	
je	**nettoie**
tu	**nettoies**
il/elle/on	**nettoie**
nous	**nettoyons**
vous	**nettoyez**
ils/elles	**nettoient**
passé composé: j'**ai nettoyé**	

envoyer (to send)	
j'	**envoie**
tu	**envoies**
il/elle/on	**envoie**
nous	**envoyons**
vous	**envoyez**
ils/elles	**envoient**
passé composé: j'**ai envoyé**	

▶ In the present tense, these verbs are conjugated like **parler,** except that **i** is used in place of **y** in the singular and the third-person plural.

iLrn
Diagnostics

21 **Un message à ma famille.** Complétez les phrases suivantes avec les verbes **envoyer** et **nettoyer.** Faites attention au choix du verbe et au choix entre le présent, le passé composé et l'infinitif.

1. Hier, j'ai _____ un e-mail à ma famille.
2. J'ai parlé de mon camarade de chambre qui ne _____ jamais notre chambre.
3. J'ai écrit «Pourquoi c'est toujours moi qui dois _____ la chambre?»
4. Lui, il s'amuse et il _____ des textos à ses amis.
5. Moi aussi, je voudrais _____ des textos et m'amuser.
6. Les bons camarades de chambre _____ leur chambre ensemble, non?

22 **À vous.** Répondez aux questions suivantes.

1. Avez-vous envoyé des textos ou des e-mails aujourd'hui? Si oui, à qui?
2. Envoyez-vous des textos chaque jour? Si oui, combien de fois par jour envoyez-vous des textos?
3. Est-ce que vos amis envoient souvent des e-mails ou des messages? Si oui, comment s'appellent ces amis? Combien de messages ou d'e-mails est-ce qu'ils envoient chaque jour?
4. Qui n'envoie jamais de lettres? Pourquoi pas?
5. Qui n'aime pas nettoyer sa chambre? Pourquoi pas?
6. Nettoyez-vous votre chambre chaque jour? Pourquoi ou pourquoi pas?

ENTRE AMIS　Le week-end

Follow the steps below to find out about your partner's weekend activities.

1. Ask if s/he goes out with friends.
2. If so, find out where s/he goes.
3. Find out if s/he gets up early or late on Sunday morning.
4. Find out when s/he cleans her room.
5. What else can you find out?

Intégration

RÉVISION

A **Mon week-end.** Que faites-vous d'habitude le week-end? Avez-vous beaucoup de temps libre?

B **Notre vie à l'université.** Posez des questions. Votre partenaire va répondre. Attention au présent et au passé composé.

MODÈLE: parler français avec tes amis pendant le cours de français

> VOUS: **Est-ce que tu parles français avec tes amis pendant le cours de français?**
>
> VOTRE PARTENAIRE: **Oui, je parle français avec eux.** ou **Non, je ne parle pas français avec eux.**

1. dormir bien quand il y a un examen
2. aller souvent à la bibliothèque après le dîner
3. écouter la radio quelquefois pendant que tu étudies
4. être absent(e) le mois dernier
5. jouer aux cartes avec tes amis le week-end dernier
6. faire la vaisselle d'habitude après le dîner
7. sortir avec tes amis ce soir

C **Trouvez quelqu'un qui ...** Interviewez les autres étudiants pour trouver quelqu'un qui ...

1. regarde la télé pendant qu'il étudie
2. joue de la guitare
3. a eu le temps de lire un livre la semaine dernière
4. a déjà écrit une dissertation ce semestre
5. n'a rien mangé ce matin
6. a eu la grippe l'année dernière
7. a nettoyé sa chambre le week-end dernier
8. ne sort jamais le dimanche soir
9. envoie souvent des e-mails à ses professeurs

D **À l'écoute.** Marc parle de son week-end. Écoutez et décidez si les phrases suivantes sont vraies ou fausses.

Track 2-16

1. Marc aime bien regarder la télé.
2. Marc a fait du sport ce week-end.
3. Marc ne sort jamais le week-end.
4. D'habitude Marc ne se couche pas trop tard.
5. Marc n'a pas travaillé dimanche.

E À vous. Répondez aux questions.

1. Que fait-on pour s'amuser le week-end sur votre campus?
2. Qu'est-ce que la plupart des étudiants font le dimanche soir?
3. Avez-vous regardé la télévision hier soir? Si oui, combien de temps avez-vous passé devant la télévision?
4. Quelle est la dernière fois que vous avez dîné au restaurant? Combien de temps avez-vous passé à table?
5. Est-ce que vous êtes sportif (sportive)? Si oui, à quel sport jouez-vous?
6. Quelle est la dernière fois que vous avez nettoyé votre chambre?

NÉGOCIATIONS

Hier, d'habitude et pendant le week-end.
Interviewez votre partenaire pour trouver les renseignements qui manquent *(missing information)*. La copie de votre partenaire est dans l'Appendice D.

Communication and Communities. To learn more about the culture presented in this chapter, go to the *Premium Website* and click on the Web Search Activities.

Also see the *Entre amis* Video Program and Video Worksheet in the *Cahier*.

MODÈLE: **Est-ce que Valérie va au cours de français d'habitude?**
Est-ce qu'Alain a fumé hier?

A			
NOM	**HIER**	**D'HABITUDE**	**PENDANT LE WEEK-END**
Valérie	OUI	aller au cours de français _____	NON
Chantal	déjeuner avec ses amis _____	se lever tôt _____	OUI
Sophie	NON	OUI	faire ses devoirs _____
Alain	fumer _____	NON	lire des livres _____
David	nettoyer sa chambre _____	être absent _____	NON
Jean-Luc	NON	OUI	sortir avec ses amis _____

Be careful to choose between the past and the present.

REPÈRES:	LE MAROC	L'ALGÉRIE	LA TUNISIE
Superficie:	446.550 km², un peu plus grand que la Californie	environ 2.381.741 km², un peu plus de trois fois le Texas	163.610 km²; un peu plus grand que la Géorgie
Population:	environ 31 millions	environ 34 millions	environ 10 millions
Ethnicité:	99% Arabes-Berbères	Arabes-Berbères, 1% Européens	98% Arabes, 1% Européens, 1% autres
Capitale:	Rabat	Alger	Tunis
Langues:	arabe, français, berbère	arabe, français, berbère	arabe, français

Vocabulaire: sont devenus *became,* guerre *war*

LECTURE 1

A Étude du vocabulaire. Étudiez les phrases suivantes et choisissez *(choose)* les mots anglais qui correspondent aux mots français en caractères gras *(bold print)*: *stay up-to-date, net surfer, toward, is bored, less than, late, since.*

1. **Depuis** son retour à Angers, Thomas est heureux. Il n'a pas été content à Paris.
2. Il n'y a rien à faire; Karine **s'ennuie**.
3. D'habitude le train arrive à 18h, mais il a 15 minutes **de retard**. Il va arriver à 18h15.
4. Pour trouver le cinéma, il faut aller **vers** le centre commercial.
5. Je suis vieux! J'ai 30 ans et tous mes amis ont **moins de** 25 ans.
6. Ils **se tiennent au courant** parce qu'ils lisent un journal tous les jours.
7. Les personnes qui utilisent l'Internet s'appellent des **internautes**.

B Parcourez l'article et le tableau. Skim the article and table and ask yourself the *W-questions* listed in **La méthodo.** Then, using your answers, summarize what you think the article is about.

TUNISIE: L'OFFRE DE LOISIRS POUR LA JEUNESSE

Depuis qu'elle est revenue[1] s'installer en Tunisie après six ans d'études de commerce en France, Sonia s'ennuie ferme et le dit: «Les films arrivent avec des mois de retard. Dans les galeries, on rencontre toujours les mêmes personnes…» Même si[2] 80% des programmes de développement de l'État sont orientés vers les jeunes, en particulier pour l'éducation et les loisirs, moins de 2% des 15-29 ans disent[3] fréquenter les maisons de la culture. Les cinémas sont rares: Tunis ne compte plus que[4] 12 salles (contre 62 en 1960), Sousse et Sfax une seule chacune. …Pour voir le dernier film américain ou écouter un nouvel album, les jeunes ont plutôt tendance à privilégier[5] la myriade de magasins où l'on vend des CD et DVD piratés. Et puis il y a la télévision…

À première vue, l'offre de loisirs peut paraître[6] mal adaptée aux attentes[7] de la jeunesse. Mais «Quand on cherche, on trouve», dit Nabil, étudiant en médecine. Ses amis et lui se tiennent au courant de tous les événements sur Facebook. Exposition privée dans un appartement, pièce de théâtre encore confidentielle, projection de court-métrage[8]… Si l'offre culturelle souffre d'un manque[9] de médiatisation, rien n'échappe[10] aux internautes. «Pour nous, les loisirs riment[11] surtout avec sociabilité, ajoute Nabil… Certains vont au restaurant et en boîte[12] tous les week-ends. Ils voyagent. Les autres se contentent d'aller au café, de jouer aux cartes et de se faire un ciné de temps en temps.»

---

[1]*came back* / [2]*Even if* / [3]*say* / [4]*only has* / [5]*to favor* / [6]*may seem* / [7]*expectations* [8]*short film* / [9]*suffers from a lack* / [10]*escapes* / [11]*go with* / [12]*clubs*

Les cinq activités privilégiées des 15–29 ans		Lieux préférés des 15–29 ans pendant leurs loisirs			
			Tunisie	Algérie	Maroc
Internet	35,07%				
Regarder la télévision	25,07%	Chez eux/chez leurs parents	54,27%	61%	54,5%
Rencontrer des amis	14,97%	Café	14,10%	15,2%	18,20%
Écouter de la musique	12,78%	Rue	13,34%	17,7%	19,0%
Faire du sport	12,11%	Bibliothèque	3,56%	1,50%	2,40%
Ils aiment passer leurs vacances …		Maison de jeunes ou de la culture	1,78%	0,50%	0,60%
en famille	45%	Centres de loisirs	1,34%	1,60%	1,80%
avec des amis	38%	Cinémas	1,27%	1,50%	1,80%
au sein d'une association ou d'un club	15%	Discothèques	0,71%	0,50%	0,90%
		Associations et organisations	0,50%	0,50%	0,70%

From *Jeune Afrique*, No. 2567 du 21 au 27 mars 2010. Copyright Jeune Afrique. Used with permission.
Source: Euromad Jeunesse (décembre 2008).

C Vrai ou faux? Décidez si les phrases suivantes sont vraies ou fausses. Si une phrase est fausse, corrigez-la.

1. Les jeunes Tunisiens vont souvent aux maisons de la culture.
2. Les villes de Tunisie ont beaucoup de cinémas.
3. Les jeunes Tunisiens aiment les activités sociales.
4. Les jeunes Tunisiens n'utilisent pas beaucoup l'Internet.

D Questions. Regardez le tableau et répondez aux questions.

1. Quelles sont les activités préférées des jeunes Tunisiens?
2. Avec qui est-ce que les jeunes Tunisiens passent leurs vacances?
3. Quels sont les endroits que les jeunes en Afrique du Nord (le Maghreb) fréquentent?

 Cultural Activities

Réalités culturelles
Le Maghreb

Le Maghreb est le nom donné en France à l'ensemble des trois pays du nord-ouest de l'Afrique: **le Maroc, l'Algérie** et **la Tunisie**. La France a colonisé l'Algérie en 1830. Plus tard, la Tunisie (1881) et le Maroc (1912) sont devenus des protectorats français. Ces deux pays sont indépendants depuis 1956. L'Algérie a gagné son indépendance en 1962, après une guerre avec la France.

E **Familles de mots.** Essayez de deviner le sens des mots suivants.

1. étudier, étudiant(e), étude
2. offrir, offre
3. se contenter, contentement, content(e)
4. médiatiser, médias, médiatisation

F **Discussion.**

1. Identify three aspects of Tunisian culture mentioned in the article that are similar to or different from American culture.
2. Is the situation regarding the availability of leisure activities for young people in Tunisia depicted favorably or unfavorably in the article? Explain your answer.

LECTURE II

A **Étude du vocabulaire.** Étudiez les phrases suivantes et choisissez les mots anglais qui correspondent aux mots français en caractères gras: *skip, be quiet, will hold myself, rights, out loud, whatever, claim.*

1. La Constitution des États-Unis parle des **droits** et des responsabilités.
2. Il y a des pays qui **prétendent** que la liberté de la presse est importante, mais en réalité cette liberté n'existe pas.
3. Quand on passe un examen, les étudiants **sautent** souvent les questions difficiles.
4. J'ai envie de jouer à quelque chose: aux cartes, aux échecs, **n'importe quoi.**
5. Lisez le paragraphe **à voix haute.** Nous voulons vous écouter.
6. Nous pouvons parler ou **nous taire.**
7. Je **me tiendrai** à 10 bonnes résolutions; 11 c'est trop.

Les droits imprescriptibles[1] du lecteur

Daniel Pennac, né à Casablanca au Maroc en 1944, a été enseignant. Il a travaillé dans le sud de la France et à Paris. Il écrit souvent sur ses expériences dans l'enseignement. L'extrait suivant est tiré de Comme un roman, *un livre qui a eu beaucoup de succès en France.*

En matière de lecture, nous autres "lecteurs" nous nous accordons tous les droits, à commencer par ceux que nous refusons aux jeunes gens que nous prétendons initier à la lecture.

Le *bovarysme* signifie un état d'insatisfaction.

1. Le droit de ne pas lire.
2. Le droit de sauter les pages.
3. Le droit de ne pas finir un livre.
4. Le droit de relire.
5. Le droit de lire n'importe quoi.
6. Le droit au bovarysme (maladie textuellement transmissible).
7. Le droit de lire n'importe où.
8. Le droit de grappiller.[2]
9. Le droit de lire à haute voix.
10. Le droit de nous taire.

Je me tiendrai au chiffre 10, d'abord parce que c'est un compte rond, ensuite parce que c'est le nombre sacré des fameux Commandements et qu'il est plaisant de le voir une fois servir à une liste d'autorisations.

Car[3] si nous voulons que mon fils, que ma fille, que la jeunesse lisent, il est urgent de leur octroyer[4] les droits que nous nous accordons.

Daniel Pennac, "Les droits imprescriptibles du lecteur", from *Comme un roman.*
© Éditions Gallimard. Reprinted with permission.

---

[1]*inalienable* / [2]*turn down pages* / [3]*Because* / [4]*grant*

B **Vrai ou faux?** Décidez si les phrases suivantes sont vraies ou fausses. Ensuite cherchez dans le texte quelque chose qui justifie chaque réponse.

1. "Nous autres 'lecteurs'" sont les professeurs.
2. Pennac pense qu'il est important de lire de la manière dont on désire lire.
3. Pennac a écrit dix droits parce qu'il aime le numéro 10.
4. Les adultes et les jeunes ont les mêmes (*same*) droits.

C **Discussion.** Why does Pennac feel children should have certain rights with regard to reading? Do you agree or disagree with him? Explain your answer.

RÉDACTION

> **LA MÉTHODO** When relating a series of events in the past, consider using a timeline to organize your thoughts before beginning to write.

9 h	12 h	15 h	16 h 30	18 h	20 h
tennis	déjeuner avec Vincent	étudier	nettoyer	écrire des e-mails	manger au bistro avec Nathalie

QU'EST-CE QUE TU AS FAIT HIER?

Un(e) ami(e) voudrait savoir ce que vous avez fait hier. Écrivez un e-mail pour décrire ce que vous avez fait. Dans votre e-mail:

- dites-lui bonjour
- dites deux choses que vous avez faites hier matin, deux choses que vous avez faites hier après-midi et deux choses que vous avez faites hier soir
- dites à quelle heure, où et avec qui vous avez fait chaque activité
- ajoutez (*add*) d'autres détails si vous voulez
- utilisez les expressions de temps et le passé composé

A **Avant d'écrire.** Faites une ligne chronologique avec toutes les activités que vous avez faites hier. Notez l'heure, l'endroit et avec qui vous avez fait chaque activité. Parlez uniquement des activités dont vous connaissez le verbe (*Only use verbs you already know*).

B **Écrire.** Écrivez une ébauche de votre e-mail. Suivez les indications ci-dessus (*above*). Utilisez votre ligne chronologique pour être sûr(e) que vous avez inclus tous les détails demandés.

C **Correction.** Échangez votre e-mail avec un(e) camarade de classe pour le corriger. Est-ce que l'ordre des activités est logique? Faites les corrections nécessaires.

Vocabulaire Actif

Practice some of this vocabulary with the flashcards on **iLrn**.

Instruments de musique

un accordéon *accordion*
une batterie *drums*
une flûte *flute*
une guitare *guitar*
un piano *piano*
un saxophone *saxophone*
une trompette *trumpet*
un violon *violin*

D'autres noms

un cigare *cigar*
une cigarette *cigarette*
une crêpe *crepe (pancake)*
un examen *test, exam*
un exercice *exercise*
la grippe *flu*
un robinet *faucet*

Pronoms accentués

moi *I, me*
toi *you*
lui *he, him*
elle *she, her*
soi *oneself*
nous *we, us*
vous *you*
eux *they, them*
elles *they, them (female)*

Jeux

le basket-ball (le basket) *basketball*
le bridge *bridge*
les cartes *(f. pl.) cards*
les dames *(f. pl.) checkers*
les échecs *(m. pl.) chess*
le football (le foot) *soccer*
le football américain *football*
le golf *golf*
le hockey *hockey*
un jeu *game*
la pétanque *lawn bowling, bocce*
le rugby *rugby*
le tennis *tennis*

Choses à lire ou à écrire

une bande dessinée *comic strip*
un blog *blog*

une carte postale *postcard*
une dissertation *(term) paper*
un journal *newspaper*
une lettre *letter*
un magazine *magazine*
un e-mail *e-mail*
un mot *word*
une pièce *play*
un poème *poem*
un roman *novel*
un roman policier *detective story*
un texto (SMS) *text message*

Divisions du temps

une année *year*
une fois *one time*
une journée *day*
un mois *month*
un semestre *semester*
le temps *time; weather*
les vacances *(f. pl.) vacation*

Prépositions

pendant *for; during*
sans *without*

Verbes

accompagner *to accompany*
s'amuser *to have fun*
se coucher *to go to bed*
décrire *to describe*
demander *to ask*
dormir *to sleep*
écrire *to write*
envoyer *to send*
être à *to belong to*
fermer *to close*
fumer *to smoke*
se lever *to get up*
lire *to read*
nettoyer *to clean*
oublier *to forget*
partir *to leave*
préparer (un cours) *to prepare (a lesson)*
remarquer *to notice*
sortir *to go out*
téléphoner (à qqn) *to telephone (someone)*

Expressions de temps

il y a ... ans (mois, etc.) ... *years (months, etc.) ago*
Je suis ici depuis ... mois (heures, etc.). *I've been here for ... months (hours, etc.).*
Pendant combien de temps ... ? *How long ... ?*
tout à l'heure *a little while ago; in a little while*

Adverbes de temps

déjà *already*
hier *yesterday*
hier soir *last night*
longtemps *a long time*
récemment *recently*
tard *late*
tôt *early*

D'autres adverbes

au moins *at least*
heureusement *fortunately*
rien (ne ... rien) *nothing, not anything*
tant *so much; so many*

D'autres expressions utiles

Aïe! *Ouch!*
à l'intérieur de *inside of*
À quoi jouez-vous? *What (game, sport) do you play?*
à table *at dinner, at the table*
Bonnes vacances! *Have a good vacation!*
C'est la vie! *That's life!*
chaque *each; every*
De quoi jouez-vous? *What (instrument) do you play?*
Eh bien *Well*
en vacances *on vacation*
faire du sport *to play sports*
faire du vélo *to go bike riding*
la plupart (de) *most (of)*
parce que *because*
par exemple *for example*
Pourquoi pas? *Why not?*

Références

Verbes

VERBES RÉGULIERS

Infinitif	Présent		Passé composé		Imparfait	
1. parler	je	parle	j'	ai parlé	je	parlais
	tu	parles	tu	as parlé	tu	parlais
	il/elle/on	parle	il/elle/on	a parlé	il/elle/on	parlait
	nous	parlons	nous	avons parlé	nous	parlions
	vous	parlez	vous	avez parlé	vous	parliez
	ils/elles	parlent	ils/elles	ont parlé	ils/elles	parlaient
2. finir	je	finis	j'	ai fini	je	finissais
	tu	finis	tu	as fini	tu	finissais
	il/elle/on	finit	il/elle/on	a fini	il/elle/on	finissait
	nous	finissons	nous	avons fini	nous	finissions
	vous	finissez	vous	avez fini	vous	finissiez
	ils/elles	finissent	ils/elles	ont fini	ils/elles	finissaient
3. attendre	j'	attends	j'	ai attendu	j'	attendais
	tu	attends	tu	as attendu	tu	attendais
	il/elle/on	attend	il/elle/on	a attendu	il/elle/on	attendait
	nous	attendons	nous	avons attendu	nous	attendions
	vous	attendez	vous	avez attendu	vous	attendiez
	ils/elles	attendent	ils/elles	ont attendu	ils/elles	attendaient
4. se laver	je	me lave	je	me suis lavé(e)	je	me lavais
	tu	te laves	tu	t'es lavé(e)	tu	te lavais
	il/on	se lave	il/on	s'est lavé	il/on	se lavait
	elle	se lave	elle	s'est lavée	elle	se lavait
	nous	nous lavons	nous	nous sommes lavé(e)s	nous	nous lavions
	vous	vous lavez	vous	vous êtes lavé(e)(s)	vous	vous laviez
	ils	se lavent	ils	se sont lavés	ils	se lavaient
	elles	se lavent	elles	se sont lavées	elles	se lavaient

Impératif	Futur		Conditionnel		Subjonctif	
parle	je	parlerai	je	parlerais	que je	parle
parlons	tu	parleras	tu	parlerais	que tu	parles
parlez	il/elle/on	parlera	il/elle/on	parlerait	qu'il/elle/on	parle
	nous	parlerons	nous	parlerions	que nous	parlions
	vous	parlerez	vous	parleriez	que vous	parliez
	ils/elles	parleront	ils/elles	parleraient	qu'ils/elles	parlent
finis	je	finirai	je	finirais	que je	finisse
finissons	tu	finiras	tu	finirais	que tu	finisses
finissez	il/elle/on	finira	il/elle/on	finirait	qu'il/elle/on	finisse
	nous	finirons	nous	finirions	que nous	finissions
	vous	finirez	vous	finiriez	que vous	finissiez
	ils/elles	finiront	ils/elles	finiraient	qu'ils/elles	finissent
attends	j'	attendrai	j'	attendrais	que j'	attende
attendons	tu	attendras	tu	attendrais	que tu	attendes
attendez	il/elle/on	attendra	il/elle/on	attendrait	qu'il/elle/on	attende
	nous	attendrons	nous	attendrions	que nous	attendions
	vous	attendrez	vous	attendriez	que vous	attendiez
	ils/elles	attendront	ils/elles	attendraient	qu'ils/elles	attendent
lave-toi	je	me laverai	je	me laverais	que je	me lave
lavons-nous	tu	te laveras	tu	te laverais	que tu	te laves
lavez-vous	il/on	se lavera	il/on	se laverait	qu'il/on	se lave
	elle	se lavera	elle	se laverait	qu'elle	se lave
	nous	nous laverons	nous	nous laverions	que nous	nous lavions
	vous	vous laverez	vous	vous laveriez	que vous	vous laviez
	ils	se laveront	ils	se laveraient	qu'ils	se lavent
	elles	se laveront	elles	se laveraient	qu'elles	se lavent

VERBES RÉGULIERS AVEC CHANGEMENTS ORTHOGRAPHIQUES

Infinitif	Présent				Passé composé	Imparfait
1. manger	je	mange	nous	mangeons	j'ai mangé	je mangeais
	tu	manges	vous	mangez		
	il/elle/on	mange	ils/elles	mangent		
2. avancer	j'	avance	nous	avançons	j'ai avancé	j'avançais
	tu	avances	vous	avancez		
	il/elle/on	avance	ils/elles	avancent		
3. payer	je	paie	nous	payons	j'ai payé	je payais
	tu	paies	vous	payez		
	il/elle/on	paie	ils/elles	paient		
4. préférer	je	préfère	nous	préférons	j'ai préféré	je préférais
	tu	préfères	vous	préférez		
	il/elle/on	préfère	ils/elles	préfèrent		
5. acheter	j'	achète	nous	achetons	j'ai acheté	j'achetais
	tu	achètes	vous	achetez		
	il/elle/on	achète	ils/elles	achètent		
6. appeler	j'	appelle	nous	appelons	j'ai appelé	j'appelais
	tu	appelles	vous	appelez		
	il/elle/on	appelle	ils/elles	appellent		

Impératif	Futur	Conditionnel	Subjonctif	Autres verbes
mange mangeons mangez	je mangerai	je mangerais	que je mange que nous mangions	exiger nager neiger voyager
avance avançons avancez	j'avancerai	j'avancerais	que j'avance que nous avancions	commencer divorcer
paie payons payez	je paierai	je paierais	que je paie que nous payions	essayer
préfère préférons préférez	je préférerai	je préférerais	que je préfère que nous préférions	espérer exagérer s'inquiéter répéter
achète achetons achetez	j'achèterai	j'achèterais	que j'achète que nous achetions	lever se lever se promener
appelle appelons appelez	j'appellerai	j'appellerais	que j'appelle que nous appelions	s'appeler épeler jeter

VERBES IRRÉGULIERS

To conjugate the irregular verbs on the top of the opposite page, consult the verbs conjugated in the same manner, using the number next to the verbs. The verbs preceded by a bullet are conjugated with the auxiliary verb **être**. Of course, when the verbs in this chart are used with a reflexive pronoun (as reflexive verbs), the auxiliary verb **être** must be used in compound tenses.

Infinitif		Présent			Passé composé	Imparfait
1. aller	je	vais	nous	allons	je suis allé(e)	j'allais
	tu	vas	vous	allez		
	il/elle/on	va	ils/elles	vont		
2. s'asseoir	je	m'assieds	nous	nous asseyons	je me suis assis(e)	je m'asseyais
	tu	t'assieds	vous	vous asseyez		
	il/elle/on	s'assied	ils/elles	s'asseyent		
3. avoir	j'	ai	nous	avons	j'ai eu	j'avais
	tu	as	vous	avez		
	il/elle/on	a	ils/elles	ont		
4. battre	je	bats	nous	battons	j'ai battu	je battais
	tu	bats	vous	battez		
	il/elle/on	bat	ils/elles	battent		
5. boire	je	bois	nous	buvons	j'ai bu	je buvais
	tu	bois	vous	buvez		
	il/elle/on	boit	ils/elles	boivent		
6. conduire	je	conduis	nous	conduisons	j'ai conduit	je conduisais
	tu	conduis	vous	conduisez		
	il/elle/on	conduit	ils/elles	conduisent		
7. connaître	je	connais	nous	connaissons	j'ai connu	je connaissais
	tu	connais	vous	connaissez		
	il/elle/on	connaît	ils/elles	connaissent		
8. croire	je	crois	nous	croyons	j'ai cru	je croyais
	tu	crois	vous	croyez		
	il/elle/on	croit	ils/elles	croient		
9. devoir	je	dois	nous	devons	j'ai dû	je devais
	tu	dois	vous	devez		
	il/elle/on	doit	ils/elles	doivent		

apprendre 25 détruire 6 offrir 21 repartir 22 sortir 22
comprendre 25 devenir 28 permettre 17 revenir 28 sourire 26
couvrir 21 dormir 22 promettre 17 revoir 29 traduire 6
découvrir 21 élire 16 réduire 6 sentir 22 valoir mieux 15
décrier 11 s'endormir 22

Impératif	Futur	Conditionnel	Subjonctif
va allons allez	j'irai	j'irais	que j'aille que nous allions
assieds-toi asseyons-nous asseyez-vous	je m'assiérai	je m'assiérais	que je m'asseye que nous nous asseyions
aie ayons ayez	j'aurai	j'aurais	que j'aie que nous ayons
bats battons battez	je battrai	je battrais	que je batte que nous battions
bois buvons buvez	je boirai	je boirais	que je boive que nous buvions
conduis conduisons conduisez	je conduirai	je conduirais	que je conduise que nous conduisions
connais connaissons connaissez	je connaîtrai	je connaîtrais	que je connaisse que nous connaissions
crois croyons croyez	je croirai	je croirais	que je croie que nous croyions
dois devons devez	je devrai	je devrais	que je doive que nous devions

Infinitif	Présent				Passé composé	Imparfait
10. dire	je	dis	nous	disons	j'ai dit	je disais
	tu	dis	vous	dites		
	il/elle/on	dit	ils/elles	disent		
11. écrire	j'	écris	nous	écrivons	j'ai écrit	j'écrivais
	tu	écris	vous	écrivez		
	il/elle/on	écrit	ils/elles	écrivent		
12. envoyer	j'	envoie	nous	envoyons	j'ai envoyé	j'envoyais
	tu	envoies	vous	envoyez		
	il/elle/on	envoie	ils/elles	envoient		
13. être	je	suis	nous	sommes	j'ai été	j'étais
	tu	es	vous	êtes		
	il/elle/on	est	ils/elles	sont		
14. faire	je	fais	nous	faisons	j'ai fait	je faisais
	tu	fais	vous	faites		
	il/elle/on	fait	ils/elles	font		
15. falloir		il faut			il a fallu	il fallait
16. lire	je	lis	nous	lisons	j'ai lu	je lisais
	tu	lis	vous	lisez		
	il/elle/on	lit	ils/elles	lisent		
17. mettre	je	mets	nous	mettons	j'ai mis	je mettais
	tu	mets	vous	mettez		
	il/elle/on	met	ils/elles	mettent		
18. mourir	je	meurs	nous	mourons	je suis mort(e)	je mourais
	tu	meurs	vous	mourez		
	il/elle/on	meurt	ils/elles	meurent		
19. naître	je	nais	nous	naissons	je suis né(e)	je naissais
	tu	nais	vous	naissez		
	il/elle/on	naît	ils/elles	naissent		
20. nettoyer	je	nettoie	nous	nettoyons	j'ai nettoyé	je nettoyais
	tu	nettoies	vous	nettoyez		
	il/elle/on	nettoie	ils/elles	nettoient		
21. ouvrir	j'	ouvre	nous	ouvrons	j'ai ouvert	j'ouvrais
	tu	ouvres	vous	ouvrez		
	il/elle/on	ouvre	ils/elles	ouvrent		

Impératif	Futur	Conditionnel	Subjonctif
dis disons dites	je dirai	je dirais	que je dise que nous disions
écris écrivons écrivez	j'écrirai	j'écrirais	que j'écrive que nous écrivions
envoie envoyons envoyez	j'enverrai	j'enverrais	que j'envoie que nous envoyions
sois soyons soyez	je serai	je serais	que je sois que nous soyons
fais faisons faites	je ferai	je ferais	que je fasse que nous fassions
—	il faudra	il faudrait	qu'il faille
lis lisons lisez	je lirai	je lirais	que je lise que nous lisions
mets mettons mettez	je mettrai	je mettrais	que je mette que nous mettions
meurs mourons mourez	je mourrai	je mourrais	que je meure que nous mourions
nais naissons naissez	je naîtrai	je naîtrais	que je naisse que nous naissions
nettoie nettoyons nettoyez	je nettoierai	je nettoierais	que je nettoie que nous nettoyions
ouvre ouvrons ouvrez	j'ouvrirai	j'ouvrirais	que j'ouvre que nous ouvrions

Infinitif	Présent				Passé composé	Imparfait
22. partir*	je	pars	nous	partons	je suis parti(e)*	je partais
	tu	pars	vous	partez		
	il/elle/on	part	ils/elles	partent		
23. pleuvoir		il pleut			il a plu	il pleuvait
24. pouvoir	je	peux**	nous	pouvons	j'ai pu	je pouvais
	tu	peux	vous	pouvez		
	il/elle/on	peut	ils/elles	peuvent		
25. prendre	je	prends	nous	prenons	j'ai pris	je prenais
	tu	prends	vous	prenez		
	il/elle/on	prend	ils/elles	prennent		
26. rire	je	ris	nous	rions	j'ai ri	je riais
	tu	ris	vous	riez		
	il/elle/on	rit	ils/elles	rient		
27. savoir	je	sais	nous	savons	j'ai su	je savais
	tu	sais	vous	savez		
	il/elle/on	sait	ils/elles	savent		
28. venir	je	viens	nous	venons	je suis venu(e)	je venais
	tu	viens	vous	venez		
	il/elle/on	vient	ils/elles	viennent		
29. voir	je	vois	nous	voyons	j'ai vu	je voyais
	tu	vois	vous	voyez		
	il/elle/on	voit	ils/elles	voient		
30. vouloir	je	veux	nous	voulons	j'ai voulu	je voulais
	tu	veux	vous	voulez		
	il/elle/on	veut	ils/elles	veulent		

***Dormir, sentir,** and **servir** are conjugated with **avoir** in the passé composé. **Partir, sortir,** and the reflexive **s'endormir** are conjugated with **être.**

The inverted form of **je peux is **puis-je … ?**

Impératif	Futur	Conditionnel	Subjonctif
pars partons partez	je partirai	je partirais	que je parte que nous partions
—	il pleuvra	il pleuvrait	qu'il pleuve
— — —	je pourrai	je pourrais	que je puisse que nous puissions
prends prenons prenez	je prendrai	je prendrais	que je prenne que nous prenions
ris rions riez	je rirai	je rirais	que je rie que nous riions
sache sachons sachez	je saurai	je saurais	que je sache que nous sachions
viens venons venez	je viendrai	je viendrais	que je vienne que nous venions
vois voyons voyez	je verrai	je verrais	que je voie que nous voyions
veuille voulons veuillez	je voudrai	je voudrais	que je veuille que nous voulions

Appendices

A list of International Phonetic Alphabet symbols

Voyelles

Son	Exemples	Pages: *Entre amis*
[i]	**i**l, **y**	96, 312
[e]	**et**, parl**é**, **ai**m**er**, ch**ez**	35, 40, 62, 404
[ɛ]	m**è**re, n**ei**ge, **ai**me, t**ê**te, ch**è**re, b**e**lle	35, 62, 437
[a]	l**a**, f**e**mme	62
[wa]	t**oi**, tr**oi**s, qu**oi**, v**oy**age	62
[ɔ]	f**o**lle, b**o**nne	196
[o]	**eau**, ch**au**d, n**o**s, ch**o**se	196, 404
[u]	v**ou**s, **aoû**t	166
[y]	**u**ne, r**u**e, **eu**	166, 168
[ø]	d**eu**x, v**eu**t, bl**eu**, ennuy**eu**se	370
[œ]	h**eu**re, v**eu**lent, s**œu**r	370
[ə]	l**e**, s**e**rons, f**ai**sons	62, 341, 436
[ɑ̃]	**an**, l**en**t, ch**am**bre, **en**semble	96
[ɔ̃]	m**on**, n**om**, s**on**t	40, 96
[ɛ̃]	m**ain**, f**aim**, exam**en**, **im**portant, v**in**, ch**ien**, s**ym**phonie, br**un***, parf**um***	96

*Some speakers still pronounce the nasal vowel [œ̃] in words like **un** and **brun.**

Consonnes

Son	Exemples	
[p]	**p**ère, ju**p**e	405
[t]	**t**oute, gran**d** ami, quan**d** est-ce que ...	69, 110, 151, 405
[k]	**c**omment, **qu**i	222
[b]	ro**b**e, **b**ien	405
[d]	**d**eux, ren**d**ent	405
[g]	**g**are, lon**gu**e, se**c**ond	352, 405
[f]	**f**ou, **ph**armacie, neu**f**	69
[s]	mer**c**i, profe**ss**eur, fran**ç**ais, tenni**s**, démocra**t**ie	69, 222
[ʃ]	**ch**at, **sh**ort	222

[v]	vous, neuf ans	69
[z]	zéro, rose	69, 110, 222
[ʒ]	je, âge, nageons	40, 222
[l]	lire, ville	340
[R]	rue, sœur	253
[m]	mes, aime, comment	96
[n]	non, américaine, bonne	96
[ɲ]	montagne	222

Semi-consonnes

Son	**Exemples**	
[j]	fille, travail, chien, voyez, yeux, hier	312, 340
[w]	oui, week-end	
[ɥ]	huit, tuer	341

Professions

The following professions are in addition to those taught in Ch. 4, p. 115.

agent *m.* **d'assurances** insurance agent
agent *m.* **de police** police officer
agent *m.* **de voyages** travel agent
agent *m.* **immobilier** real-estate agent
artisan *m.* craftsperson
assistant(e) social(e) social worker
avocat(e) lawyer
banquier *m.* banker
boucher/bouchère butcher
boulanger/boulangère baker
caissier/caissière cashier
chanteur/chanteuse singer
charcutier/charcutière pork butcher, delicatessen owner
chauffeur *m.* driver
chercheur/chercheuse researcher
chirurgien(ne) surgeon
commerçant(e) shopkeeper
commercial(e) *m./f.* salesperson
conférencier/conférencière lecturer
conseiller/conseillère counsellor; advisor
cuisinier/cuisinière cook
dentiste *m./f.* dentist
douanier/douanière customs officer
électricien(ne) electrician
épicier/épicière grocer
expert-comptable *m.* CPA
facteur/factrice letter carrier
femme de ménage *f.* cleaning lady
fleuriste *m./f.* florist
garagiste *m./f.* garage owner; mechanic

homme/femme politique politician
hôtelier/hôtelière hotelkeeper
hôte/hôtesse de l'air *f.* flight attendant
instituteur/institutrice elementary school teacher
jardinier/jardinière gardener
joueur/joueuse (de golf, etc.) (golf, etc.) player
maire *m.* mayor
mannequin *m.* fashion model
mécanicien(ne) mechanic
militaire *m.* serviceman/servicewoman
moniteur/monitrice (de ski) (ski) instructor
musicien(ne) musician
opticien(ne) optician
PDG *m./f.* CEO (chairperson)
pasteur *m.* (Protestant) minister
peintre *m./f.* painter
photographe *m./f.* photographer
pilote *m.* pilot
plombier *m.* plumber
pompier *m.* firefighter
prêtre *m.* priest
psychologue *m./f.* psychologist
rabbin *m.* rabbi
religieuse *f.* nun
reporter *m.* reporter
restaurateur/restauratrice restaurant owner
savant *m.* scientist; scholar
sculpteur *m.* sculptor
serveur/serveuse waiter/waitress
traducteur/traductrice translator
vétérinaire *m./f.* vet

Glossary of Grammatical Terms

Term	Definition	Example(s)
accord *(agreement)* 16, 22–23, 73	Articles, adjectives, pronouns, etc. are said to agree with the noun they modify when they "adopt" the gender and number of the noun.	*La **voisine** de Patrick est allemande. C'est **une** jeune **fille** très gentil**le**. **Elle** est partie en vacances.*
adjectif *(adjective)* 16, 22, 98	A word that describes or modifies a noun or a pronoun, specifying size, color, number, or other qualities. (See **adjectif démonstratif, adjectif interrogatif, adjectif possessif.**)	*Lori Becker n'est pas **mariée**. Nous sommes **américains**. Le professeur a une voiture **noire**. C'est une **belle** voiture.*
adjectif démonstratif *(demonstrative adjective)* 106	A noun determiner (see **déterminant**) that identifies and *demonstrates* a person or a thing.	*Regarde les couleurs de **cette** robe et de **ce** blouson!*
adjectif interrogatif *(interrogative adjective)* 117, 420	An adjective that introduces a question. In French, the word **quel** *(which or what)* is used as an interrogative adjective and agrees in gender and number with the noun it modifies.	***Quelle** heure est-il? **Quels** vêtements portez-vous?*
adjectif possessif *(possessive adjective)* 73, 80	A noun determiner that indicates *possession* or *ownership*. Agreement depends on the gender of the noun and not on the sex of the possessor, as in English *(his/her)*.	*Où est **mon** livre? Comment s'appelle **son** père?*
adverbe *(adverb)* 100, 298	An invariable word that describes a verb, an adjective, or another adverb. It answers the question *when?* (time), *where?* (place), or *how? how much?* (manner).	*Mon père conduit **lentement**.* (how?) *On va regarder un match de foot **demain**.* (when?) *J'habite **ici**.* (where?)
adverbe interrogatif *(interrogative adverb)* 151	An adverb that introduces a question about time, location, manner, number, or cause.	***Où** sont mes lunettes? **Comment** est-ce que Lori a trouvé le film? **Pourquoi** est-ce que tu fumes?*
article *(article)* 46, 65, 225	A word used to signal that a noun follows, and to specify the noun as to its *gender* and *number*, as well as whether it is general, particular, or part of a larger whole. (See **article défini, article indéfini,** and **article partitif.**)	

Term	Definition	Example(s)
article défini *(definite article)* 46, 48, 323	The definite articles in French are **le, la, l'**, and **les.** They are used to refer to a specific noun, or to things in general, in an abstract sense.	*Le professeur est dans la salle de classe. Le lait est bon pour la santé. J'aime les concerts de jazz.*
article indéfini *(indefinite article)* 48	The indefinite articles in French are **un, une,** and **des.** They are used to designate unspecified nouns.	*Lori Becker a un frère et une sœur. J'ai des amis qui habitent à Paris.*
article partitif *(partitive article)* 323	The partitive articles in French are **du, de la, de l'**, and **des.** They are used to refer to *part* of a larger whole, or to things that cannot be counted.	*Je vais acheter du fromage. Tu veux de la soupe?*
comparatif *(comparison)* 320–322	When comparing people or things, these comparative forms are used: **plus** *(more),* **moins** *(less),* **aussi** *(as … as),* and **autant** *(as much as).*	*Le métro est plus rapide que le bus. Il neige moins souvent en Espagne qu'en France. Ma sœur parle aussi bien le français que moi. Elle gagne autant d'argent que moi.*
conditionnel *(conditional)* 447	A verbal mood used when stating hypotheses or expressing polite requests.	*Tu devrais faire attention. Je voudrais une tasse de café.*
conjugaison *(conjugation)* 40	An expression used to refer to the various forms of a verb that reflect *person* (1st, 2nd, or 3rd person), *number* (singular or plural), *tense* (present, past, or future), and *mood* (indicative, subjunctive, imperative, conditional). Each conjugated form consists of a *stem* and an *ending.*	Présent: *Nous parlons français en classe.* Passé composé: *Je suis allé à Paris l'année dernière.* Imparfait: *Quand il était jeune, mon frère s'amusait beaucoup.* Futur: *Je ferai le devoir de français ce soir.* Impératif: *Ouvrez vos livres!* Subjonctif: *Il faut qu'on fasse la lessive tout de suite.* Conditionnel: *Je voudrais un verre de coca.*
contraction *(contraction)* 78, 133, 417	The condensing of two words to form one.	*C'est une photo du professeur* [**de + le**]. *Nous allons au café* [**à + le**].
déterminant *(determiner)* (See articles, adjectif démonstratif, adjectif possessif, adjectif interrogatif)	A word that precedes a noun and *determines* its quality (definite, indefinite, partitive, etc.). In French, nouns are usually accompanied by one of these determiners.	Article *(le livre);* demonstrative adjective *(cette table);* possessive adjective *(sa voiture);* interrogative adjective *(Quelle voiture?);* number *(trois crayons).*
élision *(elision)* 14, 21, 46, 258	The process by which some words drop their final vowel and replace it with an apostrophe before words beginning with a vowel sound.	*Je m'appelle Martin et j'habite près de l'église.*

Term	Definition	Example(s)
futur *(future)* 38, 136, 353	A tense used to express what *will* happen. The construction **aller** + *infinitive* often replaces the future tense, especially when referring to more immediate plans.	*Un jour, nous **irons** en France.* *Nous **allons partir** cet après-midi.*
genre *(gender)* 4, 15, 46	The term used to designate whether a noun, article, pronoun, or adjective is masculine or feminine. All nouns in French have a grammatical *gender*.	***la** table, **le** livre, **le** garçon, **la** mère*
imparfait *(imperfect)* 313, 317, 438	A past tense used to describe a setting (background information), a condition (physical or emotional), or a habitual action.	*Il **faisait** beau quand je suis parti. Je **prenais** beaucoup de médicaments quand j'**étais** jeune.*
impératif *(imperative)* 147, 293	This verbal mood is used to give commands or to make suggestions.	***Répétez** après moi! **Allons** faire une promenade.*
indicatif *(indicative)* 14, 168, 313, 353	This verbal mood is used to relate facts or supply information. **Le présent, le passé composé, l'imparfait,** and **le futur** all belong to the indicative mood.	*Je ne **prends** pas le petit déjeuner. Le directeur **partira** en vacances le mois prochain. Il **faisait** beau quand je **suis parti**.*
infinitif *(infinitive)* 36, 40, 254, 348, 353	The plain form of the verb, showing the general meaning of the verb without reflecting *tense, person,* or *number.* French verbs are often classified according to the last two letters of their infinitive forms: **-er** verbs, **-ir** verbs, or **-re** verbs.	*étudi**er**, chois**ir**, vend**re***
inversion *(inversion)* 51, 68, 151, 169	An expression used to refer to the reversal of the subject pronoun-verb order in the formation of questions.	*Parlez-vous français? Chantez-vous bien?*
liaison *(liaison)* 13, 15, 40, 65, 66, 68–69, 74, 80, 132	The term used to describe the spoken linking of the final and usually silent consonant of a word with the beginning vowel sound of the following word.	*Vous [z]êtes américain? Ma sœur a un petit [t]ami.*
mot apparenté *(cognate)* 25, 54, 94, 403	Words from different languages that are related in origin and that are similar are referred to as *cognates.*	***question** [Fr.] = question [Eng.]; **semestre** [Fr.] = semester [Eng.]*
négation *(negation)* 21, 99, 169, 173, 294, 444	The process of transforming a positive sentence into a negative one. In negative sentences the verb is placed between two words, **ne** and another word defining the nature of the negation.	*On **ne** parle **pas** anglais ici. Il **ne** neige **jamais** à Casablanca. Mon grand-père **ne** travaille **plus**. Il **n'**y a **personne** dans la salle de classe. Mon fils **n'**a **rien** dit.*

Term	Definition	Example(s)
nom *(noun)* 15, 46	The name of a person, place, thing, idea, etc. All nouns in French have a grammatical gender and are usually preceded by a determiner.	*le **livre**, la **vie**, les **étudiants**, ses **parents**, cette **photo***
nombre *(number)* 14–15, 17, 46	The form of a noun, article, pronoun, adjective, or verb that indicates whether it is *singular* or *plural*. When an adjective is said to agree with the noun it modifies in *number,* it means that the adjective will be singular if the noun is singular, and plural if the noun is plural.	***La** voiture de James **est** très petite.* ***Les** livres de français ne **sont** pas aussi chers que **les** livres de biologie.*
objet direct *(direct object)* 236, 289, 294, 408	A thing or a person bearing directly the action of a verb. (See **pronom complément d'objet direct.**)	*Thierry écrit **un poème.** Il aime **Céline.***
objet indirect *(indirect object)* 408	A person (or persons) to or for whom something is done. The indirect object is often preceded by the preposition **à** because it receives the action of the verb *indirectly.* (See **pronom complément d'objet indirect.**)	*Thierry donne une rose **à Céline.** Le professeur raconte des histoires drôles **aux étudiants.***
participe passé *(past participle)* 168, 197, 380, 438	The form of a verb used with an auxiliary to form two-part (compound) past tenses such as the **passé composé.**	*Vous êtes **allés** au cinéma. Moi, j'ai **lu** un roman policier.*
passé composé 168, 197, 317, 380	A past tense used to narrate an event in the past, to tell what happened, etc. It is used to express actions *completed* in the past. The **passé composé** is composed of two parts: an auxiliary (**avoir** or **être**) conjugated in the present tense, and the past participle form of the verb.	*Le président **a parlé** de l'économie. Nous **sommes arrivés** à 5h.*
personne *(person)* 14	The notion of *person* indicates whether the subject of the verb is speaking *(1st person),* spoken to *(2nd person),* or spoken about *(3rd person).* Verbs and pronouns are designated as being in the singular or plural of one of the three persons.	First person singular: ***Je** n'ai rien compris.* Second person plural: *Avez-**vous** de l'argent?* Third person plural: ***Elles** sont toutes les deux sénégalaises.*
plus-que-parfait *(pluperfect)* 438	A past tense used to describe an event that took place prior to some other past event. The **plus-que-parfait** is composed of two parts: an auxiliary (**avoir** or **être**) conjugated in the imperfect tense, and the past participle form of the verb.	*Il était ivre parce qu'il **avait** trop **bu.***

Term	Definition	Example(s)
préposition *(preposition)* 133, 146, 149, 203	A word (or a small group of words) preceding a noun or a pronoun that shows position, direction, time, etc. relative to another word in the sentence.	*Mon oncle qui habite **à** Boston est allé **en** France. L'hôtel est **en face de** la gare.*
présent *(present)* 15, 40	A tense that expresses an action taking place at the moment of speaking, an action that one does habitually, or an action that began earlier and is still going on.	*Il **fait** très beau aujourd'hui. Je me **lève** à 7h tous les jours.*
pronom *(pronoun)* 14, 117, 180, 201, 236, 269, 289, 294, 408, 410, 418, 422	A word used in place of a noun or a noun phrase. Its form depends on the *number* (singular or plural), *gender* (masculine or feminine), *person* (1st, 2nd, 3rd), and *function* (subject, object, etc.) of the noun it replaces.	***Tu** aimes les fraises? Oui, **je les** adore. / Irez-**vous** à Paris cet été? Non, **je** n'y vais pas. / Prenez-**vous** du sucre? Oui, **j'en** prends. / Qui **t'**a dit de partir? **Lui**.*
pronom accentué *(stress pronoun)* 180, 320	A pronoun that is separated from the verb and appears in different positions in the sentence.	*Voilà son livre à **elle**. Viens avec **moi**!*
pronom interrogatif *(interrogative pronoun)* 117, 416–417, 442–443	Interrogative pronouns are used to ask questions. They change form depending upon whether they refer to people or things and also whether they function as the subject, the direct object, or the object of a preposition of a sentence.	***Qui** est là? **Que** voulez-vous faire dans la vie? **Qu'est-ce que** vous faites? **Qu'est-ce qui** est arrivé?*
pronom complément d'objet direct *(direct object pronoun)* 236, 289, 410	A pronoun that replaces a direct object noun (a noun object not preceded by a preposition).	*Thierry aime Céline et elle **l'**aime aussi.*
pronom complément d'objet indirect *(indirect object pronoun)* 408	A pronoun that replaces an indirect object noun (a noun object preceded by the preposition **à**).	*Thierry **lui** a donné une rose.*
pronom relatif *(relative pronoun)* 63, 269, 418	A pronoun that refers or "relates" to a preceding noun and connects two clauses into a single sentence.	*Le professeur a des amis **qui** habitent à Paris. J'ai lu le livre **que** tu m'as donné.*
pronom sujet *(subject pronoun)* 14	A pronoun that replaces a noun subject.	***Ils** attendent le train. **On** parle français ici.*
sujet *(subject)* 14	The person or thing that performs the action of the verb. (See **pronom sujet**.)	*Les **étudiants** font souvent les devoirs à la bibliothèque. **Vous** venez d'où?*

Term	Definition	Example(s)
subjonctif *(subjunctive)* 383, 420	A class of tenses, used under specific conditions: (1) the verb is in the second (or subordinate) clause of a sentence; (2) the second clause is introduced by **que**; and (3) the verb of the first clause expresses advice, will, necessity, emotion, etc.	Mon père préfère que je n'*aie* pas de voiture. Le professeur veut que nous *parlions* français. Ma mère est contente que vous *soyez* ici.
superlatif *(superlative)* 323	The superlative is used to express the superior or inferior degree or quality of a person or a thing.	Le TGV est le train *le plus* rapide du monde. L'eau minérale est la boisson *la moins* chère.
temps *(tense)* 40, 168, 313, 353	The particular form of a verb that indicates the time frame in which an action occurs: present, past, future, etc.	La tour Eiffel *est* le monument le plus haut de Paris. Nous *sommes arrivés* à 5h à la gare. Je *ferai* de mon mieux.
verbe *(verb)* 15, 40, 254, 348	A word expressing action or condition of the subject. The verb consists of a stem and an ending, the form of which depends on the subject (singular, plural, 1st, 2nd, or 3rd person), the tense (present, past, future), and the mood (indicative, subjunctive, imperative, conditional).	
verbe auxiliaire *(auxiliary verb)* 160, 197, 438	The two auxiliary (or helping) verbs in French are **avoir** and **être.** They are used in combination with a past participle to form the **passé composé** and the **plus-que-parfait.**	Nous *sommes* allés au cinéma hier Nous *avons* vu un très bon film.
verbes pronominaux *(reflexive verbs)* 176, 199, 375, 378, 380	Verbs whose subjects and objects are the same. A reflexive pronoun will precede the verb and act as either the direct or indirect object of the verb. The reflexive pronoun has the same number, gender, and person as the subject.	Lori *se réveille.* Elle et James *se sont* bien *amusés* hier soir

NÉGOCIATIONS

Chapitre 1 (p. 25)

Identifications. Work with your partner to prepare a new identity. First, decide with your partner whether you are describing a man or a woman. Then, complete the second half of the following form. Ask questions of your partner, who will complete the first half of the form. Your partner will ask you other questions about the person you are describing. Answer only **oui** or **non**.

MODÈLE: **Comment vous appelez-vous? Quel est votre nom de famille?**
Êtes-vous français(e)? Êtes-vous jeune?

*The **Révision** part of the **Intégration** section of each chapter ends with an activity called **Négociations**. In this activity you will exchange information with a partner. Partner A uses the version of the activity shown in the chapter. In most cases, Partner B (and occasionally C, D, etc.) uses the version of the activity given in this appendix.*

For the last two blanks you should choose adjectives that describe the person, e.g., tall.

A

Nom de famille: _____

Prénom: _____

Nationalité: _____

B

État civil: _____

Description 1: _____

_____

Description 2: _____

_____

Les activités. Use one of the forms below to interview as many students as possible. Try to find people who answer the questions affirmatively; then write their initials in the appropriate boxes. No student's initials should be used more than twice.

MODÈLE: **Est-ce que tu détestes les hot-dogs?**

B

regarder la télé le soir	aimer étudier le français	chanter une chanson française
détester les hot-dogs	parler espagnol	aimer patiner
pleurer quelquefois	être marié(e)	travailler beaucoup
étudier l'anglais	adorer skier	jouer au golf

C

danser souvent le week-end	adorer skier	parler espagnol
jouer au ping-pong	chanter une chanson française	étudier l'anglais
travailler beaucoup	être célibataire	tomber quelquefois
pleurer quelquefois	détester les hot-dogs	aimer patiner

C'est à qui? Each of the items below belongs to one of David's relatives. Ask your partner questions to match each item with its correct owner. Complete the form with the missing information.

MODÈLE: **C'est la voiture du frère de David?**
Non, ce n'est pas la voiture de David. C'est la voiture de son père.

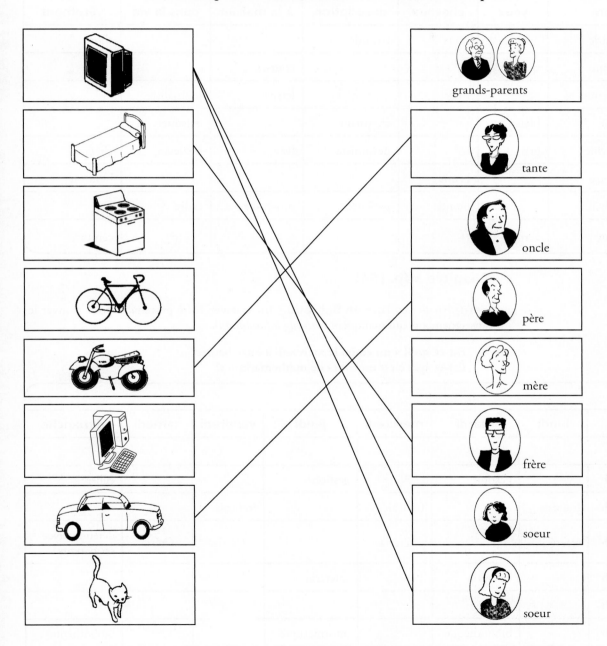

Chapitre 4 (p. 120)

Nos amis. Work with your partner to complete the forms. Ask questions to determine the information that is missing.

MODÈLE: **Est-ce que Marie a les yeux bleus?**

B

nom	yeux	cheveux	description	à la maison	dans la vie	vêtement
Marie		noirs	bavarde			short
Alain	marron			courses		
Chantal		roux		lessive	journaliste	
Éric	bleus		charmant		cuisinier	
Karine	gris		pessimiste	liste	médecin	chapeau
Pierre		bruns				blouson
Sylvie		blonds	patiente	provisions	cadre	
Jean	verts					ceinture

Chapitre 5 (p. 154)

L'emploi du temps de Sahibou. Interviewez votre partenaire pour trouver les renseignements qui manquent *(missing information)*.

MODÈLE: **Est-ce qu'il a un cours le mercredi à onze heures?**
Est-ce que c'est un cours de mathématiques?

B

	lundi	mardi	mercredi	jeudi	vendredi	samedi	dimanche
9h							
10h		gestion		gestion			église
11h	français		français		français		
12h	cafétéria		cafétéria		cafétéria	cafétéria	déjeuner avec ses parents
13h		cafétéria		cafétéria			
14h							
19h		bibliothèque		informatique			bibliothèque
20h	résidence	bibliothèque		informatique	cinéma		bibliothèque

Chapitre 6 (p. 185)

Hier, d'habitude et pendant le week-end. Interviewez votre partenaire pour trouver les renseignements qui manquent *(missing information)*.

MODÈLE: **Est-ce que Valérie va au cours de français d'habitude?**
Est-ce qu'Alain a fumé hier?

B

nom	hier	d'habitude	pendant le week-end
Valérie	écrire une dissertation _____	OUI	nettoyer sa chambre _____
Chantal	NON	NON	rester dans sa chambre _____
Sophie	être malade _____	étudier seule _____	OUI
Alain	NON	travailler après les cours _____	OUI
David	NON	OUI	jouer au basket-ball _____
Jean-Luc	passer un examen _____	envoyer des e-mails _____	NON

Chapitre 7 (p. 212)

D'où viennent-ils? Interviewez votre partenaire pour trouver les renseignements qui manquent.

MODÈLE: **D'où vient Sahibou?**
Où est-ce que Fatima est née?
Quand est-ce que Cécile est partie?

B

nom	pays d'origine	ville de naissance	départ	adresse
Sahibou		Dakar		Canada
Fatima	Maroc		en juin dernier	
Cécile	Belgique			États-Unis
Jean-Luc		Nantes	en avril dernier	
Marie	Canada	Québec		

Dînons-nous ensemble? Interviewez les autres étudiants pour trouver votre partenaire. C'est la personne qui a le même menu que vous.

MODÈLE: **Qu'est-ce que tu prends comme entrée?**
Qu'est-ce que tu vas boire?

B

	votre partenaire	vous
entrée	soupe de légumes	pâté
plat principal	saumon	bœuf
légume	épinards	riz
fromage	camembert	brie
dessert	gâteau	pâtisserie
boisson	eau minérale	eau

C

	votre partenaire	vous
entrée	soupe à l'oignon	crudités
plat principal	porc	truite
légume	frites	riz
fromage	brie	chèvre
dessert	tarte	gâteau
boisson	eau	vin blanc

D

	votre partenaire	vous
entrée	salade de tomates	soupe à l'oignon
plat principal	bœuf	poulet
légume	bœuf	frites
fromage	chèvre	emmental
dessert	fruits	gâteau
boisson	vin rouge	eau

E

	votre partenaire	vous
entrée	pâté	salade de tomates
plat principal	saumon	bœuf
légume	épinards	haricots verts
fromage	camembert	brie
dessert	fruits	glace
boisson	eau minérale	eau minérale

F

	votre partenaire	vous
entrée	crudités	soupe de légumes
plat principal	truite	poulet
légume	riz	petits pois
fromage	camembert	emmental
dessert	tarte	pâtisserie
boisson	vin blanc	eau

G

	votre partenaire	vous
entrée	soupe de légumes	pâté
plat principal	porc	bœuf
légume	frites	épinards
fromage	emmental	brie
dessert	tarte	glace
boisson	vin rouge	eau minérale

H

	votre partenaire	vous
entrée	soupe à l'oignon	crudités
plat principal	saumon	porc
légume	haricots verts	riz
fromage	chèvre	camembert
dessert	pâtisserie	glace
boisson	vin blanc	vin rouge

I

	votre partenaire	vous
entrée	salade de tomates	crudités
plat principal	poulet	truite
légume	petits pois	haricots verts
fromage	chèvre	emmental
dessert	fruits	glace
boisson	vin rouge	vin blanc

J

	votre partenaire	vous
entrée	pâté	soupe de légumes
plat principal	bœuf	saumon
légume	riz	épinards
fromage	brie	camembert
dessert	pâtisserie	gâteau
boisson	eau	eau minérale

K

	votre partenaire	vous
entrée	crudités	soupe à l'oignon
plat principal	truite	porc
légume	riz	frites
fromage	chèvre	brie
dessert	gâteau	tarte
boisson	vin blanc	eau

L

	votre partenaire	vous
entrée	soupe à l'oignon	salade de tomates
plat principal	poulet	bœuf
légume	frites	petits pois
fromage	emmental	chèvre
dessert	gâteau	fruits
boisson	eau	vin rouge

M

	votre partenaire	vous
entrée	salade de tomates	pâté
plat principal	bœuf	saumon
légume	haricots verts	épinards
fromage	brie	camembert
dessert	glace	fruits
boisson	eau minérale	eau minérale

N

	votre partenaire	vous
entrée	soupe de légumes	crudités
plat principal	poulet	truite
légume	petits pois	riz
fromage	emmental	camembert
dessert	pâtisserie	tarte
boisson	eau	vin blanc

O

	votre partenaire	vous
entrée	pâté	soupe de légumes
plat principal	bœuf	porc
légume	épinards	frites
fromage	brie	emmental
dessert	glace	tarte
boisson	eau minérale	vin rouge

P

	votre partenaire	vous
entrée	crudités	soupe à l'oignon
plat principal	porc	saumon
légume	riz	haricots verts
fromage	camembert	chèvre
dessert	glace	pâtisserie
boisson	vin rouge	vin blanc

Nos achats. Interviewez votre partenaire pour trouver les renseignements qui manquent. Il y a trois paires de cartes. Le partenaire A1 travaille avec B1, A2 avec B2, etc.

MODÈLE: **Qu'est-ce qu'on achète à la gare?**
Où est-ce qu'on achète des fleurs?

B1

achat	endroit
	gare
	supermarché
légumes	
médicaments	
	supermarché
fromage	
	librairie
chapeau	
magazine	
	épicerie
	boutique
fleurs	
	pharmacie
savon	

B2

achat	endroit
coca	
	fleuriste
	pharmacie
livre	
légumes	
	bureau de tabac
magazine	
pastilles	
	boucherie
	boulangerie
pommes	
	bureau de tabac
cadeau	
	supermarché

achat	endroit
livres	
fruits	
	bureau de tabac
	pharmacie
cadeau	
	marché
saucisses	
	boulangerie
magazine	
	charcuterie
fleurs	
	boucherie
timbres	
	grand magasin

Chapitre 10 (p. 301)

All of the vehicles in this activity are feminine.

La formule 1. Interviewez votre partenaire pour trouver les renseignements qui manquent.

MODÈLE: **Quelle sorte de véhicule est-ce que mamie conduit?**
Comment conduit-elle?

B

nom	conduire	comment?	pourquoi comme ça?
Michael Schumacher	Ferrari	à toute vitesse	
Jacques Villeneuve			C'est un pilote professionnel canadien.
Alain Prost	Renault	très vite	
tonton *(oncle)* Paul		comme un fou	
tatie *(tante)* Agnès	Harley	tranquillement	
papi *(grand-père)*			Il ne peut pas changer de vitesse.
mamie *(grand-mère)*	mobylette		Elle a peur des accidents.
votre partenaire			
vous			

Chapitre 11 (p. 327)

Hier et quand j'avais 10 ans. Since all students use the same form, it has not been reproduced here. Use the form on p. 327.

Chapitre 12 (p. 358)

Savoir ou connaître? Since all students use the same form, it has not been reproduced here. Use the form on p. 358.

Chapitre 13 (p. 391)

Il manque quelque chose. Interviewez les autres étudiants pour trouver les choses qui manquent. Il y a sept cartes différentes en tout.

MODÈLE: **Est-ce que tu as un(e) … sur ta table?**
Moi, j'ai un(e) …, mais je n'ai pas de (d') …

Chapitre 14 (p. 425)

Qu'est-ce qu'il (elle) en pense? Interviewez votre partenaire pour trouver les renseignements qui manquent.

MODÈLE: **Quelle est la réaction de Catherine?**
Pourquoi est-elle triste?

B

	ce qui arrive	sa réaction
Catherine		Elle en est triste.
Éric	Une jolie femme veut le rencontrer.	
Alain	Il y a trop de publicité à la télé.	
Pauline		Elle en est fâchée.
Estelle	Sa sœur va avoir un bébé.	
Jacques		Il le regrette.
Christophe		Il en est confus.
Nathalie	Son amie se dispute avec elle.	
Véronique	Son petit ami lui achète une bague de fiançailles.	
Pierre		Il croit que c'est dommage.

Chapitre 15 (p. 452)

Vous êtes témoin d'un accident. Vous jouerez le rôle du gendarme. Interviewez votre partenaire qui joue le rôle du témoin d'un accident. Ensuite, complétez le formulaire suivant.

B (gendarme)

Nom du témoin: _____

Adresse du témoin: _____

Numéro de téléphone du témoin: _____

Observations (date, heure, lieu, conditions météorologiques, chaussée, véhicules, chauffeur(s), description de l'accident, cause de l'accident, autres ...):

Vocabulaire

This vocabulary list includes all of the words and phrases included in the ***Vocabulaire actif*** sections of ***Entre amis***, as well as the passive vocabulary used in the text. The definitions given are limited to the context in which the words are used in this book. Entries for active vocabulary are followed by the number of the chapter in which they are introduced for the first time. If a word is formally activated in more than one chapter, a reference is given for each chapter. Some entries are followed by specific examples from the text. Expressions are listed according to their key word. In subentries, the symbol ~ indicates the repetition of the key word.

Regular adjectives are given in the masculine form, with the feminine ending in parentheses. For irregular adjectives, the full feminine form is given in parentheses.

The gender of each noun is indicated after the noun. Irregular feminine and plural forms are also noted.

The following abbreviations are used:

CP	Chapitre préliminaire				
adj.	adjective	*f.*	feminine	*n.*	noun
adv.	adverb	*f.pl.*	feminine plural	*pl.*	plural
art.	article	*inv.*	invariable	*prep.*	preposition
conj.	conjunction	*m.*	masculine	*pron.*	pronoun
fam.	familiar	*m.pl.*	masculine plural	*v.*	verb

à at, in, to 1
~ bientôt see you soon 5
~ côté next door; to the side 5
~ côté de next to, beside 5
~ demain see you tomorrow 5
~ droite (de) to the right (of) 7
~ gauche (de) to the left (of) 7
~ ... heure (s) at ... o'clock 1
~ la prochaine until next time, be seeing you 5
~ la vôtre! (here's) to yours! 2
~ l'heure on time 7
~ l'intérieur de inside 6
~ midi at noon 5
~ minuit at midnight 5
~ tout à l'heure see you in a little while 5
~ toute vitesse at top speed 10
~ travers throughout 6
~ voix haute aloud 6
être ~ to belong to 6
abord: d'~ at first 5
abri: à l'abri sheltered; **sans ~** *m.* homeless person 15
absolument absolutely 10
accepter to accept 15
accident *m.* accident 15
accompagner to accompany 6
accord *m.* agreement
  d'~ okay 5
  être d'~ (avec) to agree (with) 1, 11
accordéon *m.* accordion 6
accueillant(e) friendly
achat *m.* purchase 9
acheter to buy 9
acteur/actrice *m./f.* actor/actress 1
activité *f.* activity 11
actuellement now 14; nowadays
addition *f.* (restaurant) bill, check 8; addition
adieu *m.* (*pl.* **adieux**) farewell
adjoint/adjointe au maire *m./f.* deputy mayor
adorer to adore; to love 2
adresse *f.* address 4
aéroport *m.* airport 5
affaires *f.pl.* business 4
  homme/femme d'~ *m./f.* businessman/woman 4
âge *m.* age 3
  quel ~ avez-vous? how old are you? 3
âgé (e) old 11
agent (de police) *m.* (police) officer
  ~ de change stockbroker

agglomération *f.* urban area
agir: il s'agit de it's (*lit.* it's a matter of)
agriculteur/agricultrice *farmer* 4
agrumes *m.pl.* citrus fruits
aider to help 4
aïe! ouch! 6
ail *m.* garlic 8
aimable kind; nice 9
aimer to like; to love 2
  s' ~ to love each other 14
ainsi thus, for that reason
air: avoir l'~ to seem; to appear, to look 9
aisé(e) well-off
album *m.* album 11
alcool *m.* alcohol
Allemagne *f.* Germany 5
allemand(e) German 1
aller to go 2, 5
  ~ en ville to go into town 5
  ~ -retour *m.* round-trip ticket 12
  ~ simple *m.* one-way (ticket) 12
  allez à la porte! go to the door! CP
  allez-y! go ahead; let's go 12
  je vais très bien I'm fine 2
allô! hello! (*on the phone*) 12
alors then, therefore, so 2
amant *m.* lover
amélioration *f.* improvement
améliorer to improve
amener to bring
américain(e) American 1
ami/amie *m./f.* friend 2
amour *m.* love
amusant(e) amusing, funny; fun 11
s'amuser to have fun; to have a good time 6
  je veux m'amuser I want to have fun 10
an *m.* year 3
  Jour de l'~ *m.* New Year's Day 7
ananas *m.* pineapple
anchois *m.* anchovy 8
ancien (ancienne) former; old 4
anglais (e) English 1
Angleterre *f.* England 5
année *f.* year 5
  ~ scolaire *f.* school year 10
anniversaire *m.* birthday 7
  ~ de mariage wedding anniversary 10
annonce *f.* advertisement 14
  petites annonces want ads
annuler to cancel
août *m.* August 7
apercevoir to notice
apéritif *m.* before-dinner drink 8
appareil *m.* appliance; phone 7
appartement *m.* apartment 3
s'appeler to be named, be called 13
  comment vous appelez-vous? what is your name? 1
  je m'appelle ... my name is ... 1

appétit *m.* appetite
  Bon ~! Have a good meal! 13
apporter to bring 8
apprendre to learn; to teach 8
après after 5
après-demain day after tomorrow 12
après-midi *m.* afternoon 2
  de l'~ in the afternoon 5
  Bon ~. Have a good afternoon.
arabe *m.* Arabic 5; Arab
arbre *m.* tree
argent *m.* money 9
armée *f.* army
arrêt (d'autobus) *m.* (bus) stop 10
(s')arrêter to stop 10
arrière- great- 3
arriver to arrive 7
  qu'est-ce qui est arrivé? what happened? 14
art *m.* art 5
artiste *m./f.* artist 4
aspirine *f.* aspirin 9
s'asseoir to sit down 13
  Asseyez-vous! Sit down! CP
assez sort of, rather, enough 1
  ~ bien fairly well 2
  ~ mal rather poorly 2
  en avoir ~ to be fed up 11
assiette *f.* plate 8
assister (à) to attend 14
assurance *f.* insurance
assurer to assure; to insure 15
atout *m.* asset
attacher to attach; to put on 10
atteindre to attain
attendre to wait (for) 9
attente *f.* expectation
attentif (attentive) attentive 10
attention: faire ~ to pay attention 4
au contraire on the contrary 4
au moins at least 5
au pair au pair
  jeune fille ~ *f.* nanny 4
au: au plaisir (de vous revoir) (*I hope to*) see you again 5
  ~ revoir good-bye 1
  ~ sein de within
aucun(e) no
aujourd'hui today 4
aussi also, too 1; as 11
  ~ ... que as ... as ... 11
autant (de) as much 11
autocar *m.* tour bus 12
automne *m.* fall 7
automobiliste *m./f.* driver 15
autoroute *f.* turnpike; throughway, highway 12
autour de around 5
autre other 3

avance *f.* advance
  en ~ early 7
avancer to advance 10
avant before 5
avare miserly, stingy 4
avec with 2
avenir *m.* future
avertissement *m.* warning 14
avion *m.* airplane 7
avis *m.* opinion, advice
  à mon (à ton, etc.) ~ in my (your, etc.) opinion 11
avoir to have 3
  ~ besoin de to need 9
  ~ chaud to be hot 8
  ~ envie de to want to; to feel like 5
  ~ faim to be hungry 8
  ~ froid to be cold 8
  ~ l'air to seem, to appear, to look 9
  ~ lieu to take place 11
  ~ l'intention de to plan to 5
  ~ mal (à) to be sore, to have a pain (in) 9
  ~ peur to be afraid 8
  ~ pitié (de) to have pity (on), to feel sorry (for) 10
  ~ raison to be right 8
  ~ rendez-vous to have an appointment, meeting 4
  ~ soif to be thirsty 8
  ~ sommeil to be sleepy 8
  ~ tendance à to tend to 12
  ~ tort to be wrong; to be unwise 8
  en ~ assez to be fed up 11
  qu'est-ce que tu as? what's the matter with you? 9
avril *m.* April 7

bagages *m.pl.* luggage 7
bague *f.* ring 14
bain: salle de ~ bathroom 3
balayer to sweep
balbutier to stammer
bancaire: carte bancaire *f.* credit / debit card 9
bande dessinée *f.* comic strip 6
banlieue *f.* suburbs
banque *f.* bank 5
barquette *f.* small box; mini crate 9
bas *m.pl.* pantyhose 4
basket-ball (basket) *m.* basketball 6
baskets *f.pl.* high-top sneakers 4
bâtiment *m.* building 5
batterie *f.* drums 6
bavard(e) talkative 4
beau/bel/belle/beaux/belles handsome, beautiful 1
  il fait ~ it's nice out CP, 7
beau-frère *m.* brother-in-law 3

beau-père *m.* (*pl.* **beaux-pères**) stepfather (or father-in-law) 3

beaucoup a lot 2; much, many

beaujolais *m.* Beaujolais (*wine*) 8

beaux-parents *m.pl.* stepparents (or in-laws) 3

bébé *m.* baby 7

beige beige 4

belge Belgian 1

Belgique *f.* Belgium 5

belle-mère *f.* (*pl.* **belles-mères**) stepmother (or mother-in-law) 3

belle-sœur *f.* sister-in-law 3

bénévolat *m.* volunteerism

bénévole *m./f.* volunteer

berk! yuck! awful! 8

besoin *m.* need

    avoir ~ de to need 9

beurre *m.* butter 8

    ~ de cacahuète *m.* peanut butter 8

bibliothèque *f.* library 5

bien *m.* good 6

bien *adv.* well; fine 2

    ~ de many

    ~ que although

    ~ sûr of course 8

bientôt soon

    À bientôt. See you soon. 5

Bienvenue! Welcome! 3

bière *f.* beer 2

billet *m.* bill (*paper money*) 9; ticket 12

bise *f.* kiss 5

bistro *m.* bar and café; bistro 5

bizarre weird; funny looking 4

blague *f.* joke

    sans ~! no kidding! 14

blanc (blanche) white 4

blessé(e) wounded 15

bleu(e) blue 4

bleuet *m.* blueberry (*French-Canadian*) blond(e) blond 4

blouson *m.* windbreaker, jacket 4

bœuf *m.* beef 8

boire to drink 8

    voulez-vous ~ quelque chose? do you want to drink something? 2

boisson *f.* drink, beverage 2

boîte *f.* box, can 8; nightclub

bol *m.* bowl 13

bon (bonne) good 2

    bon après-midi good afternoon 5

    bon marché *adj. inv.* inexpensive 4

    bonne journée have a good day 1

    bonne nuit pleasant dreams 5

bonbon *m.* candy 8

bonjour hello 1

bonnet de nuit *m.* party pooper

bonsoir good evening 2

bordeaux *m.* Bordeaux (*wine*) 8

bottes *f.pl.* boots 4

boubou *m.* traditional dress for women in Senegal

bouche *f.* mouth 9

bouchée *f.* mouthful

boucherie *f.* butcher shop 9

boulangerie *f.* bakery 5

bouquet *m.* bouquet 9

bout *m.* end, goal

bouteille *f.* bottle 8

boutique *f.* (gift, clothing) shop 9

braquer to steer

bras *m.* arm 9

bridge *m.* bridge (*game*) 6

brie *m.* Brie (*cheese*) 8

brocoli *m.* broccoli 8

brosse *f.* brush

    ~ à cheveux *f.* hairbrush 13

    ~ à dents *f.* toothbrush 13

se brosser (les dents) to brush (one's teeth) 13

bruit *m.* noise 9

brûler to burn; to run through (light) 15

brun(e) brown(-haired) 4

bulle *f.* bubble

bureau *m.* (*pl.* **bureaux**) desk; office 3

    ~ de poste *m.* post office 5

    ~ de tabac *m.* tobacco shop 5

but *m.* goal

ça (cela) that 4

    ~ dépend It depends 9

    ~ m'est égal It's all the same to me

    ~ ne vous concerne pas That's no concern of yours

    ~ va? How's it going? 2

    ~ va bien (I'm) fine 2

    ~ veut dire ... it means ... CP

cachet (d'aspirine) *m.* (aspirin) tablet 9

cadeau *m.* gift 9

cadre *m.* executive 4

café *m.* coffee 2; café 5

    ~ crème *m.* coffee with cream 2

cafétéria *f.* cafeteria 5

calculatrice *f.* calculator 3

calme calm 4

camarade de chambre *m./f.* roommate 3

camembert *m.* Camembert (*cheese*) 8

campagne *f.* country(side); campaign

campus *m.* campus 5

Canada *m.* Canada 5

canadien(ne) Canadian 1

canicule *f.* heat wave

car because

carte *f.* map 12; menu 13

    ~ bancaire *f.* credit / debit card 9

    ~ de crédit *f.* credit card

    ~ postale *f.* postcard

cartes *f.pl.* cards (*game*) 6

cas: en tout ~ in any case

cassis *m.* blackcurrant

ce/cet/cette/ces this, that, these, those 4

ce sont they are, there are 3

ceinture *f.* belt 4

    ~ de sécurité *f.* safety belt, seat belt 10

cela (ça) that 9

célèbre famous 14

célibataire single, unmarried 1

celle *f.* this (that) one

celles *f.pl.* these; those

celui *m.* this (that) one

cendre *f.* ash 8

cent one hundred 3

centime *m.* centime (*1/100 of a euro*) 3

centre commercial *m.* shopping center, mall 5

cependant however

céréales *f.pl.* cereal; grains 8

certainement surely, of course 1

c'est it is, this is 1

    c'est-à-dire that is to say

    ~ gentil à vous that's nice of you 2

    ~ pour vous it's for you 1

ceux *m.pl.* these; those

CFA (=Communauté financière africaine) African Financial Community

chacun(e) each

chagrin *m.* sorrow

chaîne (de télé) *f.* (TV) channel 14

chaise *f.* chair 3

chaleur *f.* heat

chaleureusement warmly 4

chambre *f.* bedroom 3; room

    camarade de ~ *m./f.* roommate 3

champignons *m.pl.* mushrooms 8

chance *f.* luck 12

    Bonne ~! Good luck! 12

changer (de) to change 10

chanson *f.* song 2

chanter to sing 2

chanteur/chanteuse *m./f.* singer 11

chapeau *m.* (*pl.* **chapeaux**) hat 4

chaque each, every 6

charcuterie *f.* pork butcher's; delicatessen 9

charmant(e) charming 3

chat *m.* cat 3

château *m.* castle 5

chaud(e) hot 2

    avoir ~ to be hot 8

    il fait ~ it's hot (warm) CP, 4, 7

chauffage *m.* heat 13

chauffard *m.* bad driver 15

chauffeur *m.* driver 10

chaussée *f.* pavement 15

chaussette *f.* sock 4

chaussure *f.* shoe 4

chauve bald 4

chef *m.* head (*person in charge*); boss; chef

chemise *f.* shirt 4

chemisier *m.* blouse 4

chèque *m.* check 9
~ **de voyage** *m.* traveler's check 9
cher (chère) dear 2; expensive 4
chercher to look for 2
chéri(e) *m./f.* dear, honey 10
cheveux *m.pl.* hair 4
chèvre *m.* goat cheese 8
chewing-gum *m.* chewing gum 9
chez at the home of 3
~ **moi** at my house 3
~ **nous** at our house; back home 3
~ **vous** at your house 3
chic *adj. inv.* chic; stylish 4
chien *m.* dog 3
chiffre *m.* number
chimie *f.* chemistry 5
Chine *f.* China 5
chinois(e) Chinese 1
chocolat chaud *m.* hot chocolate 2
choisir to choose 12
choix *m.* choice 8
chose *f.* thing 4
pas grand-~ not much 5
quelque ~ *m.* something 2
chouette great *(fam.)* 14
chut! shh! 10
chute *f.* fall
cigare *m.* cigar 6
cimetière *m.* cemetery
cinéma *m.* movie theater 5
cinq five CP
cinquante fifty 3
circulation *f.* traffic 15
citron pressé *m.* lemonade 2
classe *f.* class
en ~ in class; to class 4
clé *f.* key 12
client/cliente *m./f.* customer 8
climatisation *f.* air conditioning 13
cliquer (sur) click on
coca *m.* Coca-Cola 2
code postal *m.* zip code 9
coin *m.* corner
coincé uptight
collant *m.pl.* tights 4
collège *m.* Jr. high school
combien (de) how many, how much 3
commander to order 8
comme like, as 2; how; since
~ **ci, ~ ça** so-so 2
~ **il (elle) était ...!** how ... he (she) was! 11
~ **si ...** as if ...
commencer to begin 7
commencez! begin! CP
comment how; what 3
~**?** what (did you say?) CP, 2
~ **allez-vous?** how are you? 2
~ **ça va?** how is it going? 2
~ **dit-on ...?** how do you say ...? CP

~ **est (sont) ...?** what is (are) ... like? 4
~ **est-ce qu'on écrit ...?** how do you spell ...? 2
~ **je vais faire?** what am I going to do? 12
~ **trouvez-vous ...?** what do you think of ...? 2
~ **vous appelez-vous?** what is your name? 1
commentaire *m.* commentary 10
commerce *m.* business 5
communication *f.* communication
complet (complète) full; complete 12
comportant consisting of
composter (un billet) to punch (a ticket) 12
compréhensif/compréhensive understanding 4
comprendre to understand; to include 8
je ne comprends pas I don't understand CP
compris(e) included; understood 8
je n'ai pas compris I didn't understand 3
comptabiliser to count
comptabilité *f.* accounting 5
compter to count
condamner: être condamné(e) to be sentenced
conducteur/conductrice driver 15
conduire to drive 10
conduite *f.* driving 10
confirmer to confirm 12
confiture *f.* jam 8
confortable comfortable 4
confus(e) ashamed; embarrassed 14
congé *m.* leave, holiday
connaissance *f.* consciousness
connaître to know; to be acquainted with, to be familiar with 10
conseil *m.* (piece of) advice 10
se consoler to console oneself 14
constamment constantly 10
constant(e) constant 10
content(e) happy 4
continuer to continue
continuez continue CP
contraire *m.* contrary, opposite
au ~ on the contrary 4, 8
contravention *f.* traffic ticket
contre against; in exchange for 15
par ~ on the other hand
corps *m.* body 9
costume *m.* suit
côté *m.* side
à ~ next door; to the side 5
à ~ de next to, beside 5
se coucher to go to bed 6
couci-couça so-so
coude *m.* elbow
couleur *f.* color 4
de quelle ~ est (sont) ...? what color is (are) ...? 4
couloir *m.* hall; corridor 5
coup *m.* :~ d'envoi kick-off
couper to cut 13

couple *m.* couple 14
cour *f.* court
couramment fluently
coureur/coureuse runner; cyclist
courir to run
courriel *m.* email (*Can.*)
cours *m.* course; class 5
course *f.* race
courses *f.pl.* errands, shopping 4
court-métrage *m.* film short
cousin/cousine *m./f.* cousin 3
couteau *m.* (*pl.* **couteaux**) knife 13
coûter to cost 9
coutume *f.* custom
couvrir to cover
craie *f.* chalk CP
cravate *f.* tie 4
crèche *f.* daycare center
crème *f.* cream 2
crêpe *f.* crepe; French pancake 8
croire to believe, to think 14
je crois que oui I think so 14
je ne crois pas I don't think so 14
croissance *f.* increase, growth
croissant *m.* croissant 8
croque-monsieur *m.* grilled ham and cheese sandwich 8
croûte *f.* crust
crudités *f.pl.* raw vegetables 8
cuiller *f.* spoon 13
cuisine *f.* cooking; food 4; kitchen 3
cuisinière *f.* stove 3

d'abord at first 5
d'accord okay 5
être ~ (avec) to agree (with) 5
dame *f.* lady 13
dames *f.pl.* checkers 6
dangereux (dangereuse) dangerous 11
dans in 2
~ **une heure** one hour from now 5
danser to dance 2
d'après according to
davantage additional, more
de (d') from, of 1
de même you too 1
de rien you're welcome 12
décalage horaire *m.* time difference 5
décembre *m.* December 7
décider to decide
décombres *m.pl.* ruins
découvrir to discover
décrire to describe 6
déçu(e) disappointed 9
dégâts *m.pl.* damage(s) 15
dégustation *f.* tasting
dehors outside
déjà already 6

déjeuner *m.* lunch 8
  petit ~ breakfast 8
déjeuner *v.* to have lunch 5
délicieux (délicieuse) delicious 8
demain tomorrow 5
  à ~ see you tomorrow 5
  après-~ day after tomorrow 12
demande *f.* request 12
  faire une ~ to make a request 12
demander to ask 6
démarrer to start 10
demi(e) half
  et ~ half past (the hour) 5
demi- (frère, sœur) step (brother, sister) 3
demi-heure *f.* half hour 7
démontrer to demonstrate
dent *f.* tooth 9
dentifrice *m.* toothpaste 9
départ *m.* departure 12
départementale *f.* departmental (local) highway 12
dépasser to pass
se dépêcher to hurry 13
dépendre to depend 9
  ça dépend (de ...) it (that) depends (on ...) 9
déprimé(e) depressed 9
depuis for 6; since 9
déranger to bother 1
  Excusez-moi de vous ~ Excuse me for bothering you 1
déraper to skid 15
dernier (dernière) last 6
  la dernière fois the last time 6
derrière behind 5
  juste ~ right behind 15
détruire to destroy 15
des some; any 3; of the
désagréable disagreeable 4
désastre naturel *m.* natural disaster 15
descendre to go down, get out of 7
désirer to want 2
désolé(e) sorry 9
dessert *m.* dessert 8
dessin animé *m.* cartoon 11
se détendre to relax 9
détester to hate, to detest 2
détruire to destroy 15
dette *f.* debt 15
deux two CP, 1
  tous (toutes) les ~ both 12
devant in front of 5
développer to develop 15
devenir to become 7
deviner to guess
devoir *m.* obligation
  devoirs *m.pl*. homework 4
devoir *v.* must, to have to, to probably be, to be supposed to; to owe 5
d'habitude usually 4

Dieu *m.* God
  Mon Dieu! My goodness! 2
dimanche *m.* Sunday 5
dîner *m.* dinner 4
dîner *v.* to eat dinner 4
diplôme *m.* diploma 12
dire to say; to tell 14
  ... veut ~ ... ... means ... 6
  vous dites you say 3
discret (discrète) discreet, reserved 4
se disputer to argue 14
dissertation *f.* (term) paper 6
divorce *m.* divorce 14
divorcé(e) divorced 1
divorcer to get a divorce 14
dix ten CP
dix-huit eighteen CP
dix-neuf nineteen CP
dix-sept seventeen CP
doigt *m.* finger
dollar *m.* dollar 9
DOM (=Département d'outre-mer) overseas department *(equivalent of a state)*
dommage *m.* pity, shame
  c'est ~ that's (it's) too bad 14
donc then; therefore
donner to give 4
  donnez-moi ... give me ... CP
dont about/of which (whom); whose 14
dormir to sleep 6
dos *m.* back 9
d'où: vous êtes ~? where are you from? 2
douche *f.* shower 12
  prendre une douche to shower
doute *m.* doubt
  sans ~ probably 3
doux (douce) mild
douzaine *f.* dozen
douze twelve CP
droit *m.* right *(entitlement)* **droit(e)** *adj.* right
  à droite (de) to the right (of) 5
  droits de l'homme human rights
  tout droit straight ahead 5
drôle funny 14
durcir to harden
durée *f.* duration; length

eau *f.* (*pl.* **eaux**) water 2
  ~ minérale mineral water 2
échanger (contre) to trade (for) 15
échapper to escape
échecs *m.pl.* chess 6
éclater to burst
école *f.* school 5
écouter to listen (to) 2
  écoutez! listen! CP
écrire to write 6

comment est-ce qu'on écrit...? how do you spell ... ? 2
  écrivez votre nom! write your name! CP
  ... s'écrit ... ... is spelled ... 2
écrivain *m.* writer 4
efficacité *f.* efficiency
égal(e) (*m.pl.* **égaux**) equal
  cela (ça) m'est ~ I don't care 5
église *f.* church 5
égratignure *f.* scratch
Eh bien ... Well then ...
élève *m./f.* pupil 4
élire to elect
elle she, it 1; her 6
elles they 1; them 6
s'éloigner to move away
e-mail *m.* email 4
s'embrasser to kiss 4, 14
émission (de télé) *f.* (TV) show 14
  ~ de téléréalité reality TV show 14
emmental *m.* Swiss cheese 8
emploi du temps *m.* schedule 5
employé/employée *m./f.* employee 4
emprunter to borrow 14
en *prep.* in 1; by, through
  ~ avance early 7
  ~ effet in fact
  ~ fouillant scouring
  ~ première (seconde) in first (second) class 12
  ~ provenance de coming from
  ~ retard late 7
  ~ tout cas in any case
  ~ voiture by car 7
en *pron.* some, of it (them); about it (them) 14
  je vous ~ prie don't mention it; you're welcome; please do 7
  vous n'~ avez pas? don't you have any? 9
enchanté(e) delighted (to meet you) 1
encore again CP; still, more 3
  ~ à boire (manger)? more to drink (eat)? 8
  ~ de ...? more ...? 8
  pas ~ not yet 2
s'endormir to fall asleep 13
endroit *m.* place 5
enfant *m./f.* child 3
enfin finally 5
s'engager to become involved
ennuyeux (ennuyeuse) boring 4
enquête *f.* quest
enseigne *f.* sign
enseigner to teach 2
ensemble together CP, 2
ensoleillé(e) sunny
ensuite next, then 5
entendre to hear 9
  s'~ (avec) to get along (with) 14
  ~ parler de to hear about 15
  entendu agreed; understood 12

entourer to surround
entraîner to lead to
entre between, among 5
~ amis between (among) friends 1
entrée f. first course, starter 8
entreprise f. business
entrer to enter 7
  ~ en collision to hit, collide 15
  entrez! come in! CP
envie: avoir ~ de to want to; to feel like 5
environ approximately 9
envoyer to send 6
épaule f. shoulder 9
épeler to spell 12
épicerie f. grocery store 5
épidémie f. epidemic 15
épinards m.pl. spinach 8
époque f. time, period 11
  à cette ~ at that time; back then 11
épouser to marry 11
équilibré(e) stable
équipe f. team 11
escale f. stop(over)
escargot m. snail 10
esclave m./f. slave
Espagne f. Spain 5
espagnol(e) Spanish 1
espérance de vie f. life expectancy
espérer to hope 8
essayer to try
essentiel: il est ~ que it is essential that 13
est m. east
est-ce que (question marker) 2
estimer to estimate 15
estomac m. stomach 9
et and 1
étage m. floor 12
étape f. stage
état m. state 5
  ~ civil marital status 1
États-Unis m.pl. United States 5
été m. summer 7
éternuer to sneeze
étoile f. star
étranger/étrangère m./f. foreigner
étranger (étrangère) foreign 12
étroit(e) narrow; close
études f.pl. studies 15
étudiant(e) m./f. student 3
étudier to study 2
être to be 1
  ~ à to belong to 6
  ~ d'accord (avec) to agree (with) 5
  ~ en train de to be in the process of 11
  ~ originaire de to be a native of 7
  vous êtes d'où? where are you from? 2
étroit(e) close
Europe f. Europe
eux m.pl. pron. they, them 6

évacuer to evacuate 15
exact(e) exact, correct
  c'est ~ that's right 13
exagérer to exaggerate 2
examen m. test, exam 6
  à un ~ on an exam 6
excellent(e) excellent 2
excuser to excuse
  excusez-moi excuse me 1
  excusez-moi (-nous, etc.) d'être en
    retard excuse me (us, etc.) for being
    late 13
exemple m. example
  par ~ for example 6
exercice m. exercise 6
exiger (que) to demand (that) 13
expédier to send
exprimer to express
extraverti(e) outgoing 4

fâché(e) angry 14
se fâcher to get angry 14
facile easy 9
façon f. way, manner 8
  sans ~ honestly, no kidding 8
façonner to shape
faculté f. : ~ des lettres College of
  Liberal Arts
faim f. hunger
  avoir ~ to be hungry 8
faire to do, to make 4
  ~ attention to pay attention 4
  ~ du pouce to hitchhike (French-Canadian)
  ~ du sport to play sports 6
  ~ la cuisine to cook 4
  ~ la lessive to do laundry 4
  ~ la sieste to take a nap 4
  ~ des provisions to do the grocery
    shopping 4
  ~ un voyage to take a trip 5
  ~ une demande to make a request 12
  ~ une promenade to take a walk; to take
    a ride 4
  il fait chaud it's hot out CP, 4, 7
  se ~ des amis to make friends 14
fait m. fact
  au ~ ... by the way ... 2
falloir (il faut) to be necessary 4, 10
famille f. family 3
fatigué(e) tired 2
faut: il ~ ... it is necessary ... 4
  il ~ que it is necessary that, (someone)
    must 13
  il ne ~ pas que (someone) must not 13
faute f. fault; mistake 15
fauteuil m. armchair 3
faux (fausse) false; wrong 2
femme f. woman 1; wife 3
  ~ au foyer housewife 4

  ~ d'affaires businesswoman 4
  ~ politique (female) politician 4
fermé(e) closed 6
fermer to close 6
  fermez le livre! close the book! CP
  fermez la porte! close the door! CP
fermier/fermière m./f. farmer 4
fête f. holiday; party 7
feu m. (pl. feux) traffic light 10; fire
feuille f. leaf/sheet (of paper) 9
feuilleton m. soap opera; series 14
février m. February 7
fiançailles f.pl. engagement 14
fiancé(e) engaged 1
fier (fière) proud
fièvre f. fever 9
filière f. field of study
fille f. girl 3; daughter 3
film m. film, movie 5
fils m. son 3
fin f. end
finir to finish 12
flamand m. Flemish 5
fleur f. flower 9
fleuriste m./f. florist 9
fleuve m. river
flûte f. flute 6
  ~! darn!; shucks! 12
fois f. one time 4, 6; times, multiplied by
  à la ~ at the same time
  deux ~ twice
  la dernière ~ the last time 6
follement in a crazy manner 10
fonctionnaire m./f. civil servant 4
football (foot) m. soccer 6
  ~ américain m. football 6
forêt f. forest 15
formation f. training
formidable great, fantastic 14
fort adv. loudly, with strength 15
fossé m. ditch
fou/folle m./f. fool; crazy person 10
fou (folle) (m.pl. fous) crazy 10
foulard m. scarf 4
fourchette f. fork 13
foyer: femme au foyer f. housewife 4
frais: il fait ~ it's cool 7
fraise f. strawberry 8
franc m. franc 9
français(e) French 1
  à la française in the French style 13
  en français in French CP
France f. France 5
francophone French-speaking
frapper to knock
  Frappez à la porte! Knock on the door! CP
freiner to brake 15
fréquenter (quelqu'un) to date (someone) 11
frère m. brother 3

frire to fry
frites *f.pl.* French fries 8
  steak-~ *m.* steak with French fries 15
froid(e) cold 2
  avoir ~ to be cold 8
  il fait ~ it's cold CP, 7
fromage *m.* cheese 5
frontière *f.* border
fruit *m.* a piece of fruit 8
fumer to smoke 6
fumeur/fumeuse *m./f.* smoker
  non-~ nonsmoker
fumeur *m.* smoking 12
  non ~ nonsmoking 12
fumeur/fumeuse *adj.* smoking 12

gagner to win; to earn
  ~ (au loto) to win (the lottery) 12
gant *m.* glove 4
garage *m.* garage 3
garçon *m.* boy 3
garder to keep; to look after 4
gare *f.* (train) station 3
gâteau *m.* (*pl.* **gâteaux**) cake 8
  petit ~ cookie
gauche *adj.* left
  à ~ (de) to the left (of) 5
gendarme *m.* (state) policeman 15
général: en ~ in general 2
généralement generally 4
généreux (généreuse) generous
genou *m.* knee 9
  genoux *m.pl.* lap, knees 13
gens *m.pl.* people 4
gentil (gentille) nice 3
  c'est ~ à vous that's nice of you 2
gestion *f.* management 5
glace *f.* ice cream 8
glissant(e) slippery 15
golf *m.* golf 6
gorge *f.* throat 9
goudron *m.* tar
goût *m.* taste
goûter to taste 13; *m.* afternoon snack
grand(e) big, tall 1
  ~ magasin *m.* department store 9
  pas grand-chose not much 5
grand-mère *f.* (*pl.* **grands-mères**) grandmother 3
grand-père *m.* (*pl.* **grands-pères**) grandfather 3
grands-parents *m.pl.* grandparents 3
grapiller (les pages) to turn down (the pages)
gras (grasse) fat
  faire la grasse matinée to sleep in, to sleep late
gratuit(e) free
grippe *f.* flu 6
gris(e) grey 4

grisant(e) intoxicating
gros (grosse) fat; large 1
grossir to put on weight 12
guerre *f.* war 7
  en temps de ~ in wartime
guitare *f.* guitar 6
gymnase *m.* gymnasium 5
gymnastique *f.* gymnastics 5

An asterisk indicates that no liaison or élision is made at the beginning of the word.
habile skilful
s'habiller to get dressed 13
habiter to live; to reside 2
  où habitez-vous? where do you live? 1
habitude *f.* habit
  avoir l'~ de to be used to 5
  d'~ usually 4
*****hammam** *m.* steamroom
*****haricots verts** *m.pl.* green beans 8
*****hasard** *m.* chance, luck
  par ~ by chance 15
heurter to hit 15
heure *f.* hour CP, 1; (clock) time 5
  à l'~ on time 7
  dans une ~ one hour from now 5
  il est ... heure(s) it is ... o'clock CP, 5
  tout à l'~ in a little while 5; a little while ago 6
heureusement fortunately 6
heureux (heureuse) happy 4
*****heurter** to hit, run into 15
hier yesterday 4
histoire *f.* history 4; story 14
  quelle ~! what a story! 14
hiver *m.* winter 7
*****hockey** *m.* hockey 6
homme *m.* man 1
  ~ d'affaires businessman 4
  ~ politique politician 4
horaire *m.* timetable 12
*****hors** except; out of
*****hors-d'œuvre** *m. inv.* appetizer 8
hôtel *m.* hotel 1
hôtesse de l'air *f.* (female) flight attendant 11
huile (d'olive) *f.* (olive) oil
*****huit** eight CP
hypermarché *m.* giant supermarket 9

ici here 4
  par ~ this way, follow me 13
idiot/idiote *m./f.* idiot 15
ignorer to not know
il he, it 1
il y a there is (are) 3
  il n'y a pas de quoi you're welcome 13
  il n'y en a plus there is (are) no more 12

  ~ ... jours ... days ago 6
  qu'est-ce qu'~ ? what's the matter? 3
île *f.* island
ils they 1
imbécile *m./f.* imbecile 15
immeuble *m.* building
impair: nombre ~ *m.* odd number
impatience *f.* impatience 9
impatient(e) impatient 4
imperméable *m.* raincoat 4
important(e) important
  il est ~ que it is important that 13
imprescriptible inalienable
incendie *m.* fire 15
incroyable *adj.* unbelievable, incredible 14
indications *f.pl.* directions 10
indiquer to tell; to indicate; to point out 12
indispensable indispensable, essential
  il est ~ que it is essential that 13
infirmier/infirmière *m./f.* nurse 4
informations *f.pl.* news 14
informatique *f.* computer science 5
informaticien/informaticienne *m./f.* programmer 4
ingénieur *m.* engineer 4
inondation *f.* flood 15
s'inquiéter to worry 13
insister to insist
  je n'insiste pas I won't insist 8
  si vous insistez if you insist 8
s'installer to move (into)
instrument *m.* instrument 6
intelligent(e) intelligent 4
intellectuel (intellectuelle) intellectual 4
intention: avoir l' ~ de to plan to 5
interdiction *f.* ban
interdit(e) forbidden
  sens ~ *m.* one-way street 10
intéressant(e) interesting 4
s'intéresser à to be interested in 14
intérêt *m.* interest 9
intérieur *m.* inside
  à l'~ de inside of 6
internaute *m./f.* net surfer
interprète *m./f.* interpreter 4
intolérant(e) intolerant 4
inutile useless 12
inviter to invite 10
Irak *m.* Iraq 5
Irlande *f.* Ireland 5
Israël *m.* Israel 5
Italie *f.* Italy 5
italien(ne) Italian 1
ivre drunk 15

jaillir to burst forth
jamais ever, never
  ne ... ~ never 4

jambe *f.* leg 9
jambon *m.* ham 8
janvier *m.* January 7
Japon *m.* Japan 5
japonais(e) *adj.* Japanese 1
jardin *m.* garden
jaune yellow 4
je I 1
jean *m.* jeans 4
se jeter to throw oneself
jeu *m.* (*pl.* **jeux**) game 6
jeudi *m.* Thursday 5
jeune young 1
jogging *m.* jogging 2
joli(e) pretty 1
jouer to play 2
   à quoi jouez-vous? what (game) do
    you play? 6
   de quoi jouez-vous? what (instrument)
    do you play? 6
jour *m.* day 2
   ~ de l'An New Year's Day 7
   quinze jours two weeks 11
journal *m.* newspaper 6
journée *f.* day
   bonne ~! have a nice day! 1
juillet *m.* July 7
juin *m.* June 7
jupe *f.* skirt 4
jurer to swear
   je te le jure I swear (to you) 14
jus *m.* juice
   ~ d'orange orange juice 2
jusqu'à *prep.* until 10
   jusqu'au bout right up till the end
juste *adv.* just; right
   ~ derrière moi right behind me 15

kilo *m.* kilogram 8
kiosque (à journaux) *m.* newsstand 9
kir *m.* kir 2

la (*see* **le**)
là there 4
laïcité *f.* separation of church and state
laid(e) ugly 1
laisser to leave; to let 10
   laisse-moi (laissez-moi) tranquille! leave me
    alone! 10
lait *m.* milk 2
lamelle *f.* strip
lancer to launch
langue *f.* language 5
laquelle (*see* **lequel**)
las (lasse) tired
lave-linge *m.* washing machine 3
lave-vaisselle *m.* dishwasher 3

laver to wash 13
   se ~ to get washed; to wash up 13
le/la/l'/les *art.* the 2; *pron.* him, her, it, them 8
leçon *f.* lesson 10
léger (légère) *adj.* light
légume *m.* vegetable 8
lent(e) slow 10
lentement slowly 10
lequel/laquelle/lesquels/lesquelles which?
   which one(s)? 14
les (*see* **le**)
lesquel(le)s (*see* **lequel**)
lessive *f.* wash; laundry 4
lettre *f.* letter 6
leur *pron.* (to) them 14
leur(s) *adj.* their 3
lever to lift; to raise 13
   se ~ to get up; to stand up 6
   Levez-vous! Get up! CP
librairie *f.* bookstore 5
libre free 5; vacant
lien *m.* tie; bond
lieu *m.* (*pl.* **lieux**) place 5
   avoir ~ to take place 11
limonade *f.* lemon-lime soda 2
lire to read 6
   lisez! read! CP
lit *m.* bed 3
litre *m.* liter 9
littérature *f.* literature 5
livre *f.* pound 9
livre *m.* book CP, 3
logement *m.* housing
   logement social low-income housing
loi *f.* law
loin (de) far (from) 5
loisir *m.* leisure activity
long (longue) long 9
longtemps a long time 6
louer to rent 12
lui he, him 6; (to) him; (to) her 14
lumière *f.* light
lundi *m.* Monday 5
lunettes *f.pl.* eyeglasses 4
lycée *m.* high school

ma (*see* **mon**)
machine à laver *f.* washing machine
Madame (Mme) Mrs., ma'am 1
Mademoiselle (Mlle) Miss 1
magasin *m.* store 4
   grand ~ department store 9
magazine *m.* magazine 6
Maghreb *m.* the three North African countries of
   Algeria, Morocco, and Tunisia
mai *m.* May 7
maigrir to lose weight 12
maillot de bain *m.* bathing suit 13

main *f.* hand 9
maintenant now 5
maire *m.* mayor 11
   adjoint/adjointe au ~ deputy mayor
mairie *f.* town (city) hall 11
mais but 2
maison *f.* house 3
maîtriser to master
majoritaire of age
mal *m.* harm; pain; evil
   avoir ~ (à) to be sore, to have a pain (in) 9
   pas ~ not bad 2
mal *adv.* poorly 2; badly
malade sick 2
maladie *f.* illness, disease
maladroit(e) clumsy 15
malgré in spite of
manger to eat 2
manque *m.* lack
manquer to miss
manteau *m.* (*pl.* **manteaux**) coat 4
marchand/marchande *m./f.* merchant 9
marché *m.* (open-air) market 9
   ~ aux puces flea market 9
mardi *m.* Tuesday 5
mari *m.* husband 3
mariage *m.* marriage; wedding 11
marié(e) married 1
se marier (avec) to marry 14
marine *f.* navy
Maroc *m.* Morocco 5
marocain(e) *adj.* Moroccan 1
marque *f.* make, brand 15
marée *f.* tide
marron *adj. inv.* brown 4
mars *m.* March 7
mas *m.* traditional house from Provence
match *m.* game 10
matin *m.* morning 2
matinée: faire la grasse ~ to sleep in late
mauvais(e) bad 4; horrible 8
   il fait ~ the weather is bad 7
mayonnaise *f.* mayonnaise 8
me me 10; (to) me 14
méchant(e) nasty; mean 4
méchoui *m.* roast lamb *(North-African specialty)*
médecin *m.* doctor 4
médiatisation *f.* media coverage
médicament *m.* medicine 9
se méfier de to watch out for
meilleur(e) better 11
   Avec mon ~ souvenir With my best regards 4
   le/la ~ the best 11
   ~ ami(e) *m./f.* best friend 1
membre *m.* member 3
même even 14; same
   de ~ you too 1
   -~(s) -self (-selves) 2
ménage *m.* housework 4

ménagère *f.* housewife 4
menu *m.* (fixed price) menu 13
merci thank you 1; (no) thanks 2
  non, ~ no, thank you 2
mercredi *m.* Wednesday 5
mère *f.* mother 2, 3
mes (*see* **mon**)
mesdames *f.pl.* ladies 13
message *m.* message
  ~ instantané instant message 6
messieurs *m.pl.* gentlemen 13
mesure *f.* (unit of) measure
météo(rologie) *f.* weather 14
météorologique *adj.* weather
mettre to put; to place; to lay 13
  Mettez ...! Put ...! CP
  ~ la table to set the table 13
  ~ le chauffage to turn on the heat 13
  se ~ à table to sit down to eat 13
mexicain(e) *adj.* Mexican 1
Mexico Mexico City
Mexique *m.* Mexico 5
miam! yum! 8
midi noon 5
le mien/la mienne mine 5
miette *f.* crumb
mieux better 11
  il vaut ~ que it is preferable that, it is better that 10
  j'aime le ~ I like best 11
militaire *m.* serviceman/ servicewoman 4
mille *inv.* one thousand 3
milliard *m.* billion 3
millier *m.* thousand
million *m.* million 3
mince thin 1
  ~! darn it! 12
minuit midnight 5
minute *f.* minute 5
moi me 1; I, me 6
  ~ aussi me too 2
  ~ non plus me neither 2
moins less 11
  au ~ at least 6
  j'aime le ~ I like least 11
  ~ le quart quarter to (the hour) 5
mois *m.* month 6
moment *m.* moment; time 2
  à quel ~ (de la journée)? at what time (of day)?
  mon, ma, mes my 3
monde *m.* world 7
  tout le ~ everybody 4
mondial(e) *adj.* world
mondialisation *f.* globalization
monnaie *f.* change, coins 9
Monsieur (M.) *m.* Mr., Sir; man 1
monter to go up; to get into 7
montre *f.* watch 4

montrer to show 14
morceau *m.* (*pl.* **morceaux**) piece 8
mort *f.* death 15
mort(e) dead
mot *m.* word 6
  ~ de passe password
  plus un ~ not one more word 10
moto *f.* motorcycle 3
mouchoir *m.* handkerchief
mouillé(e) wet
mourir to die 7
moutarde *f.* mustard 8
moyen *m.* means
moyenne *f.* average
musée *m.* museum 5
musique *f.* music 6
myrtille *f.* blueberry

nager to swim 2
naïf (naïve) naive 4
naissance *f.* birth
naître to be born 7
  je suis né(e) I was born 3
  né(e) born
nappe *f.* tablecloth 13
natalité *f.* birth
nationalité *f.* nationality 1
naturel: désastre naturel *m.* natural disaster 15
naturellement naturally 8
naviguer sur l'Internet *to surf the internet*
navire *m.* ship
ne (n') not 1
  n'importe quoi whatever
  ~ ... jamais never 4
  ~ ... pas not 1
  ~ ... personne no one, nobody, not anyone 15
  ~ ... plus no more, no longer 8
  ~ ... que only 11
  ~ ... rien nothing, not anything 6
  n'est-ce pas? right?; are you?; don't they?; etc. 2
nécessaire: il est ~ que it is necessary that 13
négritude *f.* negritude *(system of black cultural and spiritual values)*
neiger to snow 7
  il neige it's snowing CP, 7
nerveux (nerveuse) nervous 4
nettoyer to clean 6
neuf nine CP
neuf (neuve) brand-new 10
  quoi de ~? what's new? 5
neveu *m.* (*pl.* **neveux**) nephew 3
nez *m.* nose 9
  le ~ qui coule runny nose 9
ni ... ni neither ... nor
nièce *f.* niece 3
Noël *m.* Christmas 7

  le père ~ Santa Claus 1
noir(e) black 4
nom *m.* name CP, 1
  à quel ~ ...? in whose name ...? 12
  ~ de famille last name 1
nombre *m.* number 1
nommer to name
non no 1
  ~ plus neither 6
nord *m.* north
note *f.* note; grade, mark 4
notre, nos our 3
nourrir to feed, to nourish
nourriture *f.* food
nous we 1; us 10; (to) us 14
nouveau/nouvel (nouvelle) (*m.pl.* **nouveaux**) new 4
novembre *m.* November 7
nuit *f.* night 2
  Bonne ~ Pleasant dreams. 5
numéro (de téléphone) *m.* (telephone) number 4

obéir to obey 12
occidental(e) western
occupé (e) busy 6
s'occuper de to be busy with, to take care of 7
  occupe-toi de tes oignons! mind your own business! 11
octobre *m.* October 7
octroyer to grant
œil *m.* (*pl.* **yeux**) eye 9
  mon ~! my eye!, I don't believe it! 10
œuf *m.* egg 8
œuvre *f.* work
offrir to offer
oh là là! oh dear!, wow! 9
oignon *m.* onion 8
  occupe-toi de tes oignons! mind your own business! 11
oiseau *m.* bird 5
omelette *f.* omelet 8
on one, people, we, they, you 1
oncle *m.* uncle 3
onze eleven CP
optimiste optimistic 4
or *m.* gold
orange *f.* orange *(fruit)* 4
  jus d'~ *m.* orange juice 2
orange *adj. inv.* orange 4
orangina *m.* orange soda 2
ordinaire ordinary, everyday 4
ordinateur *m.* computer 3
ordre *m.* order
oreille *f.* ear 9
oriental(e) eastern
original(e) (*m.pl.* **originaux**) different; novel; original 14

ou or 1
où where 1
oublier to forget 6
ouest *m.* west
oui yes 1
ouvert(e) open 12
ouverture *f.* opening
  heures d'~ hours of business
ouvrier/ouvrière *m./f.* laborer 4
ouvrir to open
  ouvrez la porte! open the door! CP

pagne *m.* traditional cloth, skirt from Senegal
pain *m.* bread 8
  ~ de mie *m.* sandwich bread
  ~ grillé *m.* toast 8
pâle pale 15
panneau *m.* sign
pantalon *m.* (pair of) pants 4
papier *m.* paper 9
paquet *m.* package 9
par by; through 5
  ~ contre on the other hand
  ~ exemple for example 6
  ~ ici (come) this way, follow me
  ~ jour per day 5
paraître to appear
parce que because 6
pardon: ~? pardon?, what did you say? CP
  je vous demande ~ please excuse me; I beg your pardon 9
parents *m.pl.* parents; relatives 3
paresseux (paresseuse) lazy 4
parfait(e) perfect 5
parking *m.* parking lot 5
parler to speak 2
  ~ de to tell about 7
  ~ fort to speak loudly 15
part *f.* behalf, portion
  de ma ~ for me; on my behalf
partie *f.* part
partir (de) to leave (from) 6
  à ~ de from that time on
partout everywhere 15
pas no, not
  ne ... ~ not 1
  ~ du tout! not at all! 1
  ~ encore not yet 2
  ~ grand-chose not much 5
  ~ mal not bad 2
  ~ trop bien not too well 2
passé *m.* past
passer to pass
  ~ un an to spend a year 3
  ~ un test to take a test 5
se passer to happen; to take place
passionnant(e) exciting 14
pastille *f.* lozenge 9

pâte dentifrice *f.* toothpaste 9
pâté *m.* pâté *(meat spread)* 8
patiemment patiently 10
patient(e) patient 4
patiner to skate 2
patinoire *f.* skating rink 10
pâtisserie *f.* pastry shop; pastry 9
patrie *f.* homeland
patrimoine *m.* heritage
patron/patronne *m./f.* boss 4
pauvre poor 4, 11
payer to pay (for) 9
pays *m.* country 5
Pays-Bas *m.pl.* Netherlands 5
pêche *f.* fishing
pédagogie *f.* education, teacher preparation 5
peinture *f.* painting
pelouse *f.* lawn
pendant for; during 6
  ~ combien de temps ...? how long ...? 6
  ~ que while 6
penser to think 8
  qu'en penses-tu? what do you think of it (of them)? 8
perdre to lose 9
  ~ patience to lose (one's) patience 9
père *m.* father 2
père Noël *m.* Santa Claus 1
permettre to allow
  permettez-moi de me présenter allow me to introduce myself 1
  vous permettez? may I? 1
permis de conduire *m.* driver's license 10
personnage *m.* character; individual
personne *f.* person *(male or female)* 1
  ne ... ~ no one, nobody, not anyone 15
personnellement personally 10
pessimiste pessimistic 4
pétanque *f.* lawn bowling 6
petit(e) small, short 1
  ~ ami(e) *m./f.* boyfriend/girlfriend 3
  ~ déjeuner *m.* breakfast 8
  ~-fils *m.* (*pl.* petits-fils) grandson 3
  petite-fille *f.* (*pl.* petites-filles) granddaughter 3
  petits-enfants *m.pl.* grandchildren 3
  petits pois *m.pl.* peas 8
peu (de) little, few 8
  un ~ a little bit 2
peuple *m.* people
peur *f.* fear
  avoir ~ to be afraid 8
peut-être maybe; perhaps 2
phare *m.* headlight
pharmacie *f.* pharmacy 5
pharmacien/pharmacienne *m./f.* pharmacist
photo *f.* photograph 3
  sur la ~ in the picture 3
physique physical 15

piano *m.* piano 6
pièce *f.* room 3; play 6
  ~ (de monnaie) coin 9
pied *m.* foot 9
pilote *m.* pilot 11
pilule *f.* pill 9
pique-nique *m.* picnic 12
piscine *f.* swimming pool 5
pitié *f.* pity
  avoir ~ (de) to have pity, to feel sorry (for) 10
pizza *f.* pizza 2
place *f.* seat 12; room; place 7
plaire to please
  s'il vous plaît please 2
plaisanterie *f.* joke 14
plaisir *m.* pleasure
  au ~ see you again 5
  avec ~ with pleasure 2
plan *m.* map (city; house)
plancher *m.* floor 13; board
plat *m.* course, dish 8
plein(e) full
pleurer to cry 2
pleuvoir to rain 7
  il pleut it's raining CP, 7
  il pleuvait it was raining 11
  il pleuvra it will rain 12
plupart *f.* majority
  la ~ (de) most (of) 6
plus more 11
  il n'y en a ~ there is (are) no more 12
  le/la/les ~ ... the most ... 11
  moi non ~ nor I, me neither 6
  ne ... ~ no more, no longer 8
plusieurs several
poêle *f.* frying pan
poème *m.* poem 6
pois *m.pl.* : petits ~ peas 8
poisson *m.* fish 2
poivre *m.* pepper 13
police *f.* police (force)
  agent de ~ *m.* police officer 15
politique *f.* politics 2; policy
politique: homme/femme ~ *m./f.* politician 4
pomme *f.* apple 8
pomme de terre *f.* potato 8
populaire popular 11
porc *m.* pork 8
portable *m.* cell phone 7; laptop
porte *f.* door 1
porter to wear; to carry 4
portugais(e) Portuguese 5
poser to place
  ~ une question to ask a question 12
possession *f.* possession 3
postale: carte ~ *f.* postcard 4
poste *f.* post office; mail
  bureau de ~ *m.* post office 5
poster to mail 7

pouce *m.* thumb
  faire du ~ to hitchhike *(French-Canadian)*
poulet *m.* chicken 8
pour for, in order to 2
  ~ ce qui est de with respect to
pourquoi why 2
  ~ pas? why not? 6
pourvoir to provide
pouvoir *m.* power
pouvoir *v.* to be able; to be allowed 10; can
  je peux I can 9
  on peut one can 9
  pourriez-vous ...? could you ...? 12
  pouvez-vous me dire ...? can you tell me ...? 9
  puis-je ...? may I ...? 12
préciser to specify
préféré(e) favorite 5
préférence *f.* :**de ~** preferably
préférer to prefer 8
  je préfère que I prefer that 13
premier (première) first 5
  en première in first class 12
prendre to take; to eat, to drink 8
  prenez ...! take ...! CP
prénom *m.* first name 1
préparer (un cours) to prepare (a lesson) 6
près (de) near 1
  tout ~ very near 12
présenter to introduce
  je vous présente ... let me introduce you to ... 3
presque almost 14
prétendre to claim
prêter to lend 14
prie: je vous en ~ you're welcome 7
primordial(e) essential
printemps *m.* spring 7
prise de conscience *f.* awareness
privilégier to favor
prix *m.* price 12
problème *m.* problem
  Pas de problème! No problem!
prochain(e) next 5
  À la prochaine. Until next time. 5
proche near; close
produit *m.* product; article
professeur (prof) *m.* (secondary or college) teacher 1
profession *f.* profession, occupation
progrès *m.* progress 14
promenade *f.* walk; ride 4
  faire une ~ to take a walk; to take a ride 4
se promener to take a walk, ride 13
promettre to promise
  c'est promis it's a promise 10
propos: à ~ de regarding, on the subject of 8
propre clean 4; specific; own
propriétaire *m./f.* owner 10
provisions *f.pl.* groceries 4
  faire des ~ to do the grocery shopping 4

provoquer to cause 15
prudemment carefully 10
prudent(e) cautious 10
publicité *f.* publicity; commercial 14
puis then; next 4
puis-je ...? may I ...? 12
puisque since
pull-over (pull) *m.* sweater 4
pyjama *m.* (pair of) pajamas 13

quand when 4
quantité *f.* quantity
quarante forty 3
quart quarter
  et ~ quarter past, quarter after 5
  moins le ~ quarter to, quarter till 5
quatorze fourteen CP
quatre four CP, 1
quatre-vingt-dix ninety 3
quatre-vingt-onze ninety-one 3
quatre-vingt-un eighty-one 3
quatre-vingts eighty 3
que that
  ne ... ~ only 11
  ~ ...? what ...? 4
quel(le) ...? which ...? 4
  quel âge avez-vous? how old are you? 3
  quel jour est-ce? what day is it? 5
  quel(le) ...! what a ...! 2
  quelle est votre nationalité? what is your nationality? 1
  quelle heure est-il? what time is it? 5
quelque chose *m.* something 2
quelquefois sometimes 4
quelques a few; some 8
quelqu'un someone 2
  qu'est-ce que/qui what? 4
  qu'est-ce que c'est? what is this? what is it? 4
  qu'est-ce que tu aimes? what do you like? 2
  qu'est-ce que vous avez comme ...? what do you have for (in the way of) ...? 8
  qu'est-ce que vous voulez? what do you want? 2
  qu'est-ce qu'il y a ...? what is there ...? what's the matter? 3
qui who 1
qu'est-ce ~ ...? what ...? 4
quinze fifteen CP
  ~ jours two weeks 11
quoi what
  il n'y a pas de ~ don't mention it, you're welcome 13
  ~ de neuf? what's new? 5
quoique although

raconter to tell 14
radio *f.* radio 2
rafale *f.* gust (of wind)

raison *f.* reason
  avoir ~ to be right 8
raisonnable reasonable 10
ralentir to slow down 12
ramener to bring back
rapide rapid, fast 10
rapidement rapidly 10
se rappeler to remember
rapproché(e) *adj.* close
rarement rarely 4
ravager to devastate
ravi(e) delighted 14
réalité: émission de téléréalité *f.* reality tv show 14
récemment recently 6
recette *f.* recipe
recherche *f.* research
recommander to recommend 12
reculer to back up 10
récuser to exclude; to challenge
réduire to reduce
réfrigérateur *m.* refrigerator 3
refuser to refuse
regarder to watch; to look at 2
regretter to be sorry 14
  je regrette I'm sorry 8; I miss
relief *m.* relief, hilly area
remarquer to notice 6
remercier to thank 12
remplacer to replace
rencontre *f.* meeting
rencontrer to meet 5, 14
rendez-vous *m.* meeting; date 5
  avoir ~ to have an appointment, meeting
rendre to give back 9
  ~ visite à qqn to visit someone 9
renforcer to reinforce
renseignement *m.* item of information 12
(se) renseigner to inform (oneself); to find out about
rentrer to go (come) back; to go (come) home 7
renverser to turn upside-down
répandu(e) widespread
repas *m.* meal 8
repère *m.* point of reference
répéter to repeat; to practice 8
  répétez, s'il vous plaît please repeat CP
répondre (à) to answer 9
  répondez answer CP
réponse *f.* answer
se reposer to rest 13
RER *m. train to Paris suburbs* 2
réseau *m.* network
réserver to reserve 9
résidence (universitaire) *f.* dormitory 5
responsabilité *f.* responsibility 11
restaurant *m.* restaurant 5
rester to stay 5; to remain
  il vous reste ...? do you still have ...? 12

restes *m.pl.* leftovers 8
résultat *m.* result; outcome
retard *m.* delay
  en ~ late 7
retour *m.* return
  aller-~ round-trip ticket 12
retourner to go back, to return 7
rétroviseur *m.* rearview mirror 10
réunion *f.* meeting 13
réussir (à) to succeed; to pass (a test) 12
se réveiller to wake up 13
revenant *m.* ghost 14
revenir to come back 7
revoir to see again
  au ~ good-bye 1
rez-de-chaussée *m.* ground floor 12
rhume *m.* cold *(illness)* 9
riad *m.* traditional house in North Africa
riche rich 12
ridicule ridiculous 14
rien nothing
  de ~ you're welcome; don't mention it, not at all 12
  ne ... ~ nothing, not anything 6
  ~ à voir nothing to do with
rimer to go with
riz *m.* rice 8
robe *f.* dress 4; color of wine
  ~ de mariée wedding dress 11
robinet *m.* faucet 6
roi *m.* king
roman *m.* novel 6
  ~ policier detective story 6
rose *adj.* pink 4
rôti (de bœuf) *m.* (beef) roast 9
rouge red 4
rouler to roll; to move *(vehicle)*; to go 15
route *f.* route, way, road 10, 12
roux (rousse) red(-haired) 4
rue *f.* street 9
rugby *m.* rugby 6
russe Russian 1
Russie *f.* Russia 5

sa *(see* **son***)*
s'agir to be about
  il s'agit de it's a matter of
saison *f.* season 7
salade *f.* salad 8
  ~ verte green salad 8
sale dirty 4
salle *f.* room
  ~ à manger dining room 3
  ~ de bain bathroom 3
  ~ de classe classroom P, 5
  ~ de séjour living room; den 3
salon *m.* living room 3
salut! hi! 1, 2; bye (-bye) 1, 5

salutation *f.* greeting
samedi *m.* Saturday 5
sandwich *m.* sandwich 8
sans without 6
  ~ abri *m./f.* homeless person 15
  ~ blague! no kidding 14
  ~ doute probably 3
  ~ façon honestly, no kidding 8
santé *f.* health
  à votre ~! (here's) to your health!; cheers! 2
sapeur-pompier *m.* fireman
saucisse *f.* sausage 9
saumon *m.* salmon 8
sauter to skip
savoir to know 12
  je ne sais pas I don't know 2
saxophone *m.* saxophone 6
sciences *f.pl.* science 5
  ~ économiques economics 5
scolaire *adj.* school
  année ~ *f.* school year 10
scooter *m.* scooter 3
se oneself 6
sec (sèche) dry
sécheresse *f.* drought
second(e) second
  en seconde in (by) second class 12
secouer to shake 15
seize sixteen CP
séjour *m.* stay
sel *m.* salt 13
semaine *f.* week 5
semestre *m.* semester 6
Sénégal *m.* Senegal 5
Sénégalais(e) Senegalese 1
sens interdit *m.* one-way street 10
sentier *m.* path
se séparer to separate (from each other) 14
sept seven CP
septembre *m.* September 7
sérieusement seriously 10
sérieux (sérieuse) serious 10
serveur/serveuse *m./f.* waiter/waitress 8
service *m.* service
  à votre ~ at your service
serviette *f.* towel 12; napkin 13
ses *(see* **son***)*
seul(e) alone; only 5
  un ~ a single
seulement only 2
short *m.* (pair of) shorts 4
si *conj.* if 3
  s'il vous plaît please 2
si *adv.* so 10
  ~! yes! 3
sida *m.* AIDS
siècle *m.* century 10
sieste *f.* nap 4
  faire la ~ to take a nap 4

simple simple, plain 4
  aller ~ *m.* one-way ticket 12
  c'est bien ~ it's quite easy
sincère sincere 11
se situer to be situated
six six CP
skier to ski 2
skis *m.pl.* skis 13
smoking *m.* tuxedo 11
SNCF *f. French railroad system* 2
sœur *f.* sister 3
sofa *m.* sofa 3
soi oneself 6
soif: avoir ~ to be thirsty 8
soir *m.* evening 2
  ce ~ tonight 5
  tous les soirs every night 6
soirée *f.* party 13; evening
soixante sixty 3
soixante-dix seventy 3
soixante-douze seventy-two 3
soixante et onze seventy-one 3
soleil *m.* sun 7
  Il fait (du) ~ It's sunny. CP
son, sa, ses his, her, its 3
sorte *f.* kind 8
  quelle(s) ~(s) de ...? what kind(s) of ...? 8
  toutes sortes de choses all kinds of things 9
sortir to go out 6
  je vais ~ I'm going to go out 5
  sortez! leave! CP
souci *m.* worry; care 11
soucieux (soucieuse) *worried, eager*
soudain suddenly
souffler to blow
souhaiter (que) to wish; to hope (that) 13
soulagement *m.* relief
soupe *f.* soup 8
sourire *m.* smile 13
sourire *v.* to smile 13
souris *f.* mouse 5
sous under 5
  ~-sol *m.* basement 3
souvenir *m.* memory; recollection 4
se souvenir (de) to remember 13
souvent often 2
sportif (sportive) athletic 4
stagiaire *m./f.* intern
statue *f.* statue 11
steak *m.* steak
  ~-frites steak with French fries 15
stéréo *f.* stereo 3
stop *m.* stop sign 10
stressé(e) stressed 11
stupide stupid 4
sucre *m.* sugar 13
sud *m.* south
Suède *f.* Sweden 5

suédois(e) Swedish 1
Suisse *f.* Switzerland 5
suisse *adj.* Swiss 1
suite: tout de ~ right away 1
suivant(e) following, next 5
superficie *f.* area
supermarché *m.* supermarket 9
supplément *m.* extra charge; supplement 12
sur on 3
sûr(e) sure
   bien ~ of course 8
sûrement surely, definitely 14
surmonter to overcome
surveiller to watch
survivre to survive
survécu(e) survived 15
sweat-shirt *m.* sweatshirt 4

TGV *m. very fast train* 7
tabac *m.* tobacco; tobacco shop 9
   bureau de ~ tobacco shop 5
table *f.* table CP, 1
   à ~ at dinner, at the table 6
tableau *m.* chalkboard CP
taille *f.* size, height
se taire to be quiet
   tais-toi! (taisez-vous!) keep quiet! 10
tanguer to pitch (forward)
tant so much; so many 6
tante *f.* aunt 3
tapisserie *f.* tapestry
tard late 6
tarder to be a long time coming 13
tarte *f.* pie 8
tasse *f.* cup 2
taux *m.* rate
tchao bye 5
te you 10; (to) you 14
technologie de pointe *f.* high technology
tee-shirt *m.* tee-shirt 4
télécharger to download
téléphone *m.* telephone 1
   au ~ on the telephone 6
   ~ portable *m.* cell phone 7
téléphoner (à) to telephone 6
télévision (télé) *f.* television 2
   ~ numérique terrestre (TNT) digital television
témoin *m.* witness 15
tempête *f.* storm 15
temps *m.* time 6; weather 4
   emploi du ~ *m.* schedule 4
   quel ~ fait-il? what is the weather like? 4
tendance *f.* tendency, trend
   avoir ~ à to tend to 12
se tenir au courant to keep oneself up to date
tennis *m.* tennis 2
   jouer au ~ to play tennis 2
   ~ *f.pl.* tennis shoes 4

tentation *f.* temptation
terre *f.* earth, land 9
terrestre *adj.* land
tête *f.* head 9
texto *m.* text message (SMS) 6
thé *m.* tea 2
théâtre *m.* theater
Tiens! Well! Gee! 3
timbre *m.* stamp 9
toi you 4
toilettes *f.pl.* restroom 3
toit *m.* roof 5
tomate *f.* tomato 8
tomber to fall 2
ton, ta, tes your 3
tornade *f.* tornado 15
tort *m.* wrong
   avoir ~ to be wrong; to be unwise 8
tôt early 6
toujours always 4; still
toupet *m.* nerve
tour *f.* tower 11
tour *m.* turn, tour 11
tourner to turn 7
tous *pron. m.pl.* all 4
Toussaint *f.* All Saints' Day
tousser to cough 9
tout/toute/tous/toutes *adj.* all; every; the whole 12
   tous les deux (toutes les deux) both 12
   tous les soirs every night
   tout le monde everybody CP, 12
   tout le week-end all weekend (long) 5
   toute la famille the whole family 11
tout *adv.* completely; very 12
   à ~ de suite see you very soon
   ~ à l'heure a little while ago, in a little while 5
   ~ de suite right away 12
   ~ près very near 7
tout *pron. inv.* all, everything
   pas du ~ ! not at all! 1
toutefois however
train *m.* train 3
   être en ~ de to be in the process of 11
tranche *f.* slice 8
tranquille calm 10
travail (manuel) *m.* (manual) work 4
travailler to work 2
travailleur (travailleuse) hardworking 4
travers: à ~ throughout
treize thirteen CP
tremblement de terre *m.* earthquake 15
trente thirty 3
très very 1
tricot *m.* knitting; sweater
triste sad 4
trois three CP, 1
trompette *f.* trumpet 6

trop (de) too much, too many 3
trouver to find, to be of the opinion 2
   se ~ to be located
   où se trouve (se trouvent) ...? where is (are) ...? 5
   vous trouvez? do you think so? 2
truite *f.* trout 8
tu you *(familiar)* 1
tuer to kill 15

un(e) one CP, 1; one, a, an 3
union *f.* :~ douanière customs union
unique unique
   enfant ~ *m./f.* only child
université *f.* university 1
universitaire *(adj.)* university 5

vacances *f.pl.* vacation 6
   bonnes ~! have a good vacation! 6
   en ~ on vacation 6
vague *f.* wave
vaisselle *f.* dishes 4
valeur *f.* value
valise *f.* suitcase
valoir mieux (il vaut mieux) to be better 10
vanille *f.* :glace à la ~ *f.* vanilla ice cream 8
vaut: il ~ mieux que it is preferable that, it is better that 13
véhicule *m.* vehicle 10
vélo *m.* bicycle 3
   faire du ~ to go bike riding 6
vendeur/vendeuse *m./f.* salesman/ saleswoman 4
vendre to sell 9
vendredi *m.* Friday 5
venir to come 7
   d'où venez-vous? where do you come from? 7
   je viens de ... I come from ... 2
   ~ de ... to have just ... 7
   ~ en tête to come first, in the first place
vent *m.* wind
   il fait du ~ it's windy CP, 7
véranda *f.* porch 3
vérifier to verify; to check 12
vérité *f.* truth 14
verre *m.* glass 2
vers toward 5
   ~ (8 heures) approximately, around (8 o'clock) 5
verser to pour 13
vert(e) green 4
veste *f.* sportcoat 4
vêtement *m.* article of clothing 4
veuf/veuve *m./f.* widower/ widow 1
veux *(see* **vouloir***)*

viande *f.* meat 8
victime *f.* victim 7
vie *f.* life 4
  c'est la ~ that's life 6
  gagner sa ~ to earn one's living
vieux/vieil (vieille) old 1
vigne *f.* vine; vineyard
ville *f.* city 4; town
vin *m.* wine 2
vingt twenty CP
vingt-deux twenty-two CP
vingt et un twenty-one CP
violet(te) purple 4
violon *m.* violin 6
virage *m.* curve, turn (in the road) 15
visite: rendre ~ à to visit (a person) 9
visiter to visit (a place)
vite quickly 10
vitesse *f.* speed 10
  à toute ~ at top speed 10
vivement eagerly
vivre to live

voici here is; here are 3
voilà there is; there are 1
voir to see 14
  tu vas ~ you're going to see 5
  tu vois you see 11
voisin/voisine *m./f.* neighbor 11
voiture *f.* automobile 3
  en ~ by car 7
voix *f.* voice 7
  à ~ haute aloud
vol *m.* flight 12
volant *m.* steering wheel 10
volontiers gladly 2
votre, vos your 1
vôtre: à la ~! (here's) to yours!, to your health! 2
vouloir to want, to wish 10
  je veux bien gladly; yes, thanks 2
  je veux que I want 13
  je voudrais I would like 2, 13
  ... veut dire ... ... means ... CP, 6
voler to steal

vous you *(formal; familiar pl.)* 1; (to) you 14
voyage *m.* trip, voyage 5
  chèque de ~ *m.* traveler's check 9
  faire un ~ to take a trip 5
voyager to travel 2
vrai(e) true 2
vraiment really 2

week-end *m.* weekend 5
  tout le ~ all weekend (long) 5
wolof *m.* Wolof *(language)* 5

y there 7
  allez- ~ go ahead 12
  il ~ a there is (are) 3
yeux *m.pl.* eyes 4

zéro *m.* zero CP, 3
Zut! Darn! 12, 15

Vocabulaire

This vocabulary list includes only the active words and phrases listed in the **Vocabulaire actif** sections. Only those French equivalents that occur in the text are given. Expressions are listed according to the key word. The symbol ~ indicates repetition of the key word.

The following abbreviations are used:

adj.	adjective	*m.*	masculine
adv.	adverb	*m.pl.*	masculine plural
conj.	conjunction	*n.*	noun
fam.	familiar	*pl.*	plural
f.	feminine	*prep.*	preposition
f.pl.	feminine plural	*pron.*	pronoun
inv.	invariable	*v.*	verb

a, an un(e)
able: be ~ pouvoir
about de; environ
  ~ 8 o'clock vers 8 heures
  ~ it (them) en
  hear ~ entendre parler de
absolutely absolument
accept accepter
accident accident *m.*
accompany accompagner
according to d'après
accordion accordéon *m.*
accounting comptabilité *f.*
acquainted: be ~ with connaître
activity activité *f.*
actor/actress acteur/actrice *m./f.*
address *n.* adresse *f.*
adore adorer
advance *v.* avancer
advertisement annonce *f.*
advice (piece of) conseil *m.*
afraid: be ~ avoir peur
after après
afternoon après-midi *m.*
  have a good ~ bon après-midi
  in the ~ de l'après-midi
again encore
against contre
age âge *m.*

ago il y a …
agree (with) être d'accord (avec)
  agreed entendu
ahead: go ~ allez-y
  straight ~ tout droit
air conditioning climatisation *f.*
airplane avion *m.*
airport aéroport *m.*
all *pron./adj.* tout (toute/tous/toutes)
  ~ weekend (long) tout le week-end
  not at ~! pas du tout!
allow permettre
  ~ me to introduce myself permettez-moi de me présenter
almost presque
alone seul(e)
  leave me ~! laisse-moi (laissez-moi) tranquille!
already déjà
also aussi
always toujours
  not ~ pas toujours
American *adj.* américain(e)
amusing *adj.* amusant(e)
anchovy anchois *m.*
and et
angry fâché(e)
  get ~ se fâcher
answer *n.* réponse *f.*

answer *v.* répondre (à)
anyone quelqu'un
  not ~ ne … personne
anything quelque chose *m.*
  not ~ ne … rien
apartment appartement *m.*
appear avoir l'air
appetizer hors-d'œuvre *m.inv.*
apple pomme *f.*
appointment rendez-vous *m.*
  have an ~ avoir rendez-vous
approximately environ; vers *(time)*
April avril *m.*
Arabic arabe *m.*
argue se disputer
arm bras *m.*
armchair fauteuil *m.*
around environ; vers *(time)*; autour de *(place)*
  ~ (8 o'clock) vers (8 heures)
arrive arriver
art art *m.*
artist artiste *m./f.*
as aussi, comme
  ~ … ~ aussi … que
  ~ much autant (de)
ashamed confus(e)
ask demander
  ~ a question poser une question
asleep: fall ~ s'endormir

aspirin tablet cachet d'aspirine *m.*
assure assurer
at à
  ~ first d'abord
  ~ least au moins
  ~ midnight à minuit
  ~ noon à midi
  ~ ... o'clock à ... heure(s)
  ~ the home of chez
  ~ what time (of day)? à quel moment (de la journée)?
athletic sportif (sportive)
attach attacher
attend assister (à)
attention: pay ~ faire attention à
attentive attentif (attentive)
August août *m.*
aunt tante *f.*
automobile voiture *f.*
autumn automne *m.*
away: right ~ tout de suite
awful! berk!

baby bébé *m.*
back *n.* dos *m.*
back *adv.:* go ~ retourner; rentrer
  ~ then à cette époque
  come ~ revenir, rentrer
  give ~ rendre
back up *v.* reculer
bad mauvais(e)
  ~ driver chauffard *m.*
  not ~ pas mal
  that's (it's) too ~ c'est dommage
  the weather is ~ il fait mauvais
badly mal
bakery boulangerie *f.*
bald chauve
ball (dance) bal *m.*
bank banque *f.*
bar and café bistro *m.*
basement sous-sol *m.*
basketball basket-ball (basket) *m.*
bathing suit maillot de bain *m.*
bathroom salle de bain *f.*
be être
  ~ a long time coming tarder
  ~ able pouvoir
  ~ acquainted with, familiar with connaître
  ~ afraid avoir peur
  ~ born naître
  ~ cold avoir froid
  ~ fed up en avoir assez
  ~ hot avoir chaud
  ~ hungry avoir faim
  ~ in the process of être en train de
  ~ interested in s'intéresser à
  ~ located se trouver

~ necessary falloir (il faut)
~ of the opinion trouver
~ probably, supposed devoir
~ right avoir raison
~ sleepy avoir sommeil
~ sore avoir mal (à)
~ sorry regretter
~ thirsty avoir soif
~ wrong, unwise avoir tort
beans haricots *m.pl.*
Beaujolais *(wine)* beaujolais *m.*
beautiful beau/bel/belle/beaux/belles
because parce que
become devenir
bed lit *m.*
  go to ~ se coucher
bedroom chambre *f.*
beef bœuf *m.*
beer bière *f.*
before avant
begin commencer
behind derrière; en retard
  right ~ juste derrière
beige beige
Belgian belge
Belgium Belgique *f.*
believe (in) croire (à)
  I don't ~ it! mon œil!
belong to être à
belt ceinture *f.*
  safety ~, seat ~ ceinture de sécurité *f.*
beside à côté (de)
best *adv.* mieux; *adj.* le/la meilleur(e)
  ~ friend meilleur(e) ami(e) .
  ~ regards meilleures salutations
  I like ~ j'aime le mieux (le plus); je préfère
better *adv.* mieux; *adj.* meilleur(e)
  it is ~ that il vaut mieux que
between entre
  ~ friends entre amis
beverage boisson *f.*
bicycle vélo *m.*
big grand(e), gros(se)
bill *n. (paper money)* billet *m.; (restaurant check)* addition *f.*
billion milliard *m.*
bird oiseau *m.*
birthday anniversaire *m.*
bistro bistro *m.*
black noir(e)
  ~ currant liqueur crème de cassis *f.*
blond blond(e)
blouse chemisier *m.*
blue bleu(e)
body corps *m.*
book livre *m.*
bookstore librairie *f.*
boots bottes *f. pl.*
Bordeaux *(wine)* bordeaux *m.*

boring ennuyeux (ennuyeuse)
born né(e)
  be ~ naître
borrow emprunter
boss patron (patronne) *m./f.*
both tous (toutes) les deux
bother déranger
bottle bouteille *f.*
bowl *n.* bol *m.*
bowling: lawn ~ pétanque *f.*
box boîte *f.*
boy garçon *m.*
boyfriend petit ami *m.*
brake *v.* freiner
brand *n.* marque *f.*
brand-new neuf (neuve)
bread pain *m.*
breakfast petit déjeuner *m.*
bridge *(game)* bridge *m.*
Brie *(cheese)* brie *m.*
bring apporter
broccoli brocoli *m.*
brother frère *m.*
brother-in-law beau-frère *m. (pl.* beaux-frères)
brown brun(e); marron *inv.*
brush *n.* brosse *f.*
  tooth ~ brosse à dents *f.*
brush *v.* se brosser
building bâtiment *m.*
burn brûler
business affaires *f.pl.,* commerce *m.*
  mind your own ~! occupe-toi de tes oignons!
businessman/woman homme/femme d'affaires *m./f.*
busy occupé(e)
  be ~ with s'occuper de
but mais
butcher shop boucherie *f.*
  pork butcher's charcuterie *f.*
butter beurre *m.*
  peanut ~ beurre d'arachide *m.*
buy acheter
by par
  ~ car en voiture
  ~ chance par hasard
  ~ the way ... au fait ...
bye salut; tchao

café café *m.,* bistro *m.*
cafeteria cafétéria *f.*
cake gâteau *m. (pl.* gâteaux)
calculator calculatrice *f.*
call appeler, téléphoner
called: be ~ s'appeler
calm calme, tranquille
camembert *(cheese)* camembert *m.*
campus campus *m.*

can *n.* boîte *f.*
can (be able to) *v.* pouvoir
Canada Canada *m.*
Canadian canadien(ne)
candy bonbon *m.*
car voiture *f.*
    by ~ en voiture
card carte *f.*
    credit ~ carte de crédit
    debit ~ carte bancaire
    post ~ carte postale
cards *(game)* cartes *f. pl.*
care *n.* souci *m.*
    take ~ of s'occuper de
care *v.*: I don't ~ cela (ça) m'est égal
carefully prudemment
carry porter
cartoon dessin animé *m.*
cat chat *m.*
cause *v.* provoquer
cautious prudent(e)
cell phone portable *m.*
centime centime *m.*
century siècle *m.*
cereal céréales *f.pl.*
certain sûr(e)
certainly tout à fait; certainement
chair chaise *f.*
chalk craie *f.*
chalkboard tableau *m.*
chance hasard *m.*
    by ~ par hasard
change *n.* monnaie *f.*
change *v.* changer (de)
channel: TV ~ chaîne (de télé) *f.*
charge: extra ~ supplément *m.*
charming charmant(e)
cheap bon marché *adj. inv.*
check chèque *m.*
    ~ (restaurant bill) addition *f.*
    traveler's ~ chèque de voyage *m.*
check *v.* vérifier
checkers dames *f.pl.*
cheese fromage *m.*
chemistry chimie *f.*
chess échecs *m.pl.*
chewing gum chewing-gum *m.*
chic chic *adj. inv.*
chicken poulet *m.*
child enfant *m./f.*
China Chine *f.*
Chinese chinois(e)
chocolate: hot ~ chocolat chaud *m.*
choice choix *m.*
choose choisir
Christmas Noël *m.*
church église *f.*
cigar cigare *m.*
cigarette cigarette *f.*

city ville *f.*
civil servant fonctionnaire *m./f.*
class cours *m.*, classe *f.*
    in ~ en cours
    in first ~ en première classe
classroom salle de classe *f.*
clean *adj.* propre
clean *v.* nettoyer
close *adj.* près (de)
close *v.* fermer
closed fermé(e)
clothing (article of) vêtement *m.*
clumsy maladroit(e)
coat manteau *m.* (*pl.* manteaux)
Coca-Cola coca *m.*
coffee café *m.*
coin pièce (de monnaie) *f.*
cold *(illness)* *n.* rhume *m.*
cold *adj.* froid(e)
    be ~ avoir froid
    it's ~ il fait froid
collide entrer en collision; heurter
color couleur *f.*
    what ~ is (are) …? de quelle couleur
        est (sont) …?
come venir
    ~ back revenir, rentrer
    ~ in! entrez!
    where do you ~ from? d'où venez-vous?
comfortable confortable
comic strip bande dessinée *f.*
commentary commentaire *m.*
commercial *n.* publicité *f.*
complete complet (complète)
completely tout *inv. adv.*; complètement
computer ordinateur *m.*
    ~ science informatique *f.*
confirm confirmer
console oneself se consoler
constant constant(e)
constantly constamment
contrary contraire *m.*
    on the ~ au contraire
cooking cuisine *f.*
cool: it's ~ il fait frais
corner coin *m.*
corridor couloir *m.*
cost *v.* coûter
cough *v.* tousser
could you …? pourriez-vous …?
country pays *m.*
course *(classroom)* cours *m.*; *(meal)* plat *m.*
    first ~ entrée *f.*
    of ~ certainement, bien sûr
cousin cousin/cousine *m./f.*
crazy fou (folle)
    ~ person fou/folle *m./f.*
    in a ~ manner follement
cream crème *f.*

credit card carte de crédit *f.*
croissant croissant *m.*
cry *v.* pleurer
cup tasse *f.*
curve virage *m.*
custom coutume *f.*
customer client/cliente *m./f.*
cut *v.* couper
cyclist coureur (cycliste) *m.*

damage dégâts *m. pl.*
dance *n.* bal *m.*
dance *v.* danser
dangerous dangereux (dangereuse)
darn it! mince!; zut!
date *n.* date *f.*; rendez-vous *m.*
date (someone) *v.* fréquenter (quelqu'un)
daughter fille *f.*
day jour *m.*
    ~ after tomorrow après-demain
    have a good ~ bonne journée
    New Year's ~ Jour de l'An *m.*
    what ~ is it? quel jour est-ce?
dead mort(e)
dear *n.* chéri/chérie *m./f.*
dear *adj.* cher (chère)
death mort *f.*
debit card carte bancaire *f.*
debt dette *f.*
December décembre *m.*
definitely sûrement, certainement
delicatessen charcuterie *f.*
delicious délicieux (délicieuse)
delighted ravi(e)
    ~ to meet you enchanté(e)
demand (that) exiger (que)
department store grand magasin *m.*
departmental (local) highway départementale *f.*
departure départ *m.*
depend dépendre
    it (that) depends ça dépend
depressed déprimé(e)
describe décrire
desk bureau *m.* (*pl.* bureaux)
dessert dessert *m.*
destroy détruire
detective story roman policier *m.*
detest détester
to destroy détruire
devastate ravager
develop développer
die mourir
different original(e) (*m.pl.* originaux);
    différent(e)
dining room salle à manger *f.*
dinner dîner *m.*
    at ~ à table
    have ~ dîner *v.*

diploma diplôme *m.*
directions indications *f.pl.*
dirty sale
disagreeable désagréable
disappointed déçu(e)
disaster: natural disaster désastre naturel *m.*
discreet discret (discrète)
dish plat *m.*
dishes vaisselle *f.*
   do the ~ faire la vaisselle
dishwasher lave-vaisselle *m.*
divorce *n.* divorce *m.*
divorce *v.* divorcer
divorced divorcé(e)
do faire
   ~ the grocery shopping faire les provisions
   what am I going to ~? comment je vais faire?
doctor médecin *m.*, docteur *m.*
dog chien *m.*
dollar dollar *m.*
door porte *f.*
dormitory résidence (universitaire) *f.*
dozen douzaine *f.*
dream: pleasant dreams bonne nuit
dress *n.* robe *f.*
   wedding ~ robe de mariée *f.*
dressed: get ~ s'habiller
drink *n.* boisson *f.*
   before-dinner ~ apéritif *m.*
drink *v.* boire, prendre
   do you want to ~ something? voulez-vous boire quelque chose?; quelque chose à boire?
drive *n.: to take a ~* faire une promenade en voiture
drive conduire
driver automobiliste *m./f.*, conducteur/ conductrice *m./f.*, chauffeur *m.*
   ~'s license permis de conduire *m.*
driving *n.* conduite *f.*
drums batterie *f.*
drunk *adj.* ivre
during pendant

each *adj.* chaque
   ~ (one) chacun(e)
ear oreille *f.*
early tôt; en avance
earn one's living gagner sa vie
earth terre *f.*
earthquake tremblement de terre *m.*
easy facile; simple
eat manger; prendre
   ~ dinner dîner
   ~ lunch déjeuner
economics sciences économiques *f.pl.*
education pédagogie *f.*

egg œuf *m.*
eight huit
eighteen dix-huit
eighty quatre-vingts
eighty-one quatre-vingt-un
eleven onze
email e-mail *m.*
embarrassed confus(e)
employee employé/employée *m./f.*
end *n.* fin *f.*
engaged fiancé(e)
engagement fiançailles *f.pl.*
engineer ingénieur *m.*
England Angleterre *f.*
English anglais(e)
enough assez
enter entrer
epidemic épidémie *f.*
errands courses *f.pl.*
essential essentiel(le)
   it is ~ that il est essentiel que
estimate *v.* estimer
evacuate évacuer
even même
evening soir *m.*
   good ~ bonsoir
   have a good ~ bonne soirée
ever jamais
every chaque; tout (toute/tous/toutes)
   ~ night tous les soirs
everybody tout le monde
everything tout *pron. inv.*
everywhere partout
exaggerate exagérer
exam examen *m.*
   on an ~ à un examen
example exemple *m.*
   for ~ par exemple
excellent excellent(e)
exciting passionnant(e)
excuse: ~ me je vous demande pardon; excusez-moi
executive cadre *m.*
exercise exercice *m.*
expensive cher (chère)
eye œil *m. (pl.* yeux)
   my ~! mon œil!
eyeglasses lunettes *f.pl.*

fall *n.* automne *m.*
fall *v.* tomber
   ~ asleep s'endormir
false faux (fausse)
familiar: be ~ with connaître
family famille *f.*
famous célèbre
fantastic formidable
far (from) loin (de)
farmer agriculteur/agricultrice *m./f.*

fast rapide
fat gros(se), gras(se)
father père *m.*
father-in-law beau-père *m. (pl.* beaux-pères)
faucet robinet *m.*
fault faute *f.*
favorite préféré(e)
fear peur
February février *m.*
fed up: be ~ en avoir assez
feel sentir, se sentir
   ~ like avoir envie de
   ~ sorry (for someone) avoir pitié (de)
fever fièvre *f.*
few peu (de)
   a ~ quelques
fifteen quinze
fifty cinquante
film film *m.*
finally enfin
find *v.* trouver
fine bien
   I'm ~ je vais très bien; ça va bien
finish *v.* finir
fire incendie *f.*
first premier (première)
   at ~ d'abord
   ~ name prénom *m.*
   in ~ class en première classe
fish *n.* poisson *m.*
five cinq
flea market marché aux puces *m.*
Flemish flamand *m.*
flight vol *m.*
flight attendant *(female)* hôtesse de l'air *f.*
flood *n.* inondation *f.*
floor *(of a building)* étage *m.; (of a room)* plancher *m.*
   ground ~ rez-de-chaussée *m.*
florist fleuriste *m./f*
flower fleur *f.*
flu grippe *f.*
fluently couramment
flute flûte *f.*
follow: ~ me par ici
following suivant(e)
food cuisine *f.*
fool fou/folle *m./f.*
foot pied *m.*
football football américain *m.*
for depuis; pendant; pour
foreign étranger (étrangère)
forest forêt *f.*
forget oublier
fork fourchette *f.*
former *adj.* ancien(ne)
fortunately heureusement
forty quarante
four quatre
fourteen quatorze

franc franc *m.*
France France *f.*
free libre
French français(e)
  ~ fries frites *f.pl.*
  in ~ en français
  in the ~ style à la française
  steak with ~ fries steak frites *m.*
Friday vendredi *m.*
friend ami/amie *m./f.*
  make friends se faire des amis
from de
front: in ~ of devant
fruit fruit *m.*
fun *adj.* amusant(e)
  have ~ s'amuser
funny amusant(e), drôle

game jeu *m. (pl.* jeux); match *m.*
garage garage *m.*
garlic ail *m.*
Gee! Tiens!
general: in ~ en général
generally généralement
generous généreux (généreuse)
German allemand(e)
Germany Allemagne *f.*
get obtenir, recevoir
  ~ along (with) s'entendre (avec)
  ~ angry se fâcher
  ~ dressed s'habiller
  ~ into monter
  ~ out of descendre
  ~ up, stand up se lever
  ~ washed, wash up se laver
ghost revenant *m.*
gift cadeau *m.*
girl fille *f.*
girlfriend petite amie *f.*
give donner
  ~ back rendre
gladly volontiers; je veux bien
glass (drinking) verre *m.*
glasses (eye) lunettes *f.pl.*
glove gant *m.*
go (in a vehicle) aller, rouler
  ~ across traverser
  ~ ahead allez-y
  ~ back retourner, rentrer
  ~ down descendre
  ~ into town aller en ville
  ~ out sortir
  ~ to bed se coucher
  ~ up monter
goat cheese chèvre *m.*
golf golf *m.*
good bon (bonne)
  ~ evening bonsoir
  ~ morning bonjour

  have a ~ afternoon bon après-midi
  have a ~ day bonne journée
  have a ~ time s'amuser
good-bye au revoir
grade note *f.*
grains céréales *f.pl.*
grandchildren petits-enfants *m.pl.*
granddaughter petite-fille *f. (pl.* petites-filles)
grandfather grand-père *m. (pl.* grands-pères)
grandmother grand-mère *f. (pl.* grands-mères)
grandparents grands-parents *m.pl.*
grandson petit-fils *m. (pl.* petits-fils)
great formidable; chouette *(fam.)*
great-grandfather arrière-grand-père *m.*
green vert(e)
  ~ beans haricots verts *m.pl.*
grey gris(e)
groceries provisions *f.pl.*
  do the grocery shopping faire les provisions
grocery store épicerie *f.*
guess *v.* deviner
guitar guitare *f.*
gymnasium gymnase *m.*
gymnastics gymnastique *f.*

hair cheveux *m.pl.*
  hairbrush brosse à cheveux *f.*
half *adj.* demi(e)
  ~ past … il est … heure(s) et demie
hall couloir *m.*
ham jambon *m.*
hand main *f.*
handsome beau/bel/belle/beaux/belles
happen arriver, se passer
happy heureux (heureuse); content(e)
hardworking travailleur (travailleuse)
hat chapeau *m.*
hate *v.* détester
have avoir
  do you still ~ …? il vous reste …?
  ~ a pain (in) avoir mal (à)
  ~ an appointment, date avoir rendez-vous
  ~ dinner dîner
  ~ fun s'amuser
  ~ just venir de
  ~ lunch déjeuner
  ~ pity avoir pitié (de)
  ~ to devoir
  what do you ~ for (in the way) of
    …? qu'est-ce que vous avez comme …?
he *pron.* il; lui
head tête *f.*
health: (here's) to your ~! à votre santé!
hear entendre
  ~ about entendre parler de
heat chauffage *m.*
hello bonjour; bonsoir; salut
  ~ ! *(on the phone)* allô!
help *v.* aider

her *pron.* elle; la; (to ~ lui)
her *adj.* son, sa, ses
here ici
  ~ is, ~ are voici
hi! salut!
high-top sneakers baskets *f.pl.*
highway autoroute *f.*
  departmental (local) ~ départementale *f.*
him *pron.* le; (to ~) lui
his *adj.* son, sa, ses
history histoire *f.*
hockey hockey *m.*
holiday fête *f.*
home maison *f.*
  at the ~ of chez
  go (come) ~ rentrer
homeless person sans abri *m./f.*
homework devoirs *m.pl.*
honestly sans façon
hope *v.* espérer; souhaiter (que)
horrible mauvais(e)
hose bas *m.pl.*
hot chaud(e)
  be ~ avoir chaud
  ~ chocolate chocolat chaud *m.*
  it is ~ il fait chaud
hotel hôtel *m.*
hour heure *f.*
  one ~ ago il y a une heure
  one ~ from now dans une heure
house maison *f.*
  at your ~ chez toi
housewife femme *f.* au foyer
housework ménage *m.*
  do ~ faire le ménage
how comment
  ~ are you? comment allez-vous?; (comment) ça va?
  ~ do you say …? comment dit-on …?
  ~ do you spell …? comment est-ce qu'on écrit …?
  ~ … he (she) was! comme il (elle) était …!
  ~ long? pendant combien de temps …?
  ~ many, much combien (de)
  ~ old are you? quel âge avez-vous?
hundred cent
hungry: be ~ avoir faim
hurry se dépêcher
husband mari *m.*

I *pron.* je; moi
ice cream glace *f.*
  vanilla ~ glace à la vanille *f.*
idiot idiot/idiote *m./f.*
if si
imbecile imbécile *m./f.*

impatience impatience f.
impatient impatient(e)
important important(e)
  it is ~ that il est important que
in à; dans; en
  ~ a crazy manner follement
  ~ a little while tout à l'heure
  ~ exchange for contre
  ~ general en général
  ~ order to pour
  ~ the afternoon de l'après-midi
included compris(e)
incredible incroyable
indeed tout à fait
indicate indiquer
indispensable indispensable
inexpensive bon marché inv.
inform (se) renseigner
information renseignement m.
inside intérieur m.
  ~ of à l'intérieur de
insist insister
instrument instrument m.
insure assurer
intellectual adj. intellectuel(le)
intelligent intelligent(e)
interest intérêt m.
interested: be ~ in s'intéresser à
interesting intéressant(e)
interpreter interprète m./f.
introduce présenter
  allow me to ~ myself permettez-moi de me
    présenter
invite inviter
Ireland Irlande f.
Israel Israël m.
it pron. cela, ça; il, elle
it is il est, c'est
  is it …? est-ce (que) …?
  ~ better that il vaut mieux que
  ~ cold il fait froid
  ~ cool il fait frais
  ~ essential il est essentiel
  ~ nice out il fait beau
  ~ preferable il vaut mieux
  ~ raining il pleut
  ~ snowing il neige
  ~ windy il fait du vent
Italian italien(ne)
Italy Italie f.
its adj. son, sa, ses

jacket blouson m.
jam confiture f.
January janvier m.
Japan Japon m.
Japanese japonais(e)
jeans jean m.

jogging jogging m.
juice jus m.
  orange ~ jus d'orange m.
July juillet m.
June juin m.
just: to have ~ … venir de …
just adv. juste

keep garder
key clé f
  kidding: no ~ sans façon; sans blague!
kilogram kilo m.
kind n. sorte f.
  all ~s of things toutes sortes de choses
  what ~(s) of … quelle(s) sorte(s) de …
kind adj. aimable; gentil(le)
kir kir m.
kiss v. s'embrasser
kitchen cuisine f.
knee genou m. (pl. genoux)
knife couteau m. (pl. couteaux)
knock frapper
know connaître, savoir
  I don't ~ je ne sais pas

laborer ouvrier/ouvrière m./f.
lady dame f.
language langue f.
lap n. genoux m.pl.
last dernier (dernière)
  ~ name nom de famille m.
  the ~ time la dernière fois
late tard, en retard
  be ~ être en retard
  it is ~ il est tard
lawn bowling pétanque f.
lay mettre
lazy paresseux (paresseuse)
leaf (of paper) feuille f.
learn apprendre (à)
least le/la/les moins
  at ~ au moins
  I like ~ j'aime le moins
leave laisser, partir
  ~ from partir (de)
  ~ me alone! laisse-moi (laissez-moi)
    tranquille!
  there's one left il en reste un(e)
left: to the ~ (of) à gauche (de)
leftovers des restes m. pl.
leg jambe f.
leisure activity loisir m.
lemon-lime soda limonade f.
lemonade citron pressé m.
lend prêter
length (of time) durée f.
less moins

lesson leçon f.
let laisser
  let's go allez-y, allons-y
letter lettre f.
library bibliothèque f.
license: driver's ~ permis de conduire m.
life vie f.
  that's ~ c'est la vie
lift v. lever
like v. aimer
  I would ~ je voudrais
like conj. comme
listen (to) écouter
liter litre m.
literature littérature f.
little adj. petit(e)
  ~ girl petite fille f.
little adv. peu (de)
  a ~ un peu (de)
live v. habiter
living room salon m.
long long (longue)
  a ~ time longtemps
  be a ~ time coming tarder
  how ~ …? pendant combien de temps …?
  no longer ne … plus
look regarder; (seem) avoir l'air
  ~ after garder
  ~ for chercher
lose perdre
  ~ (one's) patience perdre patience
  ~ weight maigrir
lot: a ~ (of) beaucoup (de)
love v. adorer; aimer
  ~ each other s'aimer
lozenge pastille f.
luck chance f.
  good ~! bonne chance!
  what ~! quelle chance!
lunch déjeuner m.
  have ~ déjeuner

magazine magazine m.
mail v. poster
make n. marque f.
make v. faire
  ~ a request faire une demande
  ~ friends se faire des amis
mall centre commercial m.
man homme m.; monsieur m.
management gestion f.
manner façon f.
manners étiquette f.
many beaucoup
  how ~ combien
  so ~ tant
  too ~ trop (de)
map carte f.; (city) plan m.

March mars *m.*
market marché *m.*
  flea ~ marché aux puces *m.*
  super ~ supermarché *m.*
marriage mariage *m.*
married marié(e)
marry se marier (avec); épouser
matter: what's the ~ with you? qu'est-ce que tu as?
May mai *m.*
may (be able to) pouvoir
  ~ I? vous permettez?; puis-je?
maybe peut-être
mayonnaise mayonnaise *f.*
mayor maire *m.*
me *pron.* me, moi
  ~ neither, nor I moi non plus
meal repas *m.*
  have a good ~! bon appétit!
mean *v.* vouloir dire
mean *adj.* méchant(e)
meat viande *f.*
medicine médicament *m.*
meet rencontrer
  to have met avoir connu
meeting réunion *f.*; rendez-vous *m.*
  have a ~ avoir rendez-vous
member membre *m.*
mention: don't ~ it il n'y a pas de quoi; de rien
menu *(à la carte)* carte *f.*; *(fixed price)* menu *m.*
merchant marchand/marchande *m./f.*
message: text message texto (SMS) *m.*
Mexican mexicain(e)
Mexico Mexique *m.*
midnight minuit *m.*
milk lait *m.*
million million *m.*
mind your own business! occupe-toi de tes oignons!
mine *pron.* le mien/la mienne
minute minute *f.*
mirror: rearview ~ rétroviseur *m.*
miserly avare
Miss Mademoiselle (Mlle)
mistake faute *f.*
Monday lundi *m.*
money argent *m.*
month mois *m.*
more encore, plus
  ~ ...? encore de ...?
  ~ to drink (eat)? encore à boire (manger)?
  there is no ~ il n'y en a plus
morning matin *m.*
Moroccan marocain(e)
Morocco Maroc *m.*
most (of) la plupart (de);
  the ~ le/la/les plus
mother mère *f.*
mother-in-law belle-mère *f. (pl.* belles-mères)

motorcycle moto *f.*
motorized bicycle mobylette *f.*
mouse souris *f.*
mouth bouche *f.*
movie film *m.*
  ~ theater cinéma *m.*
Mr. Monsieur (*M.*)
Mrs. Madame (Mme)
much beaucoup
  as ~ autant (de)
  how ~ combien
  not ~ pas grand-chose
  so ~ tant (de)
  too ~ trop (de)
museum musée *m.*
mushrooms champignons *m.pl.*
music musique *f.*
must devoir; il faut
  (someone) ~ not il ne faut pas
mustard moutarde *f.*
my *adj.* mon, ma, mes

naive naïf (naïve)
name *n.* nom *m.*
  family (last) ~ nom de famille
  in whose ~ ...? à quel nom ...?
  my ~ is ... je m'appelle ...
  what is your ~? comment vous appelez-vous?
named: be ~ s'appeler
nap sieste *f.*
  take a ~ faire la sieste
napkin serviette *f.*
nasty méchant(e)
nationality nationalité *f.*
  what is your ~? quelle est votre nationalité?
natural disaster désastre naturel *m.*
naturally naturellement
near près (de)
  very ~ tout près
necessary nécessaire
  it is ~ il faut, il est nécessaire (que)
need *v.* avoir besoin de
neighbor voisin/voisine *m./f.*
neither: me ~ moi non plus
  ~ ... nor ni ... ni
nephew neveu *m. (pl.* neveux)
nervous nerveux (nerveuse)
never jamais (ne ... jamais)
new nouveau/nouvel (nouvelle) (nouveaux); neuf (neuve)
  ~ Year's Day Jour de l'An *m.*
  what's ~? quoi de neuf?
news informations *f.pl.*
newspaper journal *m.*
newsstand kiosque à journaux *m.*
next *adv.* ensuite, puis; *adj.* prochain(e); suivant(e)

  ~ door à côté
  ~ to à côté de
nice aimable; gentil(le)
  have a ~ day bonne journée
  it's ~ out il fait beau
  that's ~ of you c'est gentil à vous
niece nièce *f.*
night nuit *f.*
nine neuf
nineteen dix-neuf
ninety quatre-vingt-dix
ninety-one quatre-vingt-onze
no non
  ~ kidding! sans blague!; sans façon
  ~ longer ne ... plus
  ~ more ne ... plus
  ~ one ne ... personne
nobody ne ... personne
noise bruit *m.*
noon midi *m.*
nor: ~ I moi non plus
  neither ... ~ ni ... ni
nose nez *m.*
  runny ~ le nez qui coule
not ne (n') ... pas
  ~ anyone ne ... personne
  ~ anything ne ... rien
  ~ at all il n'y a pas de quoi, de rien; pas du tout
  ~ much pas grand-chose
  ~ yet pas encore
note note *f.*
nothing ne ... rien
notice *v.* remarquer
novel *n.* roman *m.*
novel *adj.* original(e) (originaux)
November novembre *m.*
now maintenant, actuellement
number nombre *m.*, numéro *m.*; chiffre *m.*
  telephone ~ numéro de téléphone *m.*
nurse infirmier/infirmière *m./f.*

obey obéir (à)
o'clock heure(s)
  at ... ~ à ... heure(s)
  it is ... ~ il est ... heure(s)
October octobre *m.*
of de
  ~ course bien sûr
office bureau *m. (pl.* bureaux)
  post ~ bureau de poste *m.*
officer: police ~ agent de police *m.*
often souvent
oh dear! oh là là!
okay d'accord
  if that's ~ si ça va
old âgé(e), vieux/vieil (vieille)
  how ~ are you? quel âge avez-vous?

omelet omelette *f.*
on sur
one *pron.* on
  no ~ ne ... personne
one *(number)* un (une)
one-way: ~ street sens interdit *m.*
  ~ ticket aller simple *m.*
onion oignon *m.*
only *adj.* seul(e); *adv.* seulement; ne ... que
open *v.* ouvrir
open *adj.* ouvert(e)
opening ouverture *f.*
opinion avis *m.*
  be of the ~ trouver; penser
  in my (your, etc.) ~ à mon (à ton, etc.) avis
opposite contraire *m.*
optimistic optimiste
or ou
orange *n.* orange *m.*
  ~ juice jus d'orange *m.*
  ~ soda orangina *m.*
orange *adj.* orange *inv*
order *v.* commander
order: in ~ to pour
ordinary *adj.* ordinaire
original original(e) *(m.pl.originaux)*
other autre
ouch! aïe!
our notre, nos
outgoing extraverti(e)
outside dehors
owe devoir
owner propriétaire *m./f.*

package paquet *m.*
pain: have a ~ (in) avoir mal (à)
pajamas (pair of) pyjama *m.*
pale pâle
pants (pair of) pantalon *m.*
paper papier *m.*
  (news)paper journal *m.*
  term ~ dissertation *f.*
pardon: I beg your ~ je vous demande pardon; excusez-moi
parents parents *m.pl.*
parents-in-law beaux-parents *m.pl.*
party soirée *f.;* fête *f.*
pass *(an exam)* réussir
pass *(a car)* dépasser
pastry pâtisserie *f.*
  ~ shop pâtisserie *f.*
patience: lose (one's) ~ perdre patience
patient *adj.* patient(e)
patiently patiemment
pavement chaussée *f.*
pay (for) payer
  ~ attention faire attention (à)
peanut cacahuète *f.*
  ~ butter beurre de cacahuète *m.*

peas petits pois *m.pl.*
people gens *m.pl.;* on
pepper poivre *m.*
per par
perfect parfait(e)
perhaps peut-être
period *(time)* époque *f.*
person *(male or female)* personne *f.*
personally *adv.* personnellement
pessimistic pessimiste
pharmacy pharmacie *f.*
philosophy philosophie *f.*
photograph photo *f.*
physical physique
piano piano *m.*
picnic pique-nique *m.*
pie tarte *f.*
piece morceau *m. (pl.* morceaux)
pill pilule *f.;* cachet *m.*
pilot pilote *m.*
pink rose
pity pitié *f.*
pizza pizza *f.*
place *n.* endroit *m.;* lieu *m.*
  take ~ avoir lieu
place *v.* mettre
plain simple
plan to avoir l'intention de
plate assiette *f.*
play *n.* pièce *f.*
play *v.* jouer
  ~ a game jouer à
  ~ an instrument jouer de
  ~ sports faire du sport
  ~ tennis jouer au tennis
pleasant dreams bonne nuit
please s'il vous (te) plaît
  ~ do je vous (t')en prie
pleasure plaisir *m.*
  with ~ avec plaisir
poem poème *m.*
point out indiquer
police officer agent de police *m.;* gendarme *m.*
politician homme/femme politique *m./f.*
politics politique *f.*
poor *adj.* pauvre
poorly mal
popular populaire
porch véranda *f.*
pork porc *m.*
  ~ butcher's charcuterie *f.*
post office bureau de poste *m.*
postcard carte postale *f.*
potato pomme de terre *f.*
pound *n.* livre *f.*
pour verser
practice répéter
prefer préférer
  I ~ that je préfère que

preferable: it is ~ that il vaut mieux que
prepare (a lesson) préparer (un cours)
pretty joli(e)
price prix *m.*
probably sans doute
process: be in the ~ of être en train de
program programme *m.*
  TV ~ émission (de télé) *f.*
programmer informaticien/informaticienne *m./f.*
promise *v.* promettre
  it's a ~ c'est promis
psychology psychologie *f.*
publicity publicité *f.*
punch (a ticket) composter (un billet)
pupil élève *m./f.*
purchase achat *m.*
purple violet(te)
put mettre
  ~ on attacher; mettre *(clothes)*
  ~ on weight grossir

quarter *m.* quart
  ~ past, ~ after et quart
  ~ to, ~ till moins le quart
question question *f.*
  ask a ~ poser une question
quickly vite; rapidement
quiet: keep ~! tais-toi! (taisez-vous!)

race course *f.*
radio radio *f.*
rain pleuvoir
  it's raining il pleut
raincoat imperméable *m.*
raise *v.* lever
rapid rapide
rapidly rapidement
rare *(undercooked)* saignant(e)
rarely rarement
rather assez
  ~ poorly assez mal
read lire
reality TV show émission de téléréalité *f.*
really vraiment; sans façon
reasonable raisonnable
recently récemment
recommend recommander
red rouge
  ~ -haired roux (rousse)
refrigerator réfrigérateur *m.*
regarding à propos de
relatives parents *m.pl.*
remain rester
remember se souvenir (de)
rent *v.* louer

repeat répéter
request *n.* demande *f.*
  make a ~ faire une demande
reserve *v.* réserver
reside habiter
responsibility responsabilité *f.*
rest *v.* se reposer
restaurant restaurant *m.*
restroom toilettes *f.pl.*
return *v.* retourner, revenir, rentrer
rice riz *m.*
rich riche
ride: take a ~ se promener; faire une
  promenade en voiture
  ~ a bike faire du vélo
ridiculous ridicule
right *n.* droit *m.*
right *adj.* droit(e); exact(e)
  be ~ avoir raison
  ~ ? n'est-ce pas?
  ~ away tout de suite
  ~ behind juste derrière
  that's ~ c'est exact
  to the ~ (of) à droite (de)
ring *n.* bague *f.*
road route *f.*
roast (of beef) rôti (de bœuf) *m.*
roll *v.* rouler
roof toit *m.*
room chambre *f.;* salle *f.;* pièce *f.*
  bath~ salle de bain *f.*
  bed~ chambre *f.*
  class~ salle de classe *f.*
  dining~ salle à manger *f.*
roommate camarade de chambre *m./f.*
round-trip ticket aller-retour *m.*
rugby rugby *m.*
run courir
  ~ a stop sign brûler un stop
  ~ into heurter
runner coureur/coureuse
Russia Russie *f.*
Russian russe

sad triste
salad salade *f*
  (green) ~ salade (verte) *f*
salesman/saleswoman
  vendeur/vendeuse *m./f.*
salmon saumon *m.*
salt sel *m.*
sandwich sandwich *m.*
Santa Claus *m.* père Noël
Saturday samedi *m.*
sausage saucisse *f*
saxophone saxophone *m.*
say dire
scarf foulard *m.*

schedule emploi du temps *m.*
school école *f*
  high ~ lycée *m.*
science sciences *f.pl.*
  computer ~ informatique *f*
scooter scooter *m.*
season saison *f*
seat place *f.*
seatbelt ceinture de sécurité *f.*
second second(e), deuxième
  in ~ class en seconde
see voir
  (I hope to) ~ you again au plaisir (de vous
    revoir)
  ~you in a little while à tout à l'heure
  ~ you soon à bientôt
  ~ you tomorrow à demain
seem avoir l'air
-self(-selves) -même(s)
sell vendre
semester semestre *m.*
send envoyer
Senegal Sénégal *m.*
Senegalese sénégalais(e)
separate *v.* séparer
  ~ from each other se séparer
September septembre *m.*
series *(TV)* feuilleton *m.*
serious sérieux (sérieuse)
seriously sérieusement
service: at your ~ à votre service
serviceman/woman militaire *m.*
set: ~ the table mettre la table
seven sept
seventeen dix-sept
seventy soixante-dix
seventy-one soixante et onze
seventy-two soixante-douze
shake *v.* secouer
she *pron.* elle
sheet (of paper) feuille *f.*
shh! chut!
shirt chemise *f.*
shoe chaussure *f.*
shop *(clothing)* boutique *f.*
  tobacco ~ (bureau de) tabac *m.*
shopping courses *f.pl.*
  ~ center centre commercial *m.*
short petit(e)
shorts (pair of) short *m.*
shoulder épaule *f*
show *v.* montrer; émission *f.*
  reality TV ~ émission de téléréalité
shower *n.* douche *f*
shower *v.* se doucher
sick malade
since depuis
sincere sincère
sing chanter

singer chanteur/chanteuse *m./f.*
single célibataire
Sir Monsieur (*M.*)
sister sœur *f.* sister-in-law belle-sœur *f. (pl.*
  belles-sœurs)
sit down s'asseoir
  ~ to eat se mettre a table
six six
sixteen seize
sixty soixante
skate patiner
skating rink patinoire *f*
ski skier
skid déraper
skirt jupe *f*
skis skis *m.pl.*
sleep dormir
sleepy: be ~ avoir sommeil
slice tranche *f*
slippery glissant(e)
slow *adj.* lent(e)
slow down ralentir
slowly lentement
small petit(e)
smile *n.* sourire *m.*
smile *v.* sourire
smoke fumer
smoking fumeur
  non-~ non-fumeur
snail escargot *m.*
snow *v.* neiger
  it's snowing il neige
so alors, si
  ~ many tant
  ~ much tant
so-so comme ci, comme ça
soap opera feuilleton *m.*
soccer football (foot) *m.*
sock chaussette *f.*
soda: lemon-lime ~ limonade *f.*
  orange ~ orangina *m.*
sofa sofa *m.*
some *adj.* des, quelques; *pron.* en
someone quelqu'un
something quelque chose *m.*
sometimes quelquefois
son fils *m.*
song chanson *f.*
soon bientôt
sore: be ~ avoir mal (à)
sorry désolé(e)
  be ~ regretter
  feel ~ (for) avoir pitié (de)
sort of assez
soup soupe *f*
Spain Espagne *f.*
Spanish espagnol(e)
speak parler
specify préciser

speed vitesse *f.*
  at top ~ à toute vitesse
spell épeler
  how do you ~ ...? comment est-ce qu'on écrit ...?
  ... is spelled s'écrit ...
spend (a year) passer (un an)
spinach épinards *m.pl.*
spoon cuiller *f.*
sportcoat veste *f.*
spring *n.* printemps *m.*
stamp timbre *m.*
stand up se lever
start commencer; démarrer
  it's starting to get cold il commence à faire froid
starter *n.* entrée *f.*
state État *m.*
statue statue *f.*
stay rester
steak steak *m.*
  ~ with French fries steak-frites *m.*
steering wheel volant *m.*
stepbrother demi-frère *m.*
stepfather beau-père *m. (pl.* beaux-pères)
stepmother belle-mère *f (pl.* belles-mères)
stepparents beaux-parents *m.pl.*
stepsister demi-sœur *f.*
stereo stéréo *f.*
still encore; toujours
stomach estomac *m.*
stop *n.* arrêt *m.*
  bus ~ arrêt d'autobus *m.*
  ~ sign stop *m.*
stop *v.* (s')arrêter
store magasin *m.*
  department ~ grand magasin *m.*
  grocery ~ épicerie *f.*
storm *n.* tempête *f.*
story histoire *f.*
  detective ~ roman policier *m.*
stove cuisinière *f.*
straight ahead tout droit
strawberry fraise *f.*
street rue *f.*
  one-way ~ sens interdit *m.*
stressed stressé(e)
student étudiant/étudiante *m./f.*
studies études *f.pl.*
study *v.* étudier
stupid stupide
stylish chic *adj. inv.*
succeed réussir
sugar sucre *m.*
suit *n.* costume *m.*
  bathing ~ maillot de bain *m.*
suitcase valise *f.*
summer été *m.*
sun soleil *m.*

Sunday dimanche *m.*
supermarket supermarché *m.*
  giant ~ hypermarché *m.*
supplement supplément *m.*
supposed: be ~ to devoir
surely certainement, sûrement
surprise surprise *f.*
  what a good ~! quelle bonne surprise!
survive survivre
swear jurer
  I ~ (to you) je te le jure
sweater pull-over (pull) *m.*
sweatshirt sweat-shirt *m.*
Sweden Suède *f.*
Swedish suédois(e)
swim nager
swimming pool piscine *f.*
swimsuit maillot de bain *m.*
Swiss suisse
  ~ cheese emmental *m.*
Switzerland Suisse *f.*

table table *f.*
  at the ~ à table
  set the ~ mettre la table
tablecloth nappe *f.*
tablet cachet *m.*
  aspirin ~ cachet d'aspirine *m.*
take prendre
  ~ a nap faire la sieste
  ~ a test passer (un examen)
  ~ a trip faire un voyage
  ~ a walk, a ride faire une promenade
  ~ place avoir lieu
talkative bavard(e)
tall grand(e)
taste *v.* goûter
tea thé *m.*
teach enseigner
teacher professeur *m.*
  ~ preparation pédagogie *f.*
team équipe *f.*
tee-shirt tee-shirt *m.*
telephone *n.* téléphone *m.*
  on the ~ au téléphone
  ~ number numéro de téléphone *m.*
telephone *v.* téléphoner (à)
television télévision (télé) *f.*
tell indiquer, raconter, dire, parler
  can you ~ me ...? pouvez-vous me dire ...?
  ~ a story raconter une histoire
ten dix
tend to avoir tendance à
tennis tennis *m.*
  ~ shoes tennis *f.pl.*
  play ~ jouer au tennis
term paper dissertation *f.*

test examen *m.*
text message texto (SMS) *m.*
thank *v.* remercier
thanks merci
  yes, ~ je veux bien
that *adj.* ce/cet, cette, ces; *conj.* que; *pron.* ce, cela, ça; *relative pron.* qui, que
the le/la/les
theater théâtre *m.*
their leur(s)
them elles, eux; les, leur
then alors, ensuite, puis
there là, y
  over ~ là-bas
  ~ is (are) il y a; voilà
therefore alors; donc
they *pron.* ils, elles, on, eux
  ~ (these) are ce sont
thin mince
thing chose *f.*
think croire, penser, trouver
  do you ~ so? vous trouvez?
  I don't ~ so je ne crois pas
  what do you ~ of ...? Comment trouvez-vous ...?
  what do you ~ of it (of them)? qu'en penses-tu?
thirsty: be ~ avoir soif
thirteen treize
thirty trente
this *adj.* ce/cet, cette, ces
  ~ way par ici
those *adj.* ces
thousand mille *inv.*
three trois
throat gorge *f.*
throughway autoroute *f.*
Thursday jeudi *m.*
ticket billet *m.*
  one-way ~ aller simple *m.*
  round-trip ~ aller-retour *m.*
tie *n.* cravate *f.*
tights collant *m.pl.*
time temps *m.*; heure *f.*; fois *f.*
  a long ~ longtemps
  at that ~ à cette époque
  on ~ à l'heure
  the last ~ la dernière fois
  ~ difference décalage horaire *m.*
  what ~ is it? quelle heure est-il?
tired fatigué(e)
to à
  ~ the side à côté
toast pain grillé *m.*
tobacco tabac *m.*
  ~ shop (bureau de) tabac *m.*
today aujourd'hui
together ensemble
tomato tomate *f.*

tomorrow demain
   day after ~ après-demain
tonight ce soir
too aussi
   ~ many trop (de)
   ~ much trop (de)
   you ~ vous (toi) aussi
tooth dent *f.*
toothbrush brosse à dents *f.*
toothpaste dentifrice *m.*
tornado tornade *f.*
tour tour *m.*
   ~ bus autocar *m.*
towel serviette *f.*
tower tour *f.*
town ville *f.*
   ~ hall mairie *f.*
trade ... for échanger ... contre
traffic circulation *f.*
traffic light feu *m. (pl.* feux)
train train *m.*
   ~ station gare *f.*
travel voyager
traveler's check chèque de voyage *m.*
trip voyage *m.*
trout truite *f.*
true vrai(e)
truly vraiment
   yours ~ amicalement
trumpet trompette *f.*
truth vérité *f.*
try essayer
   may I ~ ...? puis-je ...?
Tuesday mardi *m.*
turn *n.* tour *m.*
turn *v.* tourner
   ~ on *(the TV)* mettre
   ~ on the heat mettre le chauffage
turnpike autoroute *f.*
tuxedo smoking *m.*
twelve douze
twenty vingt
twenty-one vingt et un
twenty-two vingt-deux
two deux

ugly laid(e)
unbelievable incroyable
uncle oncle *m.*
under sous
understand comprendre
understanding compréhensif/compréhensive
United States États-Unis *m.pl.*
university université *f.*
unmarried célibataire
until *prep.* jusqu'à
   until next time à la prochaine
unwise: be ~ avoir tort

up: get ~ se lever
us nous
useless inutile
usually d'habitude

vacation vacances *f.pl.*
   have a good ~! bonnes vacances!
   on ~ en vacances
vanilla vanille *f.*
   ~ ice cream glace à la vanille *f.*
vegetable légume *m.*
   raw vegetables crudités *f.pl.*
very très; tout
violin violon *m.*
visit *v.* visiter
   ~ someone rendre visite à qqn
voyage voyage *m.*

wait (for) attendre
waiter serveur *m.*
waitress serveuse *f.*
wake up se réveiller
walk *n.* promenade *f.*
   take a ~ se promener; faire une promenade
walk *v.* se promener
want vouloir, désirer, avoir envie de
war guerre *f.*
warmly chaleureusement
warning avertissement *m.*
wash *v.* laver; se laver
washing machine lave-linge *m.;* machine à laver *f.*
watch *n.* montre *f.*
watch *v.* regarder
water eau *f. (pl.* eaux)
   mineral ~ eau minérale
way route *f.;* façon *f.*
   by the ~ au fait
we nous
wear porter
weather météo(rologie) *f.;* temps *m.*
   the ~ is bad il fait mauvais
   what is the ~ like? quel temps fait-il?
wedding mariage *m.*
   ~ anniversary anniversaire de mariage *m.*
   ~ dress robe de mariée *f.*
Wednesday mercredi *m.*
week semaine *f.*
   per ~ par semaine
   two weeks quinze jours
weekend week-end *m.*
weight: put on ~ grossir
   lose ~ maigrir
welcome: you're ~ de rien; je vous en prie; il n'y a pas de quoi
Welcome! Bienvenue!
well *adv.* bien
   are you ~? vous allez bien?

fairly ~ assez bien
   not very ~ pas très bien
Well! Tiens!
Well then ... Eh bien ...
what *pron.* qu'est-ce que/qu'est-ce qui, que; *adj.* quel(le)
   ~? comment?; **~...!** quel(le)...!
   ~ am I going to do? Comment je vais faire?
   ~ day is it? quel jour est-ce?
   ~ (did you say)? comment?
   ~ is (are) ... like? comment est (sont) ...?
   ~ is there ...? qu'est-ce qu'il y a ...?
   ~ is this? qu'est-ce que c'est?
   ~ is your name? comment vous appelez-vous?
   ~ time is it? quelle heure est-il?
   ~'s new? quoi de neuf?
   ~'s the matter? qu'est-ce qu'il y a?
wheel: steering ~ volant *m.*
weird bizarre
when quand
where où
   ~ are you from? vous êtes (tu es) d'où?; d'où venez-vous (viens-tu)?
   ~ is (are) ...? où se trouve (se trouvent) ...?
which *adj.* quel(le); *pron.* lequel
while pendant que
   in a little ~ tout à l'heure
white blanc (blanche)
who qui
why pourquoi
   ~ not? pourquoi pas?
widower/widow veuf/veuve *m./f.*
wife femme *f.*
win gagner
   ~ the lottery gagner au loto
wind vent *m.*
   it's windy il fait du vent
windbreaker blouson *m.*
wine vin *m.*
winter hiver *m.*
wish *v.* vouloir; souhaiter
with avec
without sans
witness témoin *m.*
Wolof *(language)* wolof *m.*
which *adj.* quel(le); *pron.* le(s)quel(s), laquelle (lesquelles)
word mot *m.*
work *n.* travail *m.*
   manual ~ travail manuel *m.*
work *v.* travailler
world monde *m.*
worry *n.* souci *m.*
worry *v.* s'inquiéter
wounded *adj.* blessé(e)
wow! oh là là!

write écrire
wrong faux (fausse)
   be ~ avoir tort

year an *m.*; année *f.*
   school ~ année scolaire
yellow jaune
yes oui; si!

yesterday hier
yet encore
   not ~ pas encore
you *pron.* tu, vous; te, vous; toi, vous; ~too
   de même
young jeune
your *adj.* ton, ta, tes; votre, vos
(here's) to yours! à la vôtre!

yuck! berk!
yum! miam!

zero zéro
zip code code postal *m.*

Index

In the following index, the symbol (v) refers to lists of vocabulary within the lessons. The symbol (g) refers to the sections titled *Il y a un geste* that explain gestures used with the indicated phrase.

Canada

Québec

Nouveau-Brunswick

Québec

Montréal

St-Pierre-et-Miquelon

Amérique du Nord

États-Unis

Maine

Nouvelle-Angleterre

Nouvelle-Écosse

Louisiane

Océan Atlantique

La Nouvelle-Orléans

Haïti

Les Antilles

Port-au-Prince

Guadeloupe

Martinique

Océan Pacifique

Cayenne

Guyane française

Amérique du Sud

Wallis et Futuna

Polynésie française

Vanuatu

Tahiti

Australie

Nouvelle-Calédonie

Le monde francophone